Luminos is the Open Access monograph publishing program from UC Press. Luminos provides a framework for preserving and reinvigorating monograph publishing for the future and increases the reach and visibility of important scholarly work. Titles published in the UC Press Luminos model are published with the same high standards for selection, peer review, production, and marketing as those in our traditional program. www.luminosoa.org

Intersectional Incoherence

GLOBAL KOREA

This series is made possible through the generous support of the UC Berkeley Center for Korean Studies and the Yonsei University Department of Korean Language and Literature BK21Plus Program.

1. *Parameters of Disavowal: Colonial Representation in South Korean Cinema*, by Jinsoo An
2. *Rules of the House: Family Law and Domestic Disputes in Colonial Korea*, by Sungyun Lim
3. *Migrant Conversions: Transforming Connections Between Peru and South Korea*, by Erica Vogel
4. *Political Moods: Film Melodrama and the Cold War in the Two Koreas*, by Travis Workman
5. *Intersectional Incoherence: Zainichi Literature and the Ethics of Illegibility*, by Cindi Textor

Intersectional Incoherence

Zainichi Literature and the Ethics of Illegibility

Cindi Textor

UNIVERSITY OF CALIFORNIA PRESS

University of California Press
Oakland, California

Suggested citation: Textor, C. *Intersectional Incoherence: Zainichi Literature and the Ethics of Illegibility*. Oakland: University of California Press, 2024.
DOI: https://doi.org/10.1525/luminos.208

Library of Congress Cataloging-in-Publication Data

Names: Textor, Cindi L., author.
Title: Intersectional incoherence : Zainichi literature and the ethics of illegibility / Cindi Textor.
Other titles: Global Korea ; 5.
Description: Oakland, California : University of California Press, [2024] | Series: Global Korea; 5 | Includes bibliographical references and index.
Identifiers: LCCN 2024026586 (print) | LCCN 2024026587 (ebook) | ISBN 9780520398726 (paperback) | ISBN 9780520398733 (ebook)
Subjects: LCSH: Japanese literature—Korean authors—History and criticism. | BISAC: SOCIAL SCIENCE / Ethnic Studies / Asian Studies | HISTORY / Asia / Korea
Classification: LCC PL725.2.K67 T49 2024 (print) | LCC PL725.2.K67 (ebook) | DDC 895.609/8957—dc23/eng/20240712

LC record available at https://lccn.loc.gov/2024026586
LC ebook record available at https://lccn.loc.gov/2024026587

33 32 31 30 29 28 27 26 25 24
10 9 8 7 6 5 4 3 2 1

For MSR

CONTENTS

Acknowledgments *ix*

Introduction: Eavesdropping on Zainichi Literature *1*

1. The Untimeliness of "Zainichi": Literary History and the Construction of Coherence *17*
2. Queer(ing) Language in Yi Kwangsu's *Mujŏng*: Gender, Sexuality, and Colonial Modernity *39*
3. The Power to Know: Kim Saryang and the World as Addressee *59*
4. Representing Radical Difference: Kim Sŏkpŏm's Korea(n) in Japan(ese) *81*
5. Speaking Intersectionally: Disability, Ethnicity, and (Non-)Representation in Kin Kakuei's *Kogoeru kuchi* *100*
6. Words that Hurt: Yi Yangji's *Yuhi* and the Embodied Subject in Transit *119*
7. What Was Zainichi Literature? Temporalities of Silence and the Incoherent Future in Yū Miri's *Hachigatsu no hate* *138*

Epilogue: Global Zainichi Literature *157*

Notes *167*

Works Cited *191*

Index *205*

ACKNOWLEDGMENTS

It is a delight to reflect on the countless moments of grace and generosity I received in the process of writing this book. My sincere thanks to everyone listed here, and to the many others I fail to mention.

Atsuko Ueda, Richard Okada, and Michael Emmerich were not only inspiring teachers and mentors, but they also planted the idea that I was cut out for graduate school, which might never have occurred to me. Robert Tierney, David Goodman, Elizabeth Oyler, and Young-Jun Lee taught me so much about reading, translation, and having my own voice.

This work would not have been possible without my language teachers over the years, especially Yukari Tokumasu, Tomiko Kuwahira, Seiichi Makino, Chung-kang Kim, Hyejin Yang, Sun-Mi Kim, Tomotaro Akizawa, Ari Sato, and Hiroko Otake.

I cannot thank my dissertation mentors enough for shepherding this project through its early stages. Davinder Bhowmik always knew what I should read next and encouraged me to wrestle with difficult problems. Heekyoung Cho gave the most pointed and constructive feedback and showed me how I could contribute across fields. Ted Mack helped me to discover who I was in conversation with and that I had something to say, and taught me to question and question and question. Thanks also to Andrea Arai, Kaori Igarashi, Christopher Lowy, Hwasook Nam, Ben Rosenberg, Sachi Schmidt-Hori, Clark Sorensen, and Kai Xie for their support during graduate school.

No one has had a greater impact on the development of this book and on my own growth as a scholar than Ko Youngran. As a mentor she was extraordinarily generous with her time and energy, pointing me in so many fascinating directions and giving me the confidence to run with ideas, even when they were half-baked.

Through Ko-san I met Watanabe Naoki, who welcomed me into his *benkyōkai*, even when I got lost and showed up an hour late. He and the others I met there were unfailingly warm, enthusiastic, and knowledgeable. Thanks especially to Hatano Setsuko, Shin Ji Young, Ryu Chung Hee, Takahashi Azusa, Lee Junghee, Kim Moran, and Kim Kyongche,

Christina Yi, Andre Haag, and Nathaniel Heneghan have helped me in so many roles: on conference panels, as collection editors, in workshops and reading groups, through their own amazing scholarship, but mostly as friends. They and the other members of the Zainichi Research Consortium have been my fellow travelers, without which this book would look very different. Thanks to Julia Clark, Jonathan Glade, Andrew Harding, Sohye Kim, Nayoung Aimee Kwon, Nicholas Lambrecht, Catherine Ryu, Koji Toba, Shoya Unoda, and Nobuko Yamasaki.

I am incredibly lucky to have brilliant and supportive colleagues at the University of Utah. Thanks to my writing buddies especially—Vanessa Brutsche, Talía Dajes, Tanya Flores, M.A. Mujeeb Khan, Jacqueline Landry, Ashton Lazarus, Jacqueline Sheean, Yunwen Su, and Mamiko Suzuki—and to Maile Arvin, Patrick Cheney, Thérèse De Raedt, Shaun Delliskave, Nathan Devir, Bryce Garner, Katharina Gerstenberger, Sae Kawase, Kim Korinek, Christopher Lewis, Shawna-Kim Lowey-Ball, Joe Metz, Ryan Moran, Alejandro Quin, David Roh, Wes Sasaki-Uemura, Janet Theiss, Bunny Torrey, Margaret Toscano, Margaret Wan, Myra Washington, and John Wynne, for making it a great place to work.

Among the many other scholars in the field who have helped shape the manuscript through energizing and generative conversations are Michael Bourdaghs, Will Bridges, Jyana Browne (with shouts out to Earl), Andrew Campana, Brett de Bary, Kyeong-Hee Choi, Matthew Felt, Aaron Gerow, Klaus Yamamoto Hammering, Christopher Hanscom, Hwang Hoduk, Kyle Ikeda, Seth Jacobowitz, Kang Yuni, Kim Jae-Yong, Jina Kim, Faye Yuan Kleeman, Kono Kensuke, David Krolikoski, Kwak Hyoungduck, Hyangjin Lee, Jin-kyung Lee, Andrea Mendoza, Marc Opper, Nam Pujin, Park Kwang Hyoun, Samuel Perry, Akito Sakasai, Kimberlee Sanders, Christopher Scott, Evelyn Shih, Satoko Shimazaki, Serk-Bae Suh, John Treat, Sarah Walsh, Travis Workman, Miya Xie, Yoon Sun Yang, Emily Jungmin Yoon, Soo Ryon Yoon, and Victoria Young.

The book benefited enormously from a manuscript workshop organized by John Lie and sponsored by the Institute of East Asian Studies at the University of California, Berkeley and the Global Korea Series at University of California Press. The nuanced and rigorous feedback I received from John Lie, Sonia Ryang, Hyewon Song, and Kathy Ragsdale was transformative. I am also grateful to Janet Poole and an anonymous reader for the time and care they put into peer review, to Catherine Osborne for copyediting, and to Enrique Ochoa-Kaup, Emily Park, Teresa Iafolla, and everyone who worked on the book for UC Press.

Research for the book was funded by a Fulbright IIE Research Grant, the Graduate School at the University of Washington, the Association for Asian Studies

Northeast Asia Council, the University of Utah University Research Committee, the University of Utah College of Humanities, and the Asia Center at University of Utah.

Chapter 2 is revised from "Queer(ing) Language in Yi Kwangsu's *Mujŏng*: Sexuality, Nation, and Colonial Modernity," *Journal of Korean Studies* 23, no. 1 (March 2018): 65–94. An earlier version of chapter 4 was published as "Representing Radical Difference: Kim Sŏkpŏm's Korea(n) in Japan(ese)," *positions: asia critique* 27, no. 3 (August 2019): 499–529. Both are reproduced courtesy of Duke University Press.

Finally, I thank my family for their love and support.

Introduction

Eavesdropping on Zainichi Literature

It was a summer evening in Tokyo when three colleagues and I were jolted from our dinner conversation by an outburst from a woman at the adjacent table in the restaurant. She was not exactly eavesdropping—more likely overhearing. Seemingly out of patience, she nearly shouted, "*Zainichi* is offensive! You should say *Zainichi Kankokujin*." The four of us had used the offending term repeatedly in the course of discussing our research, which for all of us touches on the ethnic Korean community in Japan. We referred to this community as "Zainichi" (在日), a Japanese term meaning literally nothing more than "in Japan," but commonly understood as shorthand for Koreans residing in Japan. It is true, however, as the woman noted, that "Zainichi" is also used pejoratively, despite its widespread and casual use in English-language (and often even Japanese-language) academic discourse on the subject.[1] As I do throughout this book, we used this word not without a certain ambivalence, but out of a combination of necessity and convenience. After all, we had to call our subjects *something*, even if we would have no trouble recognizing the various problems with the term—one of which had just been brought inescapably to our attention.

This book is interested in the ethical contradictions this moment encapsulates. I suspect that all of us at the table that night do the work that we do in part to combat the discursive and material injustices that silence Zainichi Koreans and other marginalized communities. But there is no way to do that work, no way to give voice to these communities, outside a language that inevitably misrepresents them. There are no neutral terms. Knowledge production, I argue, necessarily involves negotiations of the violence inherent in both the failure to represent and representation itself. Innocence is untenable.

As a case in point, the woman calling us out offered the alternative "Zainichi Kankokujin" (在日韓国人), a phrase that employs "Zainichi" as a modifier of a Japanese term for "Korean," in this case written with the sinographs preferred in the South. This longer phrase is preferred precisely because it provides this higher degree of specificity, avoiding the problem of lumping together "Zainichi Kankokujin" with "Zainichi Chōsenjin" (在日朝鮮人), the equivalent written with the sinographs preferred in the North.

However, it was this very specificity that made us unable simply to substitute "Zainichi Kankokujin" for "Zainichi" and continue our discussion. As we hastened to explain to our neighbor in the restaurant, it would be more accurate to say we study "Zainichi Kankoku-Chōsenjin," a more inclusive if unwieldy term that acknowledges the existence of both modes of naming Korea. In fact, many Koreans in Japan identify as Zainichi Chōsenjin, including at least one of us at the table. Commonly misunderstood as necessarily implying allegiance to the North Korean state, this designation offers a means of rejecting the Cold War politics of division and imagining Koreans in Japan as the legacy of a unified Korea.[2] For them, "Kankoku" is a painful reminder that they exist on one side of a hierarchical division. "Kankoku-Chōsenjin," despite its greater inclusivity, also serves as such a reminder. The ordering of the terms necessarily suggests a privileging of one over the other, even as the hyphen itself acts as a material representation of the division.

In short, although "Zainichi" has become the predominant nomenclature in English-language discourse on this group, its usage implies the existence of an internally cohesive group for which there is no name in Japanese, or even Korean. Whereas the English "Zainichi Korean" is agnostic to the politics of the divided states on the peninsula, the Japanese and Korean languages cannot help but acknowledge them, if not privilege one side or the other. To denote the entire community of ethnic Koreans in Japan regardless of citizenship or political affiliation, one occasionally sees alternative terms such as "Zainichi Korian" (在日コリアン) or "Korian-Japanīzu" (コリアン・ジャパニーズ), but these share the English term's problem of implying a sort of ethnicity-based unity that may not apply (not to mention its centering of the English-language world as global arbiter of what things are called).[3]

In Korean, one can avoid the distinction by using terms such as "Chaeil kyop'o" (재일교포) or "Chaeil tongp'o" (재일동포), both of which imply a biological kinship shared by Koreans across the world, thereby reaffirming ethnocentric or even racialized notions of Korean identity. On the other hand, to avoid "tongp'o" and "kyop'o" (literally "same womb" and "overseas brethren"), one has to specify which kind of Korean: Chosŏnin (조선인), the preferred term in North Korea, or Hangugin (한국인), the name for Korea in the South. In other words, the Korean language has the same pitfall as Japanese, albeit with more fraught political stakes. More suggestively, in contemporary Korean-language discourse on the Korean diaspora in Japan, one is increasingly likely to see "Chainich'i" (자이니치) rather than "Chaeil" precede these terms. As opposed to the shared sinographic tradition underlying both the Japanese (Zainichi) and Korean (Chaeil) readings of the characters (在日), "Chainich'i" is derived from the phonetic transliteration of the Japanese "Zainichi," or perhaps even from the English-language adoption of this term. At some level, "Zainichi" as signifier has broken free of any specific national or linguistic context. Nevertheless, the heaviness of the specific discursive histories of the term in each of those contexts is still felt acutely, as it was in the restaurant that night.

All of the above terms shift in connotation as they are transformed in the process of translation, yet they each imply an internal cohesion in the "Zainichi" (or "Chaeil," or "Korean-Japanese," or "Chainich'i") community that collapses the moment it is called into question by that same process of translation. What struck me that night is that any given term my colleagues and I might have chosen, in any of the three languages to which we had access, would have inflicted violence on some potential bystander at the next table. These words are specters of historical violence as well as painful legacies of that history lingering in the present. And, importantly, that violence not only takes the form of exclusion—as in the pejorative implication of "Zainichi," that those who bear the moniker do not belong in Japan—but also arises from misrecognition in the process of *inclusion*—as in the application of "Kankokujin" to that same community, despite many rejecting such a label.

Also inescapable that night was the conclusion that the specific valence of these words, and their potential to cause harm, are of course dependent on the positions—and respective languages—of the speaker and listener. As it happens, the woman at the next table was Japanese. Her act of attempted allyship on behalf of Zainichi Kankokujin put her in conflict with Zainichi Chōsenjin. In one sense, her endeavor to speak for the community was undermined by her position outside it, but more than that she was bound by the same problem we were: the violence embedded in the language itself. Although the Chōsen-Kankoku distinction completely collapses when one speaks, perhaps in English, of Zainichi Koreans or Zainichi full stop, it is not at all surprising that the salient dichotomy in that moment at dinner was not Japan(ese) versus Korea(n), but rather a Cold War inflected divide that saw Japan and South Korea (Kankoku) on one side and North Korea (Chōsen) on the other.[4] These were the terms in which our language(s), and the politics from which they cannot be severed, allowed us to speak.

Finally, I would be remiss not to highlight the irony I experienced at that table as an American embedded in this conversation, yet somehow always outside it. On the one hand, the ambiguity of English allows the discourse on Zainichi Koreans in Anglophone academia to decenter the North-South Cold War division, a reframing of Zainichi issues that brings with it a great deal of potential for fruitful analysis, perhaps even a transformation and expansion of what can be said about these issues in Japanese and Korean. As I hope this story illustrates, to speak of

"Zainichi," full stop, creates a fictively coherent community where none, in fact, exists. On the other hand, this tendency of English-language discourse, by its very nature, to de-emphasize the existence of two Koreas serves to elide the role of the United States in the entire fraught history of Japanese colonial contact with Korea and its continuing aftermath in the present day.

It is tempting—and easy enough, if one wishes—to see English-language interventions in discourse on Zainichi literature, culture, and history, as valuable precisely because they are removed from the Japanese and Korean language politics outlined above. The English language renders moot the dichotomies that Korean- and Japanese-language discourses cannot escape. However, as I have already suggested, this veneer of distance—or worse, "objectivity"—belies the profound entanglement of the United States and the English language itself in the very politics it conceals.

In the end, I am left with a dilemma that perhaps our neighbor in the restaurant shared. To speak *of*—much less *for*—the Zainichi community (whatever that means, and what that means is perhaps the central question posed by this book) is an inherently violent exercise, especially but not exclusively from a position outside that community. Yet at the same time, silence is also untenable, violent in itself. How, then, do we ethically engage in a conversation that is not meant for us, in which we cannot and should not be centered, but from which we can never be completely removed? As a sort of eavesdropper on Zainichi literature and criticism, what is the right moment and language in which to interject?

This book addresses these questions by attending to incoherence in Zainichi literature, where "incoherence" is deployed multivalently. In one sense, I am referring to the failure of the Zainichi community or its literary production to cohere, as the fluidity and inconsistency of the terms used to name this collective would suggest. Although I have thus far presented this incoherence in terms of the division of the Korean peninsula, the mapping of this geopolitical divide onto the Zainichi community is only a particular case of the intractable internal differences that characterize any identity community. Drawing on theories of intersectionality, my readings of Zainichi literature also think through the challenges posed by differences of gender, sexuality, disability, and language to the coherence of Zainichi as a category of analysis. At the same time, I want to conceive of the imbrications of Japanese and American imperialisms at the site of colonial Korea and its postcolonial diaspora as itself a form of intersectionality. These enmeshed imperial spheres, along with other interlocking forms of domination that intersectional discourse has illuminated, conspire to render incoherent, if not quite silent, the voices at their nexus.

Perhaps as a response to these representational challenges, the texts I take up in this book, ranging from the early years of Korean colonial modernity to the twenty-first century, contain language that is non-representational. I use "incoherence" in a second sense to describe a kind of writing that deliberately defies smooth reading, interpretation, translation, or assimilation. The radical potential of this incoherence is particularly relevant where hermeneutical approaches to Zainichi and other marginalized literatures have demanded that they represent their constitutive communities, and that they do so transparently and coherently. This refusal to be understood may be read as a response to these impossible demands. But it also creates an opportunity for readers to recognize their own involvement in the production of incoherence. I argue that the opaque, illegible, absent, and incoherent in literature offer alternative ways of ethically engaging with texts, including or especially those never meant to be understood.

THE "DEATH" OF ZAINICHI STUDIES: LITERARY TAXONOMY AND THE POLITICS OF REPRESENTATION

This is not a book about Zainichi literature. I begin with this caveat not only due to the problems with the term "Zainichi" detailed above, but also because, as I will argue, Zainichi literature fails to cohere as an object of study. Even if it did, the writers and texts I consider here would stretch the category into unwieldiness. This presents not an obstacle, but an opportunity: an opportunity to make visible the pitfalls and possibilities of literary taxonomies.

It should be mentioned, first of all, that writers and critics of Zainichi literature have been worried about its sustainability as a relevant category for at least a decade.[5] As I discuss in detail in chapter 7, the publication of the anthology *"Zainichi" bungaku zenshū* (*Collected Works of Zainichi Literature*) in 2006 brought these worries to a head. Prominent younger writers declined to have their work included, while the canonical giants of Zainichi literature, responsible for forging the genre anew in the 1960s and 1970s, had aged into their eighties. In this moment, both groups seemed to concur that perhaps Zainichi literature had run its course, albeit with sharply different levels of nostalgia.

In this respect, these Zainichi writers are hardly alone. Consider the 2019 Association for Asian Studies conference roundtable provocatively titled "The Death of Japanese Studies" and the virtual roundtable "The Rebirth of Japanese Studies" organized in response for the 2020 iteration of the conference.[6] Though differing in outlook, both conversations seemed to take for granted that Japan (or Japanese literature in particular) is a self-evidently valid object of study. Alternatively, participants worried that the erosion of disciplinary and area boundaries had contributed to the crisis alongside declining institutional support for the field.[7] Either way, it was assumed that the death under discussion is one to be mourned.

Of course, this sense of loss is not the only way to process such an ending.[8] Sinophone studies, to cite an adjacent field, begins by anticipating its own eventual irrelevance. As Shu-mei Shih explains, unlike the notion of Chinese diaspora, whose ethnocentrism leaves it unable to break loose from the totalizing and transhistorical tendencies of the Chinese nation, the Sinophone is grounded in the use of

Sinitic languages in specific times and places. In this way, "the Sinophone recedes or disappears as soon as the languages in question are abandoned, but this recession or disappearance should not be seen as a cause for lament or nostalgia."[9] Just as well, perhaps, as other such fields of inquiry and literary production have welcomed their own deaths from within, even if they have not yet died. The Francophone and the Anglophone, both more unambiguously situated as (post)colonial residues than the Sinophone, have produced "manifestos" calling for their demise.[10]

In 2007, one year after the release of *"Zainichi" bungaku zenshū*, a group of forty-four writers including Michel Le Bris, Jean Rouaud, and Édouard Glissant signed a letter to the French newspaper *Le Monde* titled "Pour une 'littérature-monde' en français" ("Toward a 'World Literature' in French"), arguing for "the end of 'francophone' literature" and a decentering of the French nation in French-language literature that the concept of the Francophone failed to achieve.[11] They suggested as a model the global and plural character of English-language literature, where "the children of the former British empire were, with complete legitimacy, taking possession of English letters."[12] World Literature in English, of course, comes with its own internal hierarchies, though perhaps it is fair to say that critiques thereof entered the spotlight much earlier.

One of the best-known examples is Salman Rushdie's 1983 essay "'Commonwealth Literature' Does Not Exist."[13] Writing in reaction to a conference on Commonwealth literature, Rushdie praises the event as a stimulating affair attended by brilliant writers from all over the English-speaking world. However, over the course of the conference, he writes, "I became quite sure that our differences were so much more significant than our similarities, that it was impossible to say what 'Commonwealth literature'—the idea which had, after all, made possible our assembly—might conceivably mean." Here Rushdie points out that the category of Commonwealth literature is held together by little more than an exclusionary logic that defines the writers under its purviews as outside English literature proper, "the great sacred thing itself." If "Commonwealth literature" is to mean anything, it can only do so via such policing of its external boundaries coupled with the suppression of its internal differences, whose significance threatens to exceed that of its similarities.

Perhaps Commonwealth literature and Francophonie are particularly egregious examples of these internal and external exclusions, but the question I want to raise here is whether these same conceptual problems are not, in fact, present in *any* possible literary taxonomy. National literatures are perhaps less subjected to this kind of scrutiny than more marginal or expansive groupings, but the notion that the similarities of writers and texts taken up under a national framework are more significant than the differences can only be prescriptive rather than descriptive. I submit that no literary taxonomy can escape this conundrum. They all, including Zainichi literature, achieve coherence (to the extent that they achieve it) through the suppression of intersectional differences that remain salient nonetheless.

In that case, should we dispense with them altogether? Why use the word "Zainichi" at all, if the only reason for doing so is the utterly unsatisfying answer above—we have to call them *something*? Rushdie suggests a better kind of answer, ironically in the very same breath he denounces Commonwealth literature for failing to cohere: this concept was, despite its flaws, "the idea which had, after all, made possible our assembly."[14] If there is a purpose to literary taxonomy, it is not in finding the correct name for a cohesive, pre-existing body of texts, but rather in *creating* such assemblies, as opportunities for certain writers, texts, and readers to collide with one another. New ways of naming and categorizing create new pathways along which such collisions can occur. Moreover, when such a pathway emerges and new texts and writers find an audience (perhaps, though not inevitably, at the expense of works previously deemed canonical), the backlash that often occurs is frequently couched in the language of "coherence," with little attention to whether the previous canon coheres, or, more importantly, to how it was *made* to cohere in the process of, rather than prior to, its interpretation.[15]

Japanese (literary) studies in particular, in the leadup to its "death," has been reconfigured to open up many productive new pathways. The field has challenged the perceived singularity and homogeneity of "Japan," not only in the Anglophone world but also in Japanese-language discourse. Pioneering works such as those of Harumi Befu and Oguma Eiji began to unpack the ideological aspects of *Nihonjinron*, the belief in Japanese cultural essentialism and uniqueness, a hegemonic set of ideas in postwar Japan.[16] These critiques spurred a wave of scholarly attention to Japan's ethnic minorities and subcultures, including studies of the Zainichi community, arguing in favor of a multiethnic or multicultural lens on Japan.[17] Of course, since their heyday in the 1990s, notions of multiculturalism have undergone extensive critiques, particularly with regard to the tendency of multiculturalism to reify essentialized difference and leave the hierarchical relationships inscribed thereon intact.[18] Indeed, the case of Japanese studies demonstrates that increased representation of Japan's multiculturalism has done little to dislodge "Japan proper" (envisioned as populated by Japanese-speaking, ethnically and culturally Japanese people) from its hegemonic position.

While so many fields and disciplines, including but not limited to Japanese studies, are either dying or refusing to die, Korean studies, on the other hand, is ascendant. Opportunities to study Korean literature and especially popular culture in English are expanding rather than contracting. Having relatively recently secured a significant presence in Anglo-American academia, Korean literary studies as a field is an exception that proves the rule. That is, even as Korean studies carves out a space alongside parallel nation-based fields of Japanese and Chinese studies, Korea's divided status necessarily entails a more ambivalent relationship with the nation-state. Moreover, many of the central themes of scholarship in Korean literary and cultural studies are inherently transnational: the cultural production of the Japanese empire, divided Cold War ideologies, migration and diaspora, and the global flows of digital and popular media. Korean studies today is also increasingly interested in multiculturalism, and Korea's own myth of ethnic homogeneity and uniqueness.[19]

One could reasonably predict that Korean studies will eventually arrive at the same point of "death" as Japanese studies, albeit belatedly. That said, to rehearse this history of the arrival of crisis and death—first to the Eurocentric canon of literary studies full stop, then to Japanese literary studies (particularly as a reflection of a monolingual and monoethnic Japan), and perhaps, eventually, to Korean literature itself—is a reflection of the imperial logic that views Korea as behind Japan, which is in turn behind the West. Of course, this logic breaks down with the recognition that the very distinction between Japanese studies and Korean studies is illusory to begin with. The two are so deeply intertwined with each other—not to mention countless other national and international languages, cultures, and powers—that one simply cannot be understood without an understanding of the other. Each field's coherence, to say nothing of their mutual exclusivity, is created by deliberately ignoring its intersectional and transnational aspects. The question remains: how to do otherwise?

TRANSNATIONALISM AND THE ETHICS OF KNOWLEDGE PRODUCTION

The search for alternatives to nation-state models for studying literatures and cultures is in large part the motivation behind what has been termed "the transnational turn," to which the discourse on the "death" of Japanese studies could be read as a kind of backlash. Zainichi studies has been deeply imbricated with broader trends toward transnational models.[20] As such, it would not be overstating the case to say that "Zainichi studies," even if it has not always been named as such across its history in English-language discourse, has both shaped and been shaped by larger debates on the ethics of knowledge production by the West about Asia, which is always already a transnational endeavor.

By the late 2000s, the nation-state area studies model had come so thoroughly under fire that one scholar was able to remark that the "myth" of Japanese cultural homogeneity had become a "straw man *par-excellence*."[21] At the same time, a new generation of English-language scholars, much more likely than their predecessors to have facility in more than one Asian language, attempted to move beyond the question of what Japan's minorities could tell us about Japan, and committed much more seriously to transnational and translingual approaches to scholarship on East Asia, especially the Japanese empire.[22] Serk-Bae Suh, Nayoung Aimee Kwon, and Christina Yi have also extended this rich analysis of imperial Japan to the postcolonial (or postimperial) Cold War reconfigurations of national, cultural, and linguistic identities, including the coalescence of the Zainichi community.[23]

Much of this work engages explicitly with postcolonial studies, particularly the problematic of Japan's exceptional location or outright absence within. On the one hand, acknowledgment of Japan's particularity as the only non-Western imperial power of the twentieth century acts as a counter to the Eurocentric impulse within postcolonial studies to view the problem of empire through the lens of the West versus the Rest. On the other hand, insistence on Japanese exceptionalism returns us to something like *Nihonjinron* itself, viewing Japan as singular and incommensurable, uniquely unique. Thus, just as the expansion of Japanese studies to encompass the minor, the multicultural, or the diasporic fails to disrupt the centrality of Japan proper, the expansion of the boundaries of postcolonial studies to include the Japanese empire is perhaps preferable to its absence, but leaves intact the hierarchies that cause the absence in the first place.

As a case in point, one of the most intriguing possibilities to emerge from this work is the Japanophone.[24] As with parallel language-centered fields, the Japanophone offers the advantages and pitfalls of arranging a constellation of texts around a former (or not-so-former) imperial sphere of influence. The Japanophone foregrounds the (post)imperial language politics of the Japanese empire and its aftermath, highlighting the possibility of literary production in the Japanese language that is not necessarily by and for the Japanese ethnonation. Yet, Japanophone literature is no less prone than the Francophone or Anglophone to falling into the trap of reinforcing the central and privileged status of the former imperial power. Even in the decades-long Japanese-language discourse on *Nihongo bungaku* (Japanese-language literature) as opposed to or in opposition to *Nihon bungaku* (Japanese literature), a division of labor has emerged. That is, *Nihongo bungaku* offers a space for the exploration of writers and texts with roots in the former colonies or at the margins of Japaneseness, whereas the field of *Nihon bungaku* continues essentially undisturbed. Furthermore, in the view of Zainichi Korean writer Kim Sŏkpŏm (who himself coined *Nihongo bungaku* as a means of distinguishing Zainichi Korean literature from Japanese literature), Japanophone studies have tended to focus on contemporary, cosmopolitan writers who move freely between Japanese and other languages, at the expense of a historical, postcolonial lens that can account for those writers who had no choice but to write in Japanese.[25] The Japanophone, then, is splintered along multiple internal hierarchies, one of which is still "Japan proper" and its others.

Perhaps the most radical attempt to redraw—or discard altogether—area and disciplinary boundaries is the emergent field of transpacific studies. Born at the nexus of Asian American and Asian studies, the transpacific framework offers a method of teasing out overlapping Japanese and American imperialisms in the Pacific region. As I will argue at length in the following chapter, it is impossible to position Zainichi literature without attending to this intersectionality of empires. Moreover, this reconfiguration of our understanding of postcolonialism in East Asia as constituted by the "complicity" of American neo-imperialism and

Asian nationalisms allows for the critical re-examination of American knowledge production itself.[26] In fact, many of the debates among early adopters of the trans-pacific lens revolve around the question of who constitutes the agent of knowledge in Asia and the Pacific, and how to shift that agency from the United States and its semi-colonial partners in East Asia to the historically marginalized and silenced voices of Southeast Asia and the Pacific Islands.[27]

However, as soon as the issue of center and margin is raised within the transpacific frame, the same anxiety around unmanageability and incoherence—present across comparative, postcolonial, and area-based literary studies—rears its ugly head. In a volume that proposes no less than "to produce the trans-Pacific as a new paradigm of Area Studies that will overcome the dominant mode of imagining East Asia and discover the grid of new regional configurations beyond the neo-imperial design,"[28] the editors issue the caveat that they must "*delimit the scope of our discussion in Northeast Asia* since we deem a broader and thicker comparison to be in demand in order to extend our discussion over East Asia at large."[29] A scope any larger than that which is already well represented is once again difficult to manage. Lisa Yoneyama echoes this sentiment in the very act of pointing out the danger of endlessly re-centering the center, even within transpacific studies: "Lest I be misunderstood, I am not proposing to solve the problems associated with the prefix *trans* by merely adding yet another subject to our research agenda."[30] Even here, in a field that is boldly and unapologetically transnational and intersectional, the object of study must be "delimited," in a way that inevitably invites the suppression of these exact forms of difference.

To issue my own caveat, let me be clear that these are exciting developments toward a more honest and ethical configuration of Anglo-American scholarship and the Asia-Pacific region. At a minimum, this work of transgressing the boundaries of fields of knowledge production has had enormous and undeniable value in terms of illuminating areas of human history, culture, and experience previously rendered invisible by the single-nation frameworks under which such knowledge was pursued for so much of postwar history in the United States. This scholarship enables my own. But the one nagging concern that remains with me is that representation—particularly representation in the service of *knowledge*—is ill-equipped to address the fundamental problems these scholars have identified. These emergent fields are at risk of being co-opted by the same kind of representational logic that drives the methodologies they are explicitly attempting to reject. That is, the postcolonial, the Japanophone, and the transpacific are in danger of becoming nothing more than new objects of study whose borders, centers, peripheries, and overall internal coherence *we* the knowledge-producers define without ever being accountable for doing so.

The anxieties plaguing area studies and adjacent fields in the post–Cold War era will not be alleviated by substituting a transnational but nevertheless internally coherent object of knowledge for the nation. The problem has always been an ethical one: that the production of national knowledge conceals its own role in producing the nation. I submit that the transnational, the postcolonial, and the transpacific are just as susceptible to this kind of violence. What is needed, then, is a more radical transformation of the ways in which we think about the question of representation and engage with the texts we study. The salient questions are not how to draw the boundaries or how to name a particular field of knowledge, but rather the question of responsibility for who is doing the knowing and to what ends.

INTERSECTIONALITY AS ETHICS AND POETICS

This question of responsibility is what necessitates an ethical theoretical orientation. By invoking ethics, I do not mean to suggest that reading literature constitutes a moral good in and of itself. Rather, I am tapping a vein of criticism that is interested in ethics as a mode of insisting on positionality and relationality, of confronting the limits of knowledge and interpretation. At the theoretical heart of much of this criticism is the thought of Emmanuel Levinas, who in his argument for ethics as "first philosophy"—ethics as underpinning ontology, not the other way around—roots his critique in the irreducible alterity of the Other.[31] For Levinas, the Other's otherness is infinite, not subject to the totalizing capture (what he calls the "imperialism") of ontological concepts, lest the Other become the Same.[32] This line of thinking, particularly as taken up by deconstructionists, has opened up modes of approaching language—or literary texts in particular—that attend to the violence inherent in assigning ontological meaning.[33]

Idelber Avelar's "The Ethics of Interpretation and the International Division of Intellectual Labor" lucidly ties this ethics-informed skepticism toward totalizing knowledge to the politics of knowledge production I have been discussing thus far. Alevar offers a concise working definition of "an ethical relation to the academic apparatus" as "*the critique of a structure one cannot but inhabit*," arguing that this kind of critical orientation is "the indispensable ethical foundation for future canon expansions, disciplinary and transdisciplinary revisions, institutional reforms, and curricular changes, as well as the necessary horizon for an ethic that could rethink the role not only of literatures in foreign languages but also of English."[34] As the case of Zainichi literary studies so clearly demonstrates, neither the critic nor the language of critique has any neutral ground on which to stand, though the English language often masquerades as such. Of particular concern for Alevar is the way this inequity engenders a division of labor, "a split reproduced in the university between national traditions expected to produce thought (philosophy, 'theory,' etc.) and those traditions expected to provide objects for the thinking learned elsewhere."[35] This refusal to see theory from outside those dominant national traditions *as theory* provides yet another illustration of how illegibility is structurally produced.[36]

Of course, to state it in these words is to run the risk of suggesting that the only such intellectual division of labor is national, when there are so many other hierarchies along which such divides can occur. This is where intersectionality is once again instructive, not only in pointing out the divisions internal to the nation, but also as a case study in whose thinking can be read as "thought." In fact, the constant calling into question of intersectionality as intellectual tradition has given rise to a posture of defensiveness, which Jennifer Nash characterizes as the primary affective valence of intersectionality scholarship.[37] Wherever conversations about intersectionality take place—activist circles, program-building efforts in the American university, journalism and media, or the pages of academic publications—the discussion anticipates its own backlash. As Nash describes the state of intersectionality in the context of women's studies, "the field retains an ambivalent relationship with the analytic, always imagining it as simultaneously promising and dangerous, the field's utopic future and its past tense."[38] The emergence of a post-intersectional turn is coterminous with or even prior to widespread adoption of the term—to say nothing of its underlying methods and orientations.

This awkward temporal positioning of intersectionality is reflected by historiographic debates over its emergence in black feminist thought. As is well known, the term "intersectionality" itself was introduced in 1989 by American legal scholar and critical race theorist Kimberlé Crenshaw,[39] but recent histories of intersectional thought have traced its roots to much earlier figures.[40] Despite this long and complex history, intersectionality has often been portrayed as the latest intellectual fad, a "buzzword" more notable for its popularity than its substance.[41] In the same way that intersectionality is dismissed as both derivative of much older thought and shallowly trendy in its newness, it is accused of being both too academic to be useful for activists on the ground, yet not rigorous enough to be useful as theory. Not only is intersectionality thrown into the dustbin with "identity politics" as a fundamentally divisive idea, it is also accused of undermining unity and solidarity within feminist and anti-racist circles themselves.

I submit that these contradictions—intersectionality's simultaneous datedness and futurity, oversimplification and excessive complexity, provinciality and lack of specificity—are themselves a product of intersectional incoherence. That is, because the women of color who have developed intersectionality (or the "matrix of domination,"[42] or the notion of interlocking oppressions[43]) are themselves subject to the structures of inequity their thought tradition identifies, for them there can be no separation between the theoretical and the object of knowledge. This is where I want to posit, perhaps rather obviously, intersectionality as a specifically *ethical* theory—to paraphrase Avelar, a critique of *structures* (plural) it cannot but inhabit. And here I hope it is clear that all of us inhabit these structures.

As such, by placing Zainichi literature in dialogue with intersectional discourse, I am by no means claiming that intersectional theory, an intellectual tradition emerging from black feminist thought in the United States and further developed in transnational feminist contexts, somehow provides the terms to explain or understand Zainichi literature. But nor do I accept that such commensurability is a requisite for this kind of dialogue to take place. Audre Lorde, one of the central intersectionality thinkers, insists that what she is theorizing is not a cohesive black female experience—again, an impossibility on its face. Instead, it is the connections that can be forged not in spite of difference, but rather through the act of embracing it.[44] For me, then, reading Zainichi literature through the lens of intersectional feminist theory is a way of being accountable for my own position as a white woman within the American academy, which is no more a monolith than the community whose literary work I am reading.

Moreover, via this ethical theoretical orientation, I want to suggest that what is needed is a more profound skepticism toward the project of explaining or understanding in the first place. To explain, to understand, to grasp a subject is inevitably to suppress its internal incoherence and tame a radical difference that demands recognition of the unknowable into a domesticated difference that can be assimilated by a stable, independent knowing subject. Thus, when I describe the theoretical framework of this book as intersectional, I certainly do not mean to imply that intersectional theory speaks from a universalized subject position. Rather, I deploy intersectionality precisely because it offers a method for starting from the particular, for speaking not in a universalized language of mutual understanding that sets out to know and control the other as object, but for articulating relational positions that such language cannot accommodate. It is a way of naming the speech that is interpreted as incoherent because it is responding to a set of incoherent demands. It is a means of implicating the structural violence of hermeneutics in producing the failure to communicate.

In fact, although intersectionality in popular vernacular is shorthand for the need to think simultaneously in terms of race and gender, it ultimately provides a vocabulary for describing problems of representation that occur at the intersection of these and other axes of power. In the words of Crenshaw:

> The problem with identity politics is not that it fails to transcend difference, as some critics charge, but rather the opposite—that it frequently conflates or ignores intragroup differences.... Feminist efforts to politicize experiences of women and antiracist efforts to politicize experiences of people of color have frequently proceeded as though the issues and experiences they detail occur on mutually exclusive terrains. Although racism and sexism readily intersect in the lives of real people, they seldom do in feminist and antiracist practices. And so, when the practices expound identity as woman or person of color as an either/or proposition, they relegate the identity of women of color to a location that *resists telling*.[45]

Intersectionality is a strategy for approaching those stories that "resist telling." It is a theory of whose narratives are *heard* by those in power: not necessarily a question of who can speak, but of how a too-blunt interpretive framework, in its insensitivity to difference, proves unable to make sense of certain voices. A hermeneutics that demands that texts be read in terms of their difference from one or another form of dominance renders those voices resisting from multiple angles at once incoherent, if never quite silent.

Thus, I follow Mecca Jamilah Sullivan in thinking of intersectionality as a reading strategy for coping with what she calls "the poetics of difference," defined as "a set of subversive aesthetic strategies that uses multiplicities of form and genre to respond to global discourses of antiracism, decolonization, feminism, and antiheterosexism."[46] Sullivan is primarily concerned with the genre-bending antinormative narratives of black feminists across the diaspora, who demand that their readers "develop queer reading practices, ways of reading that both apprehend and destabilize the workings of power continuously within and between words, phrases, lines, and sentences."[47] I hope to expand upon the poetics of difference by further interrogating the multilingual aspects of texts that demand intersectional reading practices. Whereas Sullivan and the queer black feminist writers she examines work primarily in English, challenging its normative forms, the writers I consider are in many ways writing against English as itself a global norm. Rather than genre-bending, these writers operate at the level of style, orthography, and the materiality of the text on the page, which for them are sites of the interstices of power that have rendered them silent or incoherent. Even among writers who are not overtly radical in their approach, these "subversive aesthetic strategies" are present, resisting the normativity and appropriation of Eurocentric notions of style, literariness, translatability, and certainly representation.

For these reasons, these texts are ripe for intersectional reading.[48] At its best, this kind of reading strategy can move us beyond "the hermeneutics of suspicion," beyond the demands of representational knowledge-making.[49] Instead of the violent suppression of incoherence that normative hermeneutic approaches rely on, intersectional reading asks us to linger with that which is different and perhaps even unknowable. Moreover, this kind of ethical encounter allows us to become accountable for our own implication in the text's failure to cohere. Rather than interpreting or finding meaning in these texts, then, I am more interested in thinking through what these texts can make their readers feel, think, and do as they linger with incoherence and unknowability.

STRUCTURE OF THE BOOK

I begin in chapter 1 by tracing the history of the emergence of "Zainichi" as a term as well as a mode of ethnic identification and category for literary production. I examine the continuities and disjunctures among Zainichi literature's colonial origins, the elitist and exclusive genre of Zainichi Chōsenjin literature that arose in the postwar period, and the contemporary notion of a bracketed "Zainichi" literature as untethered to the ethnonational politics of the older generation's canonical writers. In the process of unpacking these literary taxonomies, I explore the varied historical conditions under which the writers encountered in this book wrote, particularly with respect to language politics.

Chapter 2 looks at one of the earliest examples of Korean literature under Japanese colonialism, Yi Kwangsu's *Mujŏng* (*Heartless*, 1917). *Mujŏng* is generally labeled as Korea's "first modern novel." The book starts here in order to consider the emergence of intersectional burdens of representation under the conditions of colonial modernity. This was the moment when Korean writers first began to discuss the need to assimilate the Korean language to the standards of modern phonocentric vernacular. For Yi, a leading figure in this discourse, this happens to be the same moment the queer figures inhabiting his texts are becoming taboo. Chapter 1 argues that the changing rules for who could be represented, and in what language, were internally inconsistent to the point of incoherence. The queerness of Yi's novel, then, arises not so much from its depiction of same-sex love as from its experimental prose, a product of its emergence within this contradictory alliance of colonial norms.

In chapter 3, I continue to interrogate the conflicting and mutually constitutive power structures present in colonial Korea through a reading of Kim Saryang's "Kusa fukashi" ("Deep in the Grass," 1940). This text, which depicts an almost ethnographic encounter between a colonial elite and the more profoundly marginalized subjects of the Korean hinterlands, is read in conversation with Kim's critical outlook on translation and World Literature. Kim's contributions to the discourse on World Literature in the 1930s and 1940s, much like the contemporary resurgence of World Literature models, raise ethical questions around appropriation and misrecognition in the process of translation and communication. "Kusa fukashi," in turn, shows that these ethical problems exist even on an intralingual and monoethnic playing field.

Kim Sŏkpŏm, the focus of chapter 4, has written for decades about the representational impossibilities faced by postcolonial Korean writers in Japan, who can neither maintain a distance from the Japanese language nor take ownership of it. He calls this conundrum "the spellbinding of language" (*kotoba no jubaku*). I examine Kim's specific solutions to this critical impasse in his works of fiction, particularly *Karasu no shi* (*Death of a Crow*, 1957) and *Mandogi yūrei kitan* (*The Curious Tale of Mandogi's Ghost*, 1970), demonstrating that Kim is able to destabilize the Japanese language of his novels by creating dissonance and incoherence between the main text and the fragments of Korean language embedded within.

In chapter 5, I discuss Kin Kakuei's *Kogoeru kuchi* (*Frozen Mouth*, 1970), narrated by a person who stutters. Kin was among the first prominent Zainichi authors to criticize the ethnocentrism of Zainichi politics as itself participating in intersectional incoherence, precluding or assimilating representations of disability. This chapter explores the politics of speaking as they act on the novel's narrator by delineating not only how his speech disability restricts him from articulating his ethnic identity, but also, conversely, how his ethnic identity precludes him from articulating a disabled identity. Kin's stuttering narrator disrupts the flow of meaning from the visual medium of text to the reader's sonic imagination, creating an incoherent alternative to speech in which alternative modes of identification and (non)representation can be forged.

If the writers covered in the chapters above experiment with writing incoherently rather than with the goal of being understood, Yi Yangji puts the practice front and center in *Yuhi* (1988), the subject of chapter 6. The novella turns on the uncanny gap it creates between its narrating character, "Onni," a Korean woman with no Japanese ability, and the narrative itself, written almost entirely in Japanese. This leads to nonsensical moments in the text, such as the utterance, in Japanese, of the words "I cannot speak a word of Japanese." By presenting the text in pseudo-translation, Yi shifts the focus from language as conduit for communication or meaning to the inevitable aporias therein. Yi also explores the impacts of spoken and written language on the body, suggesting that the non-meaning sounds where languages overlap create a space for co-presence if not empathy.

Chapter 7 takes up the current state of Zainichi literature and the sense of crisis confronting its future. As mentioned above, contemporaneously with the release of the eighteen-volume *"Zainichi" bungaku zenshū*, discussions began to emerge as to whether the "end" of Zainichi literature was nigh. Compounding this anxiety was the refusal of high-profile writers such as Kaneshiro Kazuki and Yū Miri to have their work included. Yū's refusal, as well as her rejection of the Zainichi label, could perhaps be labeled "post-Zainichi," a play on the discourse of a "post-racial" United States—and with no less irony, given the emboldened nativist sentiments and hate speech campaigns targeted specifically at Zainichi Koreans in contemporary Japan. I conclude by arguing that Yū's use of silence, incoherence, and the abject body in *Hachigatsu no hate* (*The End of August*, 2004) offers a vision of Zainichi difference capable of articulating an unassimilated future.

In the epilogue, I consider Zainichi literature as a global, deterritorialized entity—both less coherent, and more visible, than ever before in its history. Min Jin Lee's *Pachinko* (2017), translated into dozens of languages and adapted for streaming television, has done more than any text to bring the Zainichi community into the limelight. At the same time, it also embodies the central problem this book confronts: that to represent this community—perhaps especially to a global audience from nowhere in particular—is inevitably to misrepresent it. Through a reading of *Pachinko*, I tease out how the story it tells, and the story of the Zainichi community more broadly, is profoundly intertwined with American as well as Japanese imperialism. It is only through a situated, involved, and accountable mode of reading that we can begin to see their stories as our own, even if we can never quite *know* their stories.

1

The Untimeliness of "Zainichi"

Literary History and the Construction of Coherence

I would like to begin with the very origins of Zainichi literature. This is the place to start, not for the purpose of narrating Zainichi literary history from beginning to end, but because the contested historical boundaries of Zainichi literature are emblematic of the ways that literary histories and taxonomies create the very categories they purport to represent.

In the first place, it should be noted that I apply the term *Zainichi literature* anachronistically. In subsequent chapters, I discuss colonial writers such as Yi Kwangsu and Kim Saryang under the rubric of Zainichi literature, projecting a certain continuity onto a period of the past that predates even the coining and circulation of the term *Zainichi* in reference to Koreans in Japan. The context in which these figures wrote is radically different from that of the postwar writers treated in this book. However, it should also be noted that *Zainichi literature*, as a translation of *"Zainichi" bungaku*, the bracketed term most commonly used in Japanese-language discourse today, is also anachronistic when applied to writers like Kim Sŏkpŏm and Kin Kakuei, who debuted in the 1950s and 1960s respectively. At the time their writing was usually categorized as *Zainichi Chōsenjin bungaku*, with no quotation marks, and specifying *Chōsenjin*, a subset of those who identify as Zainichi today. Among the writers treated in this book, only Yū Miri's career overlaps with the widespread usage of the more flexible and loosely defined *"Zainichi" bungaku*, and Yū is better known for her deeply ambivalent stance toward the Zainichi framework than her unproblematic inclusion within it.

Why, then, use the term *Zainichi* at all? I certainly do not wish to imply any sort of consistency across the work and careers of Yi Kwangsu, Yū Miri, and everyone in between. Nor is my purpose here to argue that these writers share a totalizing characteristic or experience in which a coherent Zainichi (or even Korean) identity could be grounded. This notion is to be thoroughly dismantled. I do not mean to delineate a literary genealogy or history, much less a new set of boundaries through which to distinguish what is Zainichi and what is not. Rather, I use *Zainichi* as an ingress into the provisional and contested nature of the literary categories that emerged and faded across the times and spaces explored in this book. If there is anything consistent throughout this history, it is the inconsistency of the terms *du jour*. The bracketed "*Zainichi*," with its visible acknowledgment that the word does not refer to anything in an ontologically stable sense, captures this as well as any term could.

In this chapter, I trace the history of how the literary production of Koreans in Japan has been categorized, paying specific attention to how the terms for such categories have implied or imposed a coherence that never existed. Unraveling these terms reveals the violence of the representational logic of literary taxonomy, particularly at the intersection of empires. Throughout this history, the language denoting "Zainichi" literature and its antecedents has been overdetermined by intersecting imperial language politics. It has borne the indelible traces of the Japanese empire and its postwar reverberations, as well as the global hegemony of the English language and, in the Cold War context, the United States. Intersectional analysis is necessary to tease out the mutually constitutive and contradictory imperial demands to which these categories were forged as a response. Yet at the same time, the categories themselves enact a similar form of violence, flattening out internal difference and excising the voices within that threaten their ostensible coherence. I will unpack the incoherence of Zainichi literature along three lines: its contested colonial origins, the "thirty-eighth parallel in Japan" that fissures the genre ideologically, and the suppressed intersectional difference that has created a semblance of coherence despite these fundamental divides.

ETHNIC, NATIONAL, REGIONAL: ZAINICHI LITERARY TAXONOMY AND COLONIAL MODERNITY

Perhaps the most overtly policed set of boundaries defining Zainichi literature are historical. Even the seemingly simple question of when Zainichi literature begins is highly contested.[1] Just as the Anglophone academic division of labor between Japanese and Korean studies placed Zainichi literature traditionally within the purview of Japanese (language) literature, there is a stark divide between prewar (*kindai*, modern) and postwar (*gendai*, contemporary) literary studies in Japanese academia that makes 1945 a sort of default starting point for Zainichi literature. Still, the elision of continuities between pre-1945 imperial Japan and its post-1945 reconfiguration has been subject to many powerful critiques.[2] Korean colonial subjects of the Japanese empire and the processes by which they became Zainichi in the postwar have often been at the center of such critiques.

It is curious, then, that established narratives of Zainichi literary history tend to go out of their way to exclude colonial-period Japanese-language writing by Koreans. Kawamura Minato, one of the main progenitors of the standard generational narrative of Zainichi literature, even admits to this arbitrary exclusion up to a point:

> If we were to define 'Zainichi Korean literature' [*Zainichi Chōsenjin bungaku*] in a broad sense, it would include all literary works by Koreans who are 'in Japan' [*zainichi*][3] (or Japanese nationals of Korean descent), without any restrictions on what language they use, the content of their works, or the names of the authors. In the broadest sense, even works penned by writers like Yi Kwangsu and Yun Tongju while they lived temporarily in Japan would be Zainichi Korean literature. . . . However, the term Zainichi Korean literature, as it is used, has a much more limited connotation.[4]

Kawamura goes on to explain that the genre as defined in the narrower sense only includes those who write Japanese-language texts under a name that is easily parsed as Korean, about Zainichi Korean characters who confront the problems of Zainichi Korean society.[5] As John Lie has described these arbitrary exclusions, "Narrow is the gate to Zainichi-ness."[6]

By this reasoning, Kawamura includes in his history of Zainichi literature two "forerunners" (*kōshi*) of the genre, Kim Saryang and Chang Hyŏkju, who were active in the Japanese metropolitan literary establishment (*bundan*) in the final years of the colonial period. However, he only discusses them in order to establish that they are properly categorized outside Zainichi Korean literature. Kim, who eventually returned to Korea and pursued a Korean-language writing career in the postwar period, is better thought of as a writer of "ethnic literature" (*minzoku bungaku*), whereas Chang, who is known for collaborating with the empire and eventually naturalizing as a Japanese citizen under the name Noguchi Minoru, is an exemplar of "colonial literature" (*shokuminchi bungaku*).[7] Thus, even if these two writers meet the long list of requirements to have their works considered Zainichi Korean literature, they are nevertheless excluded. The basis for this excision seems to be their belonging to other literary categories, which are implicitly presumed to be mutually exclusive.

A sympathetic reading of the laborious process by which Kawamura and other proponents of a narrowly-defined Zainichi literature achieve a coherent object of study via exclusion is that without this winnowing, the category ceases to mean anything in particular.[8] However, as Song Hyewŏn shows in her much more expansive literary history of the Zainichi community, the gatekeeping through which the canon of Zainichi Korean literature was defined had a powerful influence on whose texts were read, circulated, and preserved.[9] In this way, Zainichi literary history demands a reorientation: away from what the category is, and toward what the category does.

To better understand this impetus to exclude or at least marginalize colonial writers within the history of Zainichi literature, I begin by comparing the historical conditions and literary rubrics under which Yi Kwangsu and Kim Saryang wrote fiction. Both made their careers in the period of Japan's colonial rule over the Korean peninsula, 1910–45, when all of Korea was officially and literally *zainichi*: "in Japan." Both were bilingual, having studied and lived in Japan proper (*naichi*), and published in both Korean and Japanese, sometimes—but not always—about the experience of being Korean and living in Japan. Both writers were deeply concerned with language throughout their careers, and contributed to public dialogues on the place of Korean language and literature within the Japanese empire and the world at large.

Again, this is not to suggest that the two writers are "the same," nor even that the boundaries of Zainichi literature should be redrawn to be inclusive of more colonial Korean writers. Instead, I wish to explore the process by which Kim is situated comfortably, if somewhat liminally, within the category of Zainichi literature, whereas it is beyond the pale to consider Yi within that frame. In Kawamura's terms, Kim is a "forerunner," while Yi is listed as a ridiculous example of the kind of writer who would be included if the definition of Zainichi literature were expanded *ad absurdum*. The politics of this distinction, as well as its material consequences, reveal themselves through a closer examination of the ways the careers of Kim and Yi overlap and depart from each other. Thinking through the ways these writers are included or excluded from Zainichi literature and other literary rubrics illustrates the intersections and entanglements of multiple imperial hegemonies that created the conditions under which not only Zainichi, but also Korean and Japanese literatures, were formed.

As is well known, in the wake of its forced opening to the West in the nineteenth century through the signing of unequal treaties with the United States and other empires staking claims in East Asia, Japan embarked on a rapid and transformative process of modernization on Western terms. This included radical reforms of the Japanese language in order to conform to Western standards of vernacular literature. Japan's speedy industrialization and militarization, initiated as a defense against European and American imperialisms, soon enabled it to compete in the race to colonize its Asian neighbors. And in fact, its program of expansionist colonialism was pursued in part as proof of its advanced civilization and equality with the West, as protection against the colonization that Japan had so recently feared.

Perhaps the most tangible sign of Japan's "catching up" to the West was its defeat of a Western power in the Russo-Japanese war (1904–05), which resulted in the protectorate status of Japan over Korea. This disrupted Korea's own accelerated process of becoming a modern nation-state and led in turn to formal colonization in 1910. The years around the turn of the twentieth century on the Korean peninsula, from the establishment of the Great Korean Empire (Taehan Cheguk) in 1897, to the Protectorate Treaty in 1905, to annexation in 1910, were a tumultuous period of ever-changing relationships and interactions with empires both Asian and Euro-American. As with other areas colonized during this period,

Korea's colonization happened under the global imposition of Western capitalism, which functioned rhetorically in part by organizing the world into a hierarchy of more and less civilized. However, by distancing themselves from an Eastern cultural tradition centered on China in order to enact reforms aimed at "civilization and enlightenment," early Korean nationalist thinkers (including Yi Kwangsu) ended up playing into the hands of Japanese imperialists, who used these efforts to demonstrate Korea's relative lack of civilization and need for protectorate status.[10] Similarly, in lending their support to a kind of self-orientalizing pan-Asian discourse, these same thinkers had their anti-Western ideas co-opted by the Japanese empire.[11] This made it almost impossible to effectively articulate resistance to both imperialisms at once. As a result, the forging of a colonial-modern Korean national identity was inextricably bound up with the cooperation and competition of Eastern and Western imperialisms. This is one reason to view colonial and postcolonial Korea as a site of intersecting imperialisms. That is, a single-empire framework is inadequate for articulating the structure of Korean oppression.

Nowhere was this more evident than in debates on modern vernacular language and literature. Even beyond Korea, the early history of modern literature in East Asia is in many ways tantamount to the story of how what we now call literature came to be called literature in the asymmetrical process of translation. More specifically, it is the story of the emergence of literature as a conceptual framework, simultaneously with the production and definition of the terms *bungaku* (Japanese) and *munhak* (Korean). Intellectuals and literary figures on both sides of the straits raised the question of how to conform a largely sinographic writing tradition with Western norms of vernacular (national) language. At the same time, the violent process of creating sinographic "equivalents" for Western terms for modern concepts was ongoing across East Asia.[12] As with the territorial occupation and eventual annexation of the peninsula, it is impossible to tell the story of the colonization of the Korean language and literature without reference to a complex triangulation between Western and Japanese imperialisms, by turns oppositional and mutually reinforcing.

Here the case of Yi Kwangsu is instructive. Yi is broadly considered the single most important pioneer of modern Korean literature and the vernacular style in which it is written to this day. As with his Japanese contemporaries, Yi's primary motivating factor in developing a modern literary style was to improve the cultural and emotional refinement of the people, thereby strengthening the nation. In 1916, Yi laid out his thoughts on literature in an essay titled "Munhak iran hao" ("What is Literature?"), published in *Maeil sinbo*, the Japanese Governor-General's Korean-language daily. The essay discusses *munhak* in general, which Yi defines explicitly as a translation of the English term "Literature" (which appears in roman characters in the essay), but focuses specifically on *Chosŏn munhak* (Korean literature), which he defines as "literary works written by Korean writers in the Korean script."[13] Due to the strictness of this definition, and the fact that the vast majority of "literary works written by Korean writers" prior to this period were produced in literary Chinese, Yi makes the provocative claim that Korean literature "has no past, only a future."[14]

Though largely focused on the dichotomy between what he viewed as the backward Chinese literary tradition that had heavily influenced Korean literature of the past (to the extent that it ever existed) and the modern European literature that it should emulate in the future, the essay, simply by virtue of the colonial context and government organ in which it was published, cannot completely escape the crucial third term of Japan. The byline for the essay's installments even notes that Yi is writing "from Tokyo" (*Tonggyŏng esŏ*), highlighting the fact that the author, if not the piece itself, is literally *zainichi*.

In one of the few moments in which Yi mentions Japan at all, it is to emphasize his central point that literature, and the concomitant development of vernacular language, is above all a national project. He writes:

> Ever since Yamada Bimyō launched the unification of the spoken and written language (*genbun itchi*) movement about three decades ago, Japan has been using vernacular writing in literature, science, politics, essays, etc. This kind of development greatly influences a nation's culture. Therefore, new literature must be written in the purely contemporary everyday vernacular, which can be understood and used by anyone.[15]

I take up the issue of vernacular style in greater depth in chapter 2, but the key point to recognize here is that despite writing in Japan, from a moment of Japanese colonization, in a Japanese imperial publication, and in a vernacular style patterned after the very *genbun itchi* blend of sinographs and native phonetic script that he mentions here (or perhaps because of these very factors), Yi frames the Japanese case as a model to be emulated in the quest to become more Western and less Eastern, rather than a hegemonic power to be resisted in the quest to become more Korean and less Japanese.[16]

From its inception, then, Korean literature (*Chosŏn munhak*) could only come into being in a language that was heavily influenced by Chinese, Japanese, and European languages (via Japanese). It was formed both at and by the intersection of empires. And it consequently struggled to articulate its position outside the binary terms of East and West, Japanese colonizer and Korean colonized, despite the imbrication of all of the above.

Eventually, however, the national literature as civilizing mechanism that Yi called *Chosŏn munhak* and conceptualized as the literature of the Korean ethnonation (*minjok*) would come to refer to the literature of the state (*kukka*), which is to say the Japanese empire. Soon after Yi penned "Munhak iran hao" and serialized his first full-length novel (*Mujŏng*, 1917), thousands of Koreans took to the streets on March 1, 1919, demonstrating against Japanese colonial rule. The March First Movement, as it is known, resulted in thousands of casualties as Japanese forces violently repressed the demonstrations. The years that followed, however, saw a shift from "military rule" to the period of so-called "cultural rule," in which Japanese colonial policy shifted from a strategy of governing through brute force to cultural assimilation. A central pillar of the Japanese assimilation program was education reform, particularly a greater push toward Japanese language use.[17] In the 1930s, as the Japanese empire expanded rapidly into the Asian continent and the South Pacific and war efforts intensified, the assimilation of Korean subjects into Japanese imperial ideology took on greater urgency. This resulted in yet another change in strategy, from *dōka* (assimilation) to *kōminka* (imperial subjectification). Under this regime the burden was shifted: rather than Japan teaching Koreans how to be properly civilized Japanese citizens, Koreans themselves were now tasked with making the effort to become loyal Japanese subjects.[18]

War mobilization and imperialization would eventually lead to what Korean literary histories designate "the dark period" (*amhŭkki*). These years, corresponding to the early 1940s, were characterized by oppressive censorship, the shuttering of publication venues (including nearly all Korean-language magazines and newspapers), greater pressure to use the Japanese language in both public and private life, and few opportunities to write literature other than pro-war propaganda. However, this same period saw a "Korea boom" in mainland Japan, which included the entry of Korean writers into the Japanese-language literary mainstream.[19] In many ways, imperialization efforts simultaneously erased and maintained ethnic difference between mainland Japanese and colonial subjects. That is, full and equal status as Japanese citizens—perhaps even fully-formed "Japaneseness"—was extended to colonial subjects at the official level as part of an effort to reduce ethnic tensions and strengthen the empire as a whole at a time of expansionist war, though in practice discrimination continued and ethnic difference had to be maintained in order to continue justifying Japanese colonial domination of the peninsula and other occupied areas.[20]

Under these conditions, *Chosŏn munhak* (Korean literature) did not cease to exist so much as it was refigured as a regional literature (*chihō bungaku*), comparable to that of Kyushu, Okinawa, Hokkaido, and other peripheral areas of the empire. The ideological project of building the Greater East Asia Co-Prosperity Sphere in the late 1930s and early 1940s was a concrete manifestation of the utopian pan-Asianism put forth by Japanese imperialist intellectuals as a means of "overcoming" Western modernity. Within this framework, regional literatures such as *Chōsen bungaku* (*Chosŏn munhak*) maintained their particularity, but only within the generality of Japanese imperial-national literature, or *kokumin bungaku*.[21] Once again, Korean literary identity was constituted by the intersection of Japanese and Western imperialisms. Resistance to one was easily co-opted by the other.

For this brief historical moment near the end of the colonial period, the distinction between the two literatures now taxonomized as Zainichi literature and modern Korean literature essentially collapsed. Japanese-language Korean writers like Kim Saryang and Chang Hyŏkju, the two most successful in the Japanese bundan (elite literary sphere), explicitly situated themselves within the category of Korean literature pioneered by Yi Kwangsu and others who would later be canonized in modern Korean literary history. These same writers, who have been viewed ambivalently within Korean literary history due to perceived or actual pro-Japanese collaboration, were already or would soon be writing in Japanese as well. Little distinction could be made between the two groups. Moreover, the language used to distinguish between Japanese and Korean—"naichi" versus "Chōsenjin"—demonstrates the anachronism of projecting the distinction between "Japanese" and "Korean" into the past. At this particular moment, all of these writers and thinkers were Japanese, or at least literally *zainichi* (in Japan). In fact, it was only through a radical reconfiguration of the relationships among language, culture, ethnicity, and nationality in postwar Japan and the Koreas that *Zainichi* could emerge as a relevant category at all.

"THIRD NATIONALS": FORMER COLONIAL SUBJECTS AND THE INTERSECTIONAL COLD WAR

The epistemological upheavals brought about in the wake of 1945 gave rise to new categories and terms for (now former) colonial subjects, including Zainichi Koreans. The tension surrounding these terms was and is emblematic of many of the larger social and political tensions underlying this historical shift. Namely, the question of how to deal with the presence of former colonial subjects in Japan—a situation that had been a matter of course in the previous decades—was now suddenly viewed as a problem by both Japanese and occupation authorities. In this way, the assumption that Koreans do not belong in Japan (embedded in the term *Zainichi*) was enabled by a radical shift from a multicultural empire to ostensibly homogenous monoethnic (and, no less importantly, monolingual) nation-states in Japan and the Koreas in the postwar. This shift necessitated an equally radical forgetting of the "intimacies" and "terms" of the past.[22]

These ruptures, like those accompanying Korea's transition into modernity, occurred at the intersection of empires. Furthermore, this intersection is paradoxically reflected and elided by the terms, such as *Zainichi*, that emerged in this period. It is impossible to articulate the newfound need for the discursive category of Zainichi without reference to the simultaneously antagonistic and mutually reinforcing quality of US and Japanese imperialisms. More specifically, the years immediately following the unconditional Japanese surrender in 1945, when *Zainichi* first came into use, were characterized by rupture and reordering across the region, with the collapse of the Japanese empire on the one hand, and the rise of Cold War (neo-)imperialism on the other. Yet as the postwar experience of Koreans in Japan attests, many of the ethnic, cultural, and linguistic hierarchies and hybridities that emerged in the colonial period endured in the subsequent decades. Much of this paradoxical rupture within continuity was a direct result of decolonization on the peninsula and deimperialization in the Japanese archipelago occurring under military occupation by Allied forces. Because the original strategic goals of these occupations were so quickly subsumed within broader Cold War currents, many of the existing political tensions in the region stemming from the Japanese empire were deliberately forgotten at the official levels, leaving the cultural realm to piece together the haunting, fragmented narratives of empire and war.[23]

In the same way, this intersectional structure created broader obstacles to representing Korea itself, whether Zainichi or otherwise, largely because Korea as such ceased to exist. The two divided states that would come to correspond with Chōsen and Kankoku (Chosŏn and Hanguk in Korean) were established under occupations that rested on the foundations of the ruined Japanese empire. Thus, the term *Zainichi* and its underlying logic of ethnic homogeneity came into use precisely at the moment it could no longer refer to a unified ethnic homeland. Korea could not be named without naming its own splintering, its lack of internal coherence. Here again, the very language used to describe Koreans in Japan bears the indelible mark of the intersectional imperial conditions under which it was produced.

This language serves as an ever-present reminder of the necessarily incomplete processes of deimperialization and decolonization in Japan and Korea respectively as a result of Cold War military occupation. Less than two weeks after Japan's unconditional surrender on August 15, 1945, US forces began arriving on mainland Japan to begin the occupation.[24] Soon after, on September 8, 1945, US forces landed at Incheon to occupy the Korean peninsula below the 38th parallel. Notably, both of these spaces—and many more across the Asia-Pacific region—fell under the umbrella of the Allied occupation of Japan, including its colonial territories. The empire was parceled out for occupation, largely by US and Soviet forces, but in most cases, the colonies were not returned immediately to precolonial sovereignty. Some never would be.[25] The Korean peninsula is arguably in this latter group, as the territory was returned to Korean sovereignty only in the form of two competing states on either side of the dividing line established by the occupation itself (and, of course, following a devastating civil war).

This is perhaps the most conspicuous, but far from the only example of how the politics of the nascent Cold War dictated the direction of the occupation of Japan as well as its former colonies. In *naichi* Japan, the so-called "Reverse Course" of 1947 saw the priority of the occupation shift from war accountability and reform to political stability and anti-communism. Koreans who remained in Japan proper after the war (over two million at the time of the surrender, and approximately six hundred thousand at the formal conclusion of the occupation) were perceived to have leftist sympathies, and were subject to increasingly repressive policies as a result. Perhaps the most consequential such policy was the 1947 Alien Registration Law, which required non-Japanese nationals residing in Japan to register and specifically included former colonial subjects in this category. Thus, long-term Korean residents of Japan proper, who were still technically citizens of Japan, faced pressure to "repatriate" to the peninsula despite significant obstacles to doing so.[26]

One problematic term that emerged in this period, in the context of the occupation of Japan, was *daisangokujin* or "third national." Today this word is used derogatorily, much like *Zainichi* itself. Likely coined by Japanese translators for occupation authorities, the term was used to refer to Koreans and other formerly colonized people who remained in Japan in order to specify that they were non-Japanese. Presumably, the *san* or "third" in the term alludes to the fact that its referents were also non-American, with the United States and Japan constituting the two nations from which a third must be distinguished. The term's existence is indicative of the fact that the position of former colonial subjects of the Japanese empire could not be articulated except in reference to the intersection of Japanese and Western hegemonies. They were not Japanese, and not American, and their situation demanded that they grapple with both of these realities simultaneously.

Moreover, the emergence of this category in the postwar is evidence of the Japanese empire's ultimate failure to make good on its promise (or threat) that Koreans and other colonized subjects could become Japanese. The ultimate betrayal of this promise would come in 1952, when the San Francisco Peace Treaty (signed between Japan and the United States) formally revoked Japanese citizenship from Koreans in Japan, and, for lack of a unified sovereign Korea in the midst of the Korean War, rendered them stateless. Yet perhaps more suggestively, the treatment of Koreans in Japan as an intractable problem indicates a buy-in on the part of American forces to the newly arising notion that Japan (and Korea) were ethnically homogenous, in both descriptive and prescriptive senses.[27]

This constitutes yet another moment, then, in which Western imperialism (now in the form of American Cold War neo-imperialism) both competed with and enabled Japanese imperialism, leading to intersectional obstacles to representation. Under US occupation, Japanese intellectuals and cultural figures quickly came to see themselves as part of the global "colonized," even using the plight of Koreans and other subjects formerly colonized by the Japanese empire as a framework for understanding their new position.[28] This mutual experience of colonialism, broadly conceived, opened up pathways to solidarity between Japan and the areas formerly under its imperial control—at least as these Japanese thinkers saw it.[29] However, it was their broad conception of colonialism, unable to account for important historical differences between Japan and Korea, that created an impossible situation for Koreans within these new coalitions. To call attention to the legacies of Japanese imperialism was to undermine this newfound solidarity (or at least to open oneself to such an accusation), leading to immense difficulty in balancing the need to mount critiques of both Japanese and US imperialisms at the same time. This double bind created the kind of representational impossibilities that are characteristic of intersectional incoherence.[30]

Essentially, Zainichi Koreans faced the same dilemma as their colonial-period counterparts. With their citizenship status alienating them from Japan and now the Koreas (Kankoku and Chōsen), and as *daisangokujin* doubly removed from the center of power represented by American occupation authorities, writing in Japanese became the only path to representation within the broader global power structure. At the same time, however, writing in Japanese constituted a reverberation of colonial language policy under the banner of assimilation and imperialization. Particularly with opportunities to publish in Korean still extant via the newspapers and magazines put out by North Korea-backed Zainichi political organizations, it was easy to see Japanese-language writing as a sort of erasure of Zainichi Korean language, culture, and identity. Zainichi writers struggle to navigate this conundrum to this day, though perhaps none more than the second generation, who found themselves both more accepted by the Japanese literary establishment and less connected to the Korean language than anyone previously in their position. It was under these conditions that *Zainichi Chōsenjin bungaku*—Zainichi Korean literature narrowly defined—truly emerged.

THE DECEPTIVE COHERENCE OF *ZAINICHI CHŌSENJIN BUNGAKU*

If there were ever a historical period for which, either in the moment itself or in present-day hindsight, the meaning of "Zainichi" was stable and representative of a concrete and internally unified politics, it is the late 1960s and early 1970s. At this time writers like Kim Sŏkpŏm, Ri Kaisei, and Kin Kakuei, an all-male trifecta recognized in the scholarship as the core of second-generation Zainichi literature, achieved career breakthroughs.[31] Ri Kaisei even received the first Akutagawa Prize to be awarded to a Zainichi writer, while the other two were nominated. It is also arguably at this moment that such a thing as a Zainichi writer began to exist. Isogai Jirō argues as much in his version of the generational narrative of Zainichi literary history: "It was in the mid-1960s that the term *Zainichi Chōsenjin bungaku* began to circulate, and that it began to take shape as a distinct genre within Japanese-language literature."[32]

However, the historical context in which this genre came to exist shows just how unrepresentative *Zainichi Chōsenjin bungaku* was of the broader Korean community in Japan.[33] This follows naturally from the way that the genre was narrowly defined through the exclusion of those who did not conform to its stringent ideological and patriarchal norms. But what is even more striking is that even within the second-generation trifecta, there is in reality very little consistency on which to found a coherent genre, much less a claim to a coherent community whose lived experience it could represent.

In fact, in many ways the emergence of the narrowly-conceived notion of Zainichi Korean literature coincides with a broader contestation surrounding the representation of Koreans in Japan in a more straightforwardly political sense. Representation was difficult to achieve within the framework of nation-states, but the Zainichi community did have political organizations to turn to for support, recognition, and advocacy. Nevertheless, these organizations could not escape the Cold War context and the logic of ethnic homogeneity under which they were conceived. The history of Zainichi organizational politics is also deeply intertwined with the language politics of Cold War Japan and the Koreas.

The first of these organizations was the League of Koreans in Japan,[34] which was instrumental in building a visible presence and ethnic consciousness for Koreans in Japan in the early years of occupied postwar Japan. One of their stated organizational goals was Korean-language education for Koreans remaining in Japan, specifically in preparation for eventual return to the Korean peninsula. They built over five hundred Korean schools between 1945 and 1947 before they were ultimately dissolved by occupation forces in 1949 due to their leftist leanings.[35] The disbanded League of Koreans was succeeded by the United Democratic Front for Koreans in Japan (known as Minsen or Minjŏn),[36] founded in 1951 and operating largely underground and in concert with the Japanese Communist Party. However, Korean leftists' relationship with the JCP in the postwar was reminiscent of the colonial period, with the JCP insisting on inter-ethnic and international unity with the goal of achieving revolution in Japan, thus downplaying problems of ethnic hierarchy and discrimination.[37]

Thus, when the North Korean state began making overtures to Koreans in Japan as a means of building support for North Korean–Japanese diplomatic relations, supporters of Minsen were reorganized under the banner of The General Association of Korean Residents in Japan (abbreviated Ch'ongryŏn or Sōren).[38] Unlike previous organizations, Ch'ongryŏn saw its members as overseas nationals of the North Korean state, and refrained from intervening in Japanese domestic politics, purposely cutting ties with the JCP. It did continue its predecessors' preoccupation with the repatriation of Koreans in Japan, however, hence its central role in the mass repatriation of over ninety thousand Koreans to North Korea between 1959 and 1984.[39] Beyond the repatriation project, Ch'ongryŏn was the dominant presence in Zainichi organizational politics in the early postwar decades. It provided crucial financing and K-16 education for Koreans who often faced discrimination at Japanese banks and schools, though this ironically excluded poorer Zainichi Koreans.[40] It was only the middle class who could afford to avoid assimilating into Japanese society through private Korean-language schooling. Also of note, Ch'ongryŏn provided venues for Korean-language publication through newspapers and magazines.

Meanwhile, the South Korean–aligned equivalent of these organizations, The Republic of Korea Residents Union in Japan (Mindan),[41] had a much less turbulent history due to its non-communist (even anti-communist) political orientation. Mindan was established in 1948 and still exists in more or less the same form today, albeit with different goals and broader support. Because the overwhelming majority of Zainichi Koreans were on the political left and supported North Korea, Mindan failed to garner much support from the community in the early postwar years.[42] Compared to Ch'ongryŏn, which had the full backing of the North Korean state, Mindan received little support or even attention from the South Korean government. Its relevance grew, however, with the normalization of Japanese–South Korean relations, which brought increased demand for travel and cultural exchange between Japan and South Korea.

The normalization talks of the early 1960s, though they eventually brought about greater rights and representation for Zainichi Koreans, were in many ways indicative of the barriers to representation erected by Cold War politics, partially due to the factionalism they generated within and between the Zainichi organizations. Notably, normalization was brokered by the United States in order to enable further cooperation between its two major allies in the region, particularly as the Vietnam War was ramping up. One of the sticking points that engendered mass popular resistance to the treaty in Korea was the perception of favoritism in how the two countries were expected to participate in the American war effort in Vietnam: South Korea by sending troops (the second-most of any foreign power behind the United States), and Japan by fulfilling lucrative military contracts. South Korean critics of the agreement even likened it to Western "connivance" in enabling Japan to establish a protectorate over Korea in the lead-up to colonization, pointing once again to the by turns collaborative and competitive relationship between Japanese and Western imperialisms on the peninsula.[43] In Japan, on the other hand, resistance to the treaty stemmed from the aftermath of massive leftist resistance to the renewal of Anpo (the US-Japan Security Treaty) in 1960. The normalization treaty with South Korea was seen as a further entrenchment of American (neo-colonial) domination of Japan.

The position of the Zainichi community within this conflict was complicated. Opposition to the treaty was one of the few issues that brought Mindan and Ch'ongryŏn together. Although Mindan officially supported the treaty, adopting the position of the South Korean state, several of its grassroots sub-organizations participated in demonstrations against the treaty.[44] They objected on the grounds that the agreement did not go far enough to establish a permanent status in Japan for Zainichi Koreans and that South Korean negotiators had failed to give Koreans in Japan a seat at the table, in addition to broader concerns about the failure to resolve the ongoing issues of Japanese colonialism and American hegemony. Ch'ongryŏn, of course, opposed the treaty due to its recognition of the southern regime as the only legitimate sovereign entity on the peninsula. Thus, the Japan–South Korea normalization process underscored the lack of political representation for Koreans in Japan within a framework of nation-states arranged according to the Cold War world order. As the division of the peninsula was calcified by Cold War politics, the organizational divide between Mindan and Ch'ongryŏn became a proxy for the division to map onto the Zainichi community, what Ri Yuhwan has called "the thirty-eighth parallel in Japan."[45] Both organizations wished to claim the whole community, just as the states they supported wished to claim the entire peninsula. However, the reality was a splintered community, whose internal divisions were as malleable as its external boundaries.

Nevertheless, the 1965 normalization did clarify that the divided Korean peninsula was a more or less permanent state of affairs with which the Zainichi community would have to cope. The treaty expanded the rights of Koreans in Japan in the sense that it allowed them to adopt South Korean nationality, rendering them no longer stateless per se. Though sometimes referred to as citizenship, this new status did not allow Zainichi Koreans to vote or receive social benefits in South Korea, and as foreign nationals, they were barred from those privileges in Japan as well. And of course, what had perhaps been the closest status akin to citizenship for Zainichi Koreans, membership in Ch'ongryŏn, became a much more marginal position with the door to official diplomatic relations with North Korea now closed.[46]

This being the case, it is unsurprising that many younger Koreans in Japan began to conceive of Zainichi identity as a sense of hybridity or in-betweenness, and Zainichi politics as oriented toward the domestic affairs of Japan. Demographic shifts taking place in the late 1960s and early 1970s demonstrate the popularity of these ideas among the Zainichi community. Upon the establishment of Ch'ongryŏn in 1955, an estimated 75 percent of Koreans in Japan held *Chōsen-seki* status, the de facto stateless nationality that refers to the defunct unified Korean peninsula. By 1969, only a few years after normalization, those with *Kankoku-seki* status (South Korean nationality) had become the majority.[47] The latter were more likely to attend Japanese schools, use Japanese names, marry Japanese spouses, and eventually obtain Japanese citizenship, either for themselves or for their children, such that today the default lifestyle for most Koreans in Japan is to "pass" as Japanese.[48]

And yet, it was precisely at this moment that a retrenchment of anti-assimilation rhetoric and a kind of stateless ethnonationalism arose in place of the "ideology of return."[49] Without the prospect of Korean reunification on the horizon, Zainichi intellectuals saw allegiance to either of the divided states as problematic, and return—which had been until recently the *raison d'être* of Zainichi politics—impossible. Yet at the same time, assimilation and integration into Japanese society were also seen as beyond the pale. This set of dual impossibilities, in many ways self-imposed by Zainichi thought leaders themselves, is what John Lie has called "Zainichi ideology."[50]

One of the main proponents of Zainichi ideology is Kim Sŏkpŏm, the subject of chapter 4. In the dominant generational history of Zainichi literature, Kim is the quintessential "1.5-generation" figure: technically second-generation as he was born in Japan, but more closely aligned in age to the first generation. Kim's point of view on many political and cultural issues similarly straddles the generational divide. For instance, on the question of eventual return versus assimilation into Japanese society, Kim's position is perhaps the most stridently anti-assimilationist of any Zainichi intellectual alive today. He famously and publicly excoriated Ri Kaisei, his fellow Zainichi elder statesman and poster child for the second generation, for adopting South Korean citizenship in 1998. Kim argued that Ri's decision legitimized the division of the peninsula, and that Koreans in Japan were uniquely positioned to maintain a sense of identification with one Korea—hence his decision to maintain *Chōsen-seki* status to this day.[51] Though Ri's position is clearly the more popular among the Zainichi community, Kim's is dominant within the Zainichi bundan, once again demonstrating the gap between *Zainichi Chōsenjin bungaku* and the people it is read as representing.

Of course, the strident anti-Japanization—and in fact anti-citizenship—position of Zainichi ideology as Kim Sŏkpŏm espouses it has been subject to criticism, especially since the 1990s. Ri's rebuttal to Kim's open letter held that adopting South Korean citizenship granted him some measure of power in shaping peninsular politics, whereas *Chōsen-seki* status precluded any such participation.[52] In the context of Kim Dae-jung's Sunshine Policy, a softening of South Korea's stance toward the North in the late 1990s and early 2000s, this could even help move the peninsula toward actual reunification, as opposed to the strictly imaginary unified Korea enabled by the maintenance of the *Chōsen-seki* designation.

However, even as Ri and Kim disagreed publicly and vehemently on the question of *Kankoku-seki* versus *Chōsen-seki* status, both would have agreed that naturalization, the adoption of Japanese citizenship, was an unacceptable choice. In this way, both were out of sync with a growing proportion of the Zainichi community itself. By the mid-1990s, an estimated two hundred thousand Koreans had become Japanese citizens.[53] Even among those who did not choose to naturalize, the vast majority of the Zainichi community found it was perfectly acceptable, if not outright necessary as a defense against discrimination, to assimilate into Japanese society in various ways. Perhaps most consequentially, by the 1990s the younger generation overwhelmingly used Japanese names and spoke only Japanese.[54] This meant that for most members of the Zainichi community, "passing" became a sort of default mode of living in Japan. As such, it is not an uncommon story for Zainichi Koreans to have discovered their Korean identity in late adolescence or young adulthood.[55] It was only by declaring one's "real name" (*honmyō sengen*) that Koreans made their ethnicity known, and in doing so joined the ranks of the Zainichi.[56]

However, as Kang Yun'i has shown, the binary opposition of *honmyō* (real name, qua Korean name) and *tsūmei* (passing name, qua Japanese name) is more useful for delineating exclusionary boundaries between those Zainichi Koreans with a proper ethnic consciousness and those without (according to those with the power to define what that means) than it is for describing the lived experience of those navigating this terrain.[57] The emphasis placed on "real names" within the Zainichi community is derived from the history of *sōshi kaimei*, the Japanese colonial policy that required Koreans to adopt a surname and allowed them to change their given name. Irrespective of debates on how exactly *sōshi kaimei* functioned in practice, the policy is remembered as the theft of Korean names, pursued in tandem with the suppression of the Korean language writ large.[58] It would not be unfair to say that *sōshi kaimei* as the essence of colonial oppression has been tied so tightly to Zainichi identity itself that the use of "real names" has become the ultimate litmus test for commitment to ethnic causes. Given the reality that the use of Korean-sounding names exposes Zainichi Koreans to discrimination and possibly even bodily harm, "the positioning of 'real names' in binary opposition to *sōshi kaimei*, as the presumptively 'good' choice between real names and passing names, is an oppressive burden to place on those who confront these issues."[59] Especially when taking into account the growing number of Zainichi Koreans whose "real names" are not Korean-sounding,[60] the insistence on the use of typical three-character Korean names and other modes of resistance to assimilating into Japanese society is a key sign that the Zainichi bundan is out of sync with the community at large.

Perhaps not coincidentally, it was the philosopher Takeda Seiji, who self-consciously uses a Japanese-sounding pen name, whose groundbreaking *"Zainichi" to iu konkyo* (*The Foundations of "Zainichi,"* 1983) mounted the first widely-cited critique of Zainichi ideology.[61] The book is organized around the three major authors of second-generation Zainichi literature—Kim Sŏkpŏm, Ri Kaisei, and Kin Kakuei—further cementing their status as the central trifecta of the genre. However, unlike most Zainichi critics to this point, Takeda clearly prefers Kin Kakuei (who also insisted on the Japanese reading of the characters in his name) to Kim and Ri. Takeda sees in Kin a pioneer of a different kind of thinking about what it means to be Zainichi, rooted not in the ethnic essentialism and diasporic nationalism of Kim and Ri, but rather in the experience of dislocation and hybridity embodied by the not-quite-Japanese yet not-quite-Korean quality of the name "Kin Kakuei" itself. Kin's position vis-à-vis the Zainichi bundan is therefore undisputed, if somewhat marginal or transitional.[62]

But perhaps the primary way in which Kin's career represents a sort of turning point in Zainichi literature and criticism is in the introduction of intersectional concerns beyond ethnicity alone into his work—and, importantly, the criticism this garnered. For Kin these concerns took the form of living with and writing about a speech disability, and having a real impairment co-opted as metaphor for ethnic oppression. Zainichi critics did not simply ignore or downplay the aspect of disability in Kin's writing in favor of ethnic concerns, but in fact used his attention to disability as evidence of his failure to be properly engaged with ethnic issues.

For Kin's detractors, ethnic consciousness could only be demonstrated through the active elision of intersectional concerns. This pattern continued, arguably more conspicuously, in the Zainichi bundan's response to the rise of women to canonical status. In this way, Kin's career heralded the bundan's increasingly fraught relationship with the younger generation of Zainichi writers, until eventually it was the bundan's relevance that decreased, and the closely-guarded boundaries of *Zainichi Chōsenjin bungaku* that began to fray.

The ways the Zainichi literary establishment has been forced to accommodate writers like Yi Yangji and Yū Miri (the subjects of chapters 6 and 7 respectively) shows how issues of intersectionality are intimately linked to questions of literary taxonomy. It was only through the suppression of internal difference that *Zainichi Chōsenjin bungaku* could emerge as a coherent category in the first place. Perhaps it would not be going too far to say that intersectional difference is suppressed in the process of creating any such coherence. But what cannot be overlooked here is that the erasure of internal difference is a particularly fraught exercise for a community that cannot even be named without referring to its own intractable division—the internal thirty-eighth parallel. As shown above, even the three authors discussed as undisputedly Zainichi within the standard generational literary history of the genre could hardly be further apart in terms of their attitudes toward Zainichi identity and its outlook toward the (imagined) homeland. And this does not even begin to unpack the massive corpus of popular literature, writing by Zainichi women, and other writers and texts that were excluded from Zainichi literature proper in order to create the sense of stability and coherence on which the standard history relies.[63]

It is the forced reckoning in recent years with these previously suppressed voices, I would argue, that has ushered in the "brackets era," by which I mean the period in which "Zainichi" (「在日」) is written almost exclusively in quotation marks—brackets in Japanese orthography. Once again, the change in the way the genre or community is named reflects a broader shift, in this case a turn from ethnic nationalism toward a more flexible definition of what Zainichi literature is and what it is for. The question for the past few decades has been whether Zainichi literature can continue to exist as such without being exclusive in the manner of Zainichi ideology.

THE BRACKETS ERA: ZAINICHI AS FLOATING SIGNIFIER

As noted at the outset of this book, there are perils to "Zainichi," the bracketed and abbreviated mode of naming the Korean community in Japan, which might more properly be called *Zainichi Chōsen-Kankokujin*. Yet as I have already suggested, and as the complex history of terminology and language politics enumerated above indicates, the latter term—presented almost exclusively *without* brackets—suggests a reified subject position that has never existed. Indeed, in explanations and caveats preceding the use of the bracketed moniker in Japanese, scholars typically point to the need to acknowledge the fluidity and constructed nature of the category of "Zainichi" as the motivation for presenting the term in this tentative fashion.[64]

This caution around the use of the term "Zainichi" is certainly in part a response to the increased volume of voices pointing to problems with the term itself, even beyond its potentially pejorative usage. At the same time, various alternatives proposed by these voices and others come with their own set of problems and inaccuracies. *"Zainichi" Korian* has become a standard way of referring to the community of Koreans in Japan without privileging one side of the divided peninsula or the other, though it brings with it the problems of the English-language terminology from which it is derived. That is, if the advantage of *Korian* over *Kankoku-Chōsenjin* is its circumvention of the division, then the disadvantage lies in that same circumvention. The "thirty-eighth parallel in Japan" does not disappear simply because it is not named. *Korian* is also a concession to English-language hegemony. The notion that the anglophonic way of naming Korea is somehow neutral belies the long history of Eurocentric language politics outlined above.

Another alternative, proposed by the popular Zainichi writer Kaneshiro Kazuki, is "Korian-Japanīzu," which drops the "Zainichi" entirely.[65] Kaneshiro's position is that Zainichi, even outside its pejorative usage, implies non-belonging in Japan. This is because the word's literal meaning implies that a Korean presence in Japan is somehow anomalous, else *zainichi* is merely redundant. There are no "zainichi Nihonjin" (在日日本人, Japanese in Japan). There are no "zaikan Kankokujin" (在韓韓国人) or "zaisen Chōsenjin" (在鮮朝鮮人). In this way, the very word Zainichi implies a logic of ethnic homogeneity within the Japanese state (as well as the Koreas), a conflation of ethnic identity with nationality or even citizenship.[66] "Korian-Japanīzu" provides the language for imagining a multiethnic Japan, and a population of Koreans within it who are there to stay, as opposed to merely displaced and destined for return to Korea where they belong. In this way, Kaneshiro's proposed language represents a radical break from the standard thinking implied by most of the terminology applied to the Zainichi community. Of course, as with *Zainichi Korian, Korian-Japanīzu* is borrowed from anglophonic discourse, in this case specifically from a model of American hyphenated multiculturalism, bringing with it all the problems that have been thoroughly critiqued in the American context.

It should also be noted that Kaneshiro himself has expressed dissatisfaction with the term, on the grounds that it still pigeonholes him and his writing into a particular rather than universal category. He has echoed the sentiments of so many other minor, postcolonial, and marginalized writers before him in expressing his desire to be read primarily as "human" rather than through a lens based on any subcategory.[67] In the end, rather than an objection to the term *Zainichi* in particular, it is this desire to break free of any taxonomical literary framework that Kaneshiro shares with other major writers of his generation, the so-called "third generation" or "new generation." As mentioned previously, both he and Yū Miri, discussed in chapter 7, drew the ire of their elders within the Zainichi bundan by declining to have their work included in the *"Zainichi" bungaku zenshū* anthology.[68]

Clearly, at least according to standard narratives of Zainichi literary history, this new generation, with its embrace of "in-between," "both-and," and "neither-nor" identities, and its attention to social concerns outside ethnicity, is more aligned with Kin Kakuei than with Kim Sŏkpŏm and the mainstream of Zainichi ideology. Kin, while less willing to reject Zainichi identity outright, wrote profusely about the generally human and the desire for universality, which Kaneshiro's push to be read as "human" echoes. Interestingly, the same could be said of Kim Sŏkpŏm, though his attitude toward the relationship between the particular (always, for Kim, taking the form of the *minzoku*, or ethnonation) and the universal contrasts with that of Kin—in part, I would argue, due to Kin's proto-intersectional view of particularity and difference. Arguably, the central thread running through the work of Yi Kwangsu and Kim Saryang is also the negotiation of the universal and the particular.[69]

In one sense, then, the "new generation" is not doing anything new. What I would like to emphasize here is that the so-called third generation began to point out the problems with existing terminology and to search for alternatives precisely because its standard-bearers were situated in positions of internal difference from the previous generations' almost exclusively elite male representatives. At the same moment that issues of gender, class, and even the distinction between "pure" and "popular" literatures came to the fore, the ostensible coherence of Zainichi literature as a genre (and the Zainichi community more broadly) came into question. However, the history of Zainichi literature and of Koreans in Japan in general, when viewed through these kinds of intersectional lenses, reveals that this coherence was always an illusion. The appearance of coherence in the pre-"brackets era" was made possible by the *suppression* of internal difference rather than its absence. It was not that counter-narratives emerged in this historical moment, but rather that they became conspicuous and impossible to ignore. Thus, what appears to be a collapse of the genre and community's cohesion in fact retroactively calls into question the entire generational narrative that has dominated Zainichi literary historiography.

Still, there are contextual factors changing the landscape for the new generation, compared to the historical conditions faced by their elders. Japan signed onto the UN Refugee Convention in 1981, necessitating an update of its immigration laws in order to be in compliance. The immigration reforms of 1981 created a "special permanent resident" status extended to those with *Chōsen-seki* nationality as well as those who had adopted *Kankoku-seki* status. With this new designation (and further reforms enacted to comply with UN human rights treaties) came expanded rights, including access to social welfare programs.[70] A mass movement in the 1980s to refuse to be fingerprinted, as was required for all resident aliens, also forced Japan to drop this requirement for Zainichi Koreans.

However, perhaps an even larger factor in shifting Zainichi identities and outlooks than the lay of the land in Japan is the increasingly international orientation of Zainichi literature. The impact of this internationalization can be felt particularly strongly in the careers of Kaneshiro and Yū, and, not for nothing, is ultimately what brought me (and possibly my readers) to this discourse in the first place. Part of this internationalization is a return, of sorts, to increased engagement with the Korean peninsula. Yi Yangji was perhaps the first Zainichi writer to attract an audience in Korean translation in the late 1980s and early 1990s. Her Akutagawa Prize-winning novella *Yuhi*, the subject of chapter 6, narrates a failed "return," in which the titular character, like the author herself, studies abroad in Seoul in order to reconnect with her roots, only to find that the sense of belonging she seeks eludes her even in her ethnic homeland.[71]

Not long after, around the turn of the century, the Zainichi community began to garner attention in English-language discourses as well. Yū Miri's *Gold Rush* (1998) became the first full-length novel by a Zainichi writer to be translated into English, in 2002, followed by Kim Sŏkpŏm's *The Curious Tale of Mandogi's Ghost* in 2010.[72] Yukisada Isao's film adaptation of Kaneshiro's *GO* in 2001 was screened widely at international film festivals and was Japan's submission for Best Foreign Language Film at the 2002 Academy Awards. Today, with Min Jin Lee's *Pachinko* (2017) achieving bestseller status and translated into over twenty languages and adapted for streaming television, and with Yū Miri's *Tokyo Ueno Station* winning the 2020 National Book Award for Translated Literature, the existence of the Zainichi community is as close to common knowledge in the United States as it has ever been. Moreover, Zainichi writers are increasingly engaged with the United States, with stories like Kim Masumi's "Moeru Sōka" ("The Burning Grass House," 1997) and Che Sil's *Jini no pazuru* (*Jini's Puzzle*, 2016) set in Los Angeles and Oregon, respectively.

Thus, it is not only the increased attention to intersectional social factors and greater openness to integrating into Japanese society, but also the deterritorialization of the genre that sets apart the post–Cold War era in Zainichi literature. All of these factors have undermined the coherence of Zainichi literature, a coherence that, as is now clear, never actually existed. And it is this incoherence that necessitates the brackets around the term. But it is also worth pausing to consider how this acknowledgment of incoherence, fictiveness, or malleability is achieved via the brackets, as quotation marks. As noted above, most explanatory statements on the use of "Zainichi" in Japanese scholarship point precisely to the need to represent Zainichi as a fluid and non-reified mode of identity. What goes unsaid, perhaps because it is obvious, is that the quotation marks literally make the term a designation of that which has been *called* "Zainichi," regardless of whether the term is accurate or not. Taken in this literal sense, the brackets force a reckoning with the notion that it is the term itself that creates the Zainichi community rather than any particular shared experience or essence. At the same time, if the foundations of the Zainichi community rest on the term itself—that which they have been named—then perhaps the most illuminating question we could ask is *who* has called them "Zainichi."

Having already discussed this question at length in the context of Japanese-language discourse, it is instructive to trace the path of *Zainichi* in other linguistic contexts. The purely discursive nature of "Zainichi" as it is used today is perhaps nowhere more visible than in translations and transliterations of the term into English and Korean. In English, whereas the earliest works to introduce the history, politics, and culture of the Zainichi community were more likely to translate the term as "Koreans in Japan" or "Resident Koreans" (depending on their interpretation of *zainichi*), more recent interventions are more likely to use the term "Zainichi" as-is.[73] This shift in perception of the function of the term is consistent with its shift in status in Japanese to a term that has explicitly broken away from its referential or denotative sense. The term itself is more important than its literal meaning.

Similarly, in Korean-language scholarship, a spike in interest in Korean literature and culture in diaspora has coincided with increased likelihood of referring to the Zainichi community with its hangŭl transliteration, *Chainich'i*, rather than with its sinographically derived equivalent, *Chaeil*. It is possible, given the citational networks of scholarship that use *Chainich'i* versus *Chaeil*, that *Chainich'i* is not merely a transliteration of the original Japanese word, but rather a representation of the English-language transliteration that occurs outside this "original" context. What I want to suggest here is that not only has the term *Zainichi* broken free from the literal, referential sense in which it emerged, but it has also sprung loose from the Japanese *national* context altogether. It can only be understood as a transnational construct with discursive roots in the triangular positioning of Japan, Korea, and the United States—and even further afield. Moreover, just as with the increased acknowledgment of internal, intersectional difference and the contradictory politics it entails, the transnational origins and entanglements of the Zainichi community are only *belatedly* recognized in the use of "Zainichi" as an explicitly floating signifier. Both factors rendering the term *Zainichi* incoherent have been present from the outset.

As I deploy the term *Zainichi* throughout the remainder of this book, I do so while acknowledging the internal heterogeneity and transnational entanglements of the community it names and delineates. To reiterate, though I apply this name broadly, I do not mean to imply a cohesion among the disparate authors, works, and historical contexts I bring under its umbrella. Instead, *Zainichi* is allowed to remain incoherent, the connections among the people and artistic works called by that name tenuous, in hopes of demonstrating that a higher degree of comfort with incoherence and disjuncture can enable different—and perhaps less violent—forms of reading.

2

Queer(ing) Language in Yi Kwangsu's *Mujŏng*

Gender, Sexuality, and Colonial Modernity

Yi Kwangsu's *Mujŏng* (*Heartless*, 1917) is widely considered the first modern novel written in the Korean language. Despite this common understanding, *Mujŏng* has predecessors among the experimental texts of early modern and colonial Korea, but more suggestively, it comes well after the author's own literary debut years earlier—in Japanese. The complex linguistic and literary history of this moment makes it a productive starting point for a discussion of Zainichi literature, particularly as a response to intersecting empires. As I will show through my reading of *Mujŏng*, colonial Korean subjects faced intersecting hierarchies of not only nation but also gender and sexuality, each one further complicated by the epistemological shifts taking place at the site of these terms as Western and Japanese imperialisms collided with each other to contest their meanings. This is how intersectionality, deployed as a form of queer reading, can enable productive engagements with the incoherence of Yi's text and the context in which it appeared.

Perhaps not coincidentally, a kind of queer sexuality makes an intriguing appearance in Kim Tong'in's literary biography of Yi Kwangsu, who published under the pen name Ch'unwŏn, and later the Japanese name Kayama Mitsurō. Kim's "Ch'unwŏn yŏngu" ("A Study of Ch'unwŏn," 1934–35) discusses Yi's career and its relevance to the beginnings of modern Korean literature.[1] In a section on Yi's short story "Ŏrin pŏt ege" ("To My Young Friend," 1917), which Kim describes as "the first piece of Korean fiction to have been influenced by Western literature," he writes the following, quoting lines from the story:

> 'Only a brute needs intercourse to be satisfied in a male-female relationship. A civilized, sophisticated gentleman knows the ultimate satisfaction that comes from loving someone mentally, admiring their appearance as well as the elegance of their heart.'

> How he clamors for his ideal love! This is the anguished cry of a man who has suffered through a life of loneliness. Not a cry, but rather a shouted curse. He could see none of life's other problems. Only after tasting love could he think of other things; before tasting love nothing else had meaning. . . .
>
> As the target for his love, he did not desire only women. Young men would do just as well. As long as that someone would hold him to their breast, that would be enough.
>
> Thus, his first short story in the formative period of Korean New Literature took the form of 'a passionate longing for love.'[2]

One theme that emerges from this passage is the important role of "love" (*sarang*) in defining both civilization and "Korean New Literature." Love that combines both emotional and bodily aspects is the mark of a civilized person, and the longing for such a love characterizes a new kind of literature. For Yi, writing at a time when the meaning and purpose of literature were being forged and contested under colonial conditions, literature becomes inextricably bound up with emotion (*chŏng*), most often the emotions attached to love. This theory of literature is borne out not only in Yi's works of fiction but also in his seminal essay "Munhak iran hao" ("What Is Literature?," 1916), in which he states: "Human emotions are the very foundation of literature. The significance of literature derives from human emotions and human relations."[3] The essay goes on to contend that any nation lacking such a literature "will be stuck in a barbaric and primitive state."[4] In sum, for Yi, a concept of *sarang*, as the primary means of exploring *chŏng*, was an essential pillar of modernity, and modernity was the concern not only of individual subjects but also of the *minjok* (J: *minzoku*; ethnonation).

As we can see from Kim's quotation, the notion of love that informs Yi's production of Korean New Literature is never divorced from sexuality. Even as he tries to separate his civilized concept of love from that of the "brute" (*yain*), he can do so only by positing the purely physical sexuality of the latter as conversely uncivilized. In this way, Yi's concept of love as marker of civilization is homologous to heteronormativity as marker of modernity. As Foucault famously argues in *The History of Sexuality*, such norms arose from nineteenth-century European medical and psychological discourse, which created the "species" of the homosexual.[5] Building on the work of Eve Kosofsky Sedgwick, who similarly dates the rupture of the "male homosocial continuum" to the late nineteenth century,[6] J. Keith Vincent locates a requirement of Japan's modernization at the turn of the twentieth century in the heteronormativity resulting from this rupture: "As exclusive and compulsory heterosexuality became associated with an enlightened modernity, love between men was increasingly branded as either 'feudal' or immature. The resulting rupture . . . thus constituted one of the most significant markers of Japan's entrance into modernity."[7] Insofar as "modern" meant "Western," and the West had embraced heterosexuality as the norm, heteronormativity was a requirement for a claim to modernity. In Korea's case, such a modernity was mediated by Japan—as was the shift in the definition of literature noted above—which had itself been subject to the same requirement to conform to Western models.

It is ironic, then, that Yi, regarded as a central figure in the project of building a modern Korean literature and importing enlightenment discourse into colonial Korea, would seem according to Kim to have embraced a sexuality at odds with heteronormativity. "Ŏrin pŏt ege" is hardly unique among Yi's early works in its depiction of male-male desire; his Japanese-language debut work "Ai ka" ("Maybe Love," 1909) tells the story of a Korean student in Tokyo who longs for and is rejected by a Japanese male student, with at least one critic suggesting that the story was based on Yi's own feelings for a Japanese student at Meiji Gakuin.[8] Although this element of Yi's early fiction is broadly acknowledged, very little scholarship engages with it directly. One of the few critics to do so, Han Sŭng-ok, argues that the open homosexuality appearing in Yi's early short stories becomes coded in later works like *Mujŏng*, when the author, "as an enlightenmentist advocate of nationalism," had to focus on other things.[9] Sin Chiyŏn, on the other hand, views the homoerotic elements of *Mujŏng* as very much out in the open, but traces a shift occurring shortly thereafter in which Yi seems to reject same-sex love as premodern in order to align himself with sexological discourse being translated into Korean in the 1920s.[10] Though the two disagree on exactly when depictions of same-sex love stop being explicit in Yi's work, both agree that this homoeroticism was somehow incompatible with the project of building a modern Korean nation and its literature.[11]

In any case, it is clear that *Mujŏng* lies at a point of transition in Korean discourse on the relationships between sexuality, (colonial) modernity, and literature. The modernity of the work is located both in its concern with themes of individual subjectivity and romantic love and in its innovative vernacular language.[12] Its hangŭl-only text stands in stark contrast to the mixed script of the articles and essays surrounding its serialized installments on the pages of the *Maeil sinbo*, January to June 1917, an experimental style that attempts to be particularly Korean while qualifying as a properly modern vernacular mode of writing. As noted in chapter 1, Yi's own critical writing during this period, particularly "Munhak iran hao," explicitly relates the use of the vernacular to the project of building a modern but particularly Korean body of national literature.

In Yi's rhetoric on Korean literature, a binary emerges between premodern Korean tradition and Western modernity, a relationship that must always be understood as triangulated by Japanese colonization of the Korean peninsula. Standard readings of *Mujŏng* map this binary onto a romantic love triangle present in the novel.[13] The male intellectual protagonist, Yi Hyŏngsik, is torn between two love interests: Sŏnhyŏng, the modern girl student who is preparing to study in the United States, and Yŏngch'ae, the traditional daughter of his teacher and benefactor who sells herself as a *kisaeng* (courtesan) in an act of filial piety, attempting to free her father from jail.

However, this simplified schematic of the novel fails to account for the many tensions and inconsistencies embedded in the language of the novel's narrative as well as in the sexualities narrated, both of which can be productively framed as queer. This intentionally broad application of *queer* builds on David Halperin's definition of the term "not as a positivity but as a positionality, not as a thing, but as a resistance to the norm."[14] Whereas Halperin is thinking of queerness as an identity category that resists sexual norms in particular, heteronormativity is necessarily bound up within a larger network of intersecting and often contradictory norms that constitute a system of power—as we have seen in the case of Yi's colonized Korea and the broader theorization of intersectionality. Just as it is impossible for Yi to forge a new literature that is both Korean and modern under the conditions of colonialism (as the colonizing power always defines the colonized, in this case Korea, as abjectly premodern), the subjects of the novel, particularly the female characters, find it impossible to comply with the overdetermined imperatives of the overlapping forms of patriarchy operative at this transitional moment. In other words, both the linguistic and the sexual norms that govern the space of *Mujŏng* are always already impossible to embody.[15]

The incoherence of mutually reinforcing norms has been theorized by Janet Jakobsen as a "working alliance," wherein the contradictory nature of norms within a regime of normativity makes resistance more difficult rather than less.[16] Thus according to Jakobsen, "queering works most effectively when it troubles multiple norms at once, when it addresses a network of dominant norms."[17] My reading of *Mujŏng* attempts to situate the novel within just such a network, at the nexus of norms reaching well beyond the sexual and into realms of modernity, (ethno)nation, and, most importantly for my purposes here, the language of literary text. I argue that the novel is a queer text insofar as it troubles all of these norms at once. My purpose, then, is not to highlight previously overlooked homoerotic aspects of the novel but rather to tease out the inherent impossibility of the novel's compliance with sexual and other norms, especially those of written vernacular language. To read the language of *Mujŏng* as queer(ing) is to more clearly position the novel as at once troubling and troubled by an entire web of norms mediated by Japanese colonialism, its queer remainders acting as sites of potential reconfiguration of (if not resistance to) the working alliance of East Asian and Western patriarchies. Moreover, this move allows us to see the ultimate embrace of *Mujŏng* as a normative text of modern Korean literature, despite its queerness, as a testament to the incoherence of norms under the conditions of colonial modernity and postcoloniality.

OVERDETERMINED NORMS AND QUEER RESISTANCE

To explore these queer potentialities, I focus on the character of Yŏngch'ae, the kisaeng, who most embodies the paradoxes arising from the novel's views on romantic love and sexuality. Throughout the events of *Mujŏng*, Yŏngch'ae must navigate the confluence of different forms of patriarchy to which she is subjected. To oversimplify, these are, first, the Confucian patriarchy of the "three obediences" (to father, husband, and son), and second, the patriarchy inherent in modern Western heteronormativity. Thus for Yŏngch'ae, complying with the rules dictated for female sexuality always involves a negotiation between two competing sets of such rules, the modern and the premodern.

Although the most basic reading of the novel situates Yŏngch'ae solidly on the premodern, more purely or traditionally Korean, side of this binary, Yŏngch'ae's position is in fact much more fluid and complex than this schematic view of the novel suggests. In fact, it is Yŏngch'ae's father's tutelage that establishes Hyŏngsik, the novel's central character, as a modern man in the first place. Yŏngch'ae's father is described as follows:

> Scholar Pak traveled to the state of Qing and brought back dozens of different kinds of new books published in Shanghai. He got an idea of what the situation was like in the West, and conditions in Japan, and realized that Korea could not go on as it was at present; thereupon, he tried to begin a "new civilization" movement. . . . Scholar Pak immediately cut his hair short and put on black clothes, and he had his two sons do the same. At the time, cutting one's hair and wearing black clothing was a very courageous decision. It symbolized the shattering of established customs that had been followed for over four thousand years, and adopting completely new ways.[18]

As is clear from this introduction to Scholar Pak, he cannot be positioned unequivocally in the traditional camp, even when compared on the other side of the love triangle to Sŏnhyŏng's father, a practicing Christian who has studied in the United States. This is not to say that Pak is unquestionably modern, either. The contradictions inherent in his (and Yŏngch'ae's) position are illustrated by the education he gives Yŏngch'ae: "Though others laughed at him, Scholar Pak ignored them and sent his daughter to school. When she returned from school, he would teach her texts such as the *Elementary Learning* and *Biographies of Exemplary Women*, and the summer she turned twelve years old, he taught her the *Classic of Poetry* too" (no. 5). Presumably "others laugh at him" because the notion of sending a daughter to school is something new and foreign that Scholar Pak carries out as part of his "new civilization" worldview, but at the same time, Pak teaches his daughter the traditional Chinese texts that *yangban* ladies would have learned in the Chosŏn period as well. In this case, as with arguably every major character in the novel, the modern-versus-premodern binary cannot be easily applied. In fact, one of the novel's most deep-seated contradictions is its simultaneous desire for and resistance toward modernity.

This contradiction eventually ensnares Yŏngch'ae, making it impossible for her to behave morally. Her classical education demands that she seek virtue through her relationships with men: first by practicing filial piety toward her father and then, after he dies, by preserving her virginity for Hyŏngsik, the man she believes her father wished her to marry. In both cases, however, Yŏngch'ae is thwarted. When her father is wrongfully imprisoned, Yŏngch'ae models herself after "women who sold themselves in order to redeem their father's sins" in "the stories of old" (no. 15), selling herself as a kisaeng to obtain the money to support her father. Not only does she fail to get him released from prison, as she is swindled out of the selling price of her own body, her father curses her decision to become a kisaeng and starves himself to death in his rage. Yŏngch'ae is then left with the guilt of having hastened her father's death—never mind the fact that it was the very education he gave her that led her to make the decision he ends up condemning. Yŏngch'ae then spends the next seven years preserving her virginity, "following the examples of women of olden times," only to "fail" again when she is raped.[19] Hence Yŏngch'ae is confronted with actual sexual violence in addition to the violence of the impossible standards imposed on her behavior as a woman.

The impossible demands of Scholar Pak's ambivalently "traditional" worldview are further compounded by the modern norms Yŏngch'ae confronts. After she is raped, Yŏngch'ae flees to Pyongyang to end her life, which she believes to be the only moral option available to her. She is stopped by Pyŏng'uk, a woman on vacation from her studies in Japan. Pyŏng'uk makes a powerful appeal for Yŏngch'ae to live, in which she mounts an attack on traditional morals: "You have been a slave of such outdated thought, and have tasted futile suffering. Free yourself from those shackles. Awake from your dream. Be a person who lives for herself. Attain freedom" (no. 90). Yŏngch'ae comes to accept Pyŏng'uk's view of the world in lieu of the one she inherited from her father, but the novel is not willing to endorse the shift completely. Even Pyŏng'uk, the most hard-line "new woman" (*sinyŏsŏng*) in the novel, is made to see the value of "traditional" ideas.

> Pyŏng'uk learned traditional knowledge from Yŏngch'ae, and had a taste of Eastern emotions. Pyŏng'uk had disliked anything that was outdated. After coming into contact with Yŏngch'ae's thorough understanding of traditional thought, though, Pyŏng'uk realized that there were appealing aspects to even traditional thought. She even thought of studying the *Elementary Learning, Biographies of Exemplary Women*, and classical Chinese poetry and prose. She took out dust-covered books at home, such as the *Genuine Treasures of Classical Literature*, and studied these books with Yŏngch'ae, and memorized what she learned. 'This is such fun,' she would exclaim, rejoicing like a child, and she would recite the texts out loud. 'Hm,' Pyŏng'uk's father would say when he heard his daughter reciting classical texts, though it was not clear whether he was praising her, or expressing ridicule (no. 91).

In the end, the skeptical and ambivalent voice of Pyŏng'uk's father reflects the narrative tone of much of the novel—somewhere between mocking and approval—toward both the "traditional" values of Korea and the often ill-conceived efforts of the characters to turn away from them toward what is new or "civilized." The result is that multiple normative systems operate simultaneously on Yŏngch'ae and the other characters, overtly contradicting each other even as they more subtly contradict themselves.

Yŏngch'ae's queer sexuality begins to make sense as a response to—or consequence of—this incoherence. When Yŏngch'ae and her older kisaeng "sister" Wŏrhwa awaken to a heterosexual desire for men, which is linked in the text to awakening as a modern subject, they turn to each other, rather than to men, to release that desire. Their erotic relationship begins shortly after they witness a group of male students singing together. The song repeats a trope in the novel used to position characters like Scholar Pak and Hyŏngsik as being advocates for the "modern," the trope of being the lone person awake among sleepers:

> While other people on earth dream,
> I alone am awake [*na man irŏna*].
> I look up at the sky
> and sing a sad song (no. 32).

Upon hearing this song, Wŏrhwa falls for one of the students, which the novel marks as the beginning of her desire for men. This could be understood as a desire for modernity itself, always remaining unfulfilled under colonialism. Thus, as in the students' song, it becomes a source of sadness:

> When Yŏngch'ae saw how Wŏrhwa had been suffering ever since the party . . . Yŏngch'ae guessed that something had happened to Wŏrhwa. Yŏngch'ae had also begun to feel a longing for the male sex. Her face grew hot when she faced a strange man, and when she lay down alone at night, she wished that there was someone who would hold her. Once, when Yŏngch'ae and Wŏrhwa came back from a party late at night, and had gone to bed together in the same bed, Yŏngch'ae put her arms around Wŏrhwa in her sleep, and kissed her on the mouth. Wŏrhwa laughed to herself. 'So you have awakened as well [*nŏ to kkaeŏkkuna*],' she thought. 'Sadness and suffering lie ahead of you' (no. 32).

Notably, this installment contains an overlap in metaphors of awakening as a modern subject and awakening as a sexual subject, both linked to a "sadness" that arises from a desire that cannot be satisfied. This "awakened" desire presents yet another impossibility for Wŏrhwa and Yŏngch'ae, who, as we have seen, are already confronted with the impossibility of meeting the mutually exclusive requirements of the patriarchal value systems in place, particularly from their marginal position as kisaeng.

At the moment both women come face to face with the weight of this impossibility, their homoerotic relationship begins. They embrace and kiss each other in place of the men they long for. One way to read Yŏngch'ae's queer sexuality, then, is as an outlet for the tension built up by the incoherent demands of colonial modernity. With heteronormative desire for men—naturalized as a bodily response by the reference to Yŏngch'ae's face flushing—at once required and censured, Yŏngch'ae's only choice is to substitute a queer desire that both mimics and upends the normative practice that is always inaccessible to her. In a moment that strikes today's reader as ironic, the narrative claims that "it was Wŏrhwa who had given Yŏngch'ae half the strength to think of Hyŏngsik as her partner in life and to remain chaste for seven years" (no. 34) even after Wŏrhwa replaces Hyŏngsik as the object of Yŏngch'ae's desire. Thus Yŏngch'ae responds to the contradictions in normative demands for chastity by creating a contradiction of her own, protecting her virginity by engaging in a seemingly erotic practice.

Notably, at the time of *Mujŏng*'s publication, this particular kind of female-female relationship—even if it did entail eroticism—tended to be written off as platonic. In the case of Japan, schoolgirl crushes and other homosocial (and sometimes homoerotic) bonds were referred to as *dōseiai* (same-sex love), but nevertheless were not considered sexually deviant.[20] In both contexts, female-female desire is illegible as sexuality. Importantly, this illegibility does not arise from a lack of visibility or representation—the queer eroticism here is out in the open. What I want to suggest is that Wŏrhwa and Yŏngch'ae's desire for each other is not *read* as sexual. This is not simply because it is nonnormative, as male-male sexuality in this period was beginning to become legible as difference or deviation from the norm. It is the intersectional incoherence of norms surrounding gender and sexuality, as well as the dominant allegorical reading of these characters, that renders this particular difference illegible. In this respect, *Mujŏng* is a paradigmatic example of the ways that hermeneutical models demanding that texts represent a given nation ignore whatever fails to cohere into such a reading. And what fails to cohere is precisely this kind of intersectional difference.

THE QUEER POTENTIAL OF ORTHOGRAPHIC INCOHERENCE

As with sexuality, the queerness of the novel's language similarly arises from contradictory demands brought on by a transition between (and overlapping of) norms. This tension is produced as the text sets out to occupy an always already foreclosed space that is both modern and nationally Korean.[21] On the pages of the *Maeil sinbo* where *Mujŏng* was serialized, it is clear that there is not a single, standardized mode of writing in the Korean language, even within the narrow limits of a fairly highbrow publication. The serialized installments of *Mujŏng*, which use hangŭl almost exclusively, stand out on the page, whose columns are filled with *kukhanmun*. The dominant orthographic style at the time, *kukhanmun* consists largely of sinographs with Korean script filling in grammatical information, as in the Japanese mixed-script style still in use today. *Mujŏng* deviates from this standard, carving out a particular style for the genre of fiction. This stylistic experiment, which would eventually become the dominant mode of writing, must be understood in the context of a discourse on the modern vernacular. The hangŭl-only orthographic style of *Mujŏng* may have offered the best prospects for developing into the kind of vernacular written language that was required, according to Yi, to produce a modern novel in a particularly Korean medium, which

Yi saw as the basis for Korean literature.[22] That is, its deployment can be seen as an attempt to depart from the ostensibly ideographic (ergo premodern) forms of Chinese writing—including those appropriated and reworked via Japanese—and to empower a writing style with claims to being both more straightforwardly phonetic (ergo modern) and uniquely Korean, Yi's stated conditions for the written language of modern Korean literature.[23]

The problem is that, upon closer examination, both of these claims are belied by the language of *Mujŏng*. What appears to be unadulterated Korean vernacular script is always already the product of the linguistic admixture characterizing East Asia at this moment. The hangŭl orthography of the text creates a contrast between the installments of the novel and the surrounding articles and essays, perhaps in an effort to distance itself from the *hanja* (sinographs) that constituted the basis for premodern forms of Korean writing, which Yi went out of his way to exclude from the category of Korean literature, as discussed in chapter 1. This may also have had the effect of creating a greater sense of separation from Japanese, versus the mixed-orthography texts that shared a common kanji/hanja vocabulary with the language of the colonizer. However, that vocabulary is still present in the hangŭl text of *Mujŏng*, and for readers of a paper published almost exclusively in the mixed-script style, the Japanese-mediated hanja corresponding to that vocabulary must have been easy to visualize, even in the absence of the actual characters on the page.

This absence is key, because it invites a different kind of interaction with the text from its readers, who supply the hanja rather than deciphering them. On the one hand, this interpellation of the reader gestures at the production of meaning by external normative frameworks rather than the innocent representation of meaning wholly within the text. But on the other hand, in asking the reader to imagine things that are not actually there, this absence creates an ethical configuration between text and reader, a mode of interacting that allows for a sidestepping of direct representation and the violence it often entails.

Ultimately, Yi was faced with a more acute version of the same anomaly embedded in discourse on *genbun itchi*, the Japanese effort to "unify spoken and written language": a discussion that set up the West and China as two poles in a dichotomy, but could only take place in a language that already contained elements of both. All available modes of writing were already overloaded with meanings mediated by and negotiated among a multiplicity of languages and forms, none of which could be disentangled.[24] In sum, the norms governing the style of the text are internally incoherent, as are those governing Yŏngch'ae's sexuality.

In the same way, the text wriggles out of these constraints through a sort of queer practice, a deviation from the assumed norms of the language that exposes their inherent incoherence. The very first installment of the novel, even as it is presented in a strikingly "pure" hangŭl form, includes representations of English and Japanese, creating a multilingual setting for the interactions of the novel's characters. These foreign words are blended into the Korean text insofar as they are transcribed into hangŭl rather than presented in Japanese or English orthographies, but on the other hand they are marked for emphasis, distinguishing them as something other. The text simultaneously accommodates and excludes the foreign.

These instances of heteroglossia also undermine the notion of the novel's text as strictly phonetic, representing the speech of the characters in an unmediated fashion—a project that is of course impossible in the first place. Although the transcription of the Japanese and English words into hangŭl is a phonetic function of the script, many of these transcriptions are followed by parenthetical glosses of the foreign terms. These glosses create two competing layers of signs, the sounds of which could not be uttered by the same person at the same time. This structure draws attention to the nature of hangŭl as visual medium: in its most phonetic moment, setting out to represent nothing more than the non-meaning sound of a foreign sign, the text ironically emphasizes its distance from the oral. It records noiseless meaning and meaningless noise in juxtaposition. The language of the novel, from its very first page, is always more fluid, more flexible, more queer than the oversimplified frameworks of modern vernacular language can accommodate.[25]

The queer ambivalence of the language comes into its starkest relief at a moment when Yŏngch'ae's queer sexuality becomes radicalized in response to her rape. Yŏngch'ae is being assaulted by clients when Hyŏngsik and his friend Sin Usŏn arrive on the scene and stop them in the act. At that moment Usŏn declares in Japanese that they are "too late" [*mō dame da*], implying that the rape has already taken place (no. 39). The installments immediately following contain some of the most striking contradictions in the novel's linguistic and sexual norms. When those norms reach their most violent and restrictive, a queer presence that was once subtle becomes much more disruptive.

First, it is worth noting that the narrative leaves open the question of whether Yŏngch'ae was actually penetrated during her (attempted?) rape. When Usŏn comes to see Hyŏngsik the day after the rape, the narrative suggests that Usŏn may have been somewhat disingenuous when he said they were too late. The next morning, Usŏn debates whether to tell Hyŏngsik the truth:

> Sin Usŏn believed that Hyŏngsik was a man of such character that Hyŏngsik would marry Yŏngch'ae. However, if Hyŏngsik made Yŏngch'ae his wife, the scene [of the rape] would always remain in Hyŏngsik's mind and would cause him much pain and suffering. It was within Sin's power to decide whether or not Hyŏngsik would suffer. For only he [and the perpetrators] knew whether or not Yŏngch'ae was still a virgin. Sin wanted to torment Hyŏngsik for a long time by withholding this secret (no. 46).

According to this, even Yŏngch'ae does not know whether she is still a virgin, though it is possible she is simply left out of Usŏn's list of those who know—after all, it is not her "pain and suffering" that is of concern here, only Hyŏngsik's.

In any case, although this passage implies that Yŏngch'ae may not have been actually penetrated, the narrative goes on from this point referring to the rape as if this had occurred. The details of the event remain obscure.

Perhaps this ambiguity is the only way the novel can justify its contradictory stances on Yŏngch'ae's status after surviving the rape. On one hand, Yŏngch'ae must remain a sympathetic character, as she remains central to the novel's development through its final installments, and Hyŏngsik can demonstrate how enlightened he is by declaring that Yŏngch'ae's life still has value. On the other hand, Hyŏngsik does not seem to question the notion that Yŏngch'ae's rape constitutes a moral failing on her part and a debasement of her body's value, and the narrative continually censures Yŏngch'ae for having been "defiled" (*tŏryŏpda*). The only way to resolve the tension between the two positions is to allow for the possibility that Yŏngch'ae was not really raped and therefore remains a suitable object of sympathy for Hyŏngsik.

By contrast, Yŏngch'ae's own strategy for overcoming this contradiction is to die. After the rape, Yŏngch'ae resolves to throw herself in the Taedong River in Pyongyang, where her lover Wŏrhwa did the same, again suggesting a more significant romantic attachment between the two than is usually acknowledged. Yŏngch'ae's planned suicide is motivated not only by a perceived sense of guilt at her failure to preserve her virginity but also by her desire to be with Wŏrhwa once again. It is not inconceivable that this journey toward a death shared with Wŏrhwa is Yŏngch'ae's ultimate rejection of the heteronormative patriarchy that has finally subjected her to one of its most grotesque form of violence.

Ironically, Yŏngch'ae's "death" becomes her greatest source of power in the novel, despite the fact that she never actually carries out her suicide, unbeknownst to Hyŏngsik and the reader until later in the novel. The specter of Yŏngch'ae's raped and bleeding body haunts Hyŏngsik. In fact, even before she departs for Pyongyang, Yŏngch'ae begins to turn her attack around, transforming her "tainted" blood into a weapon. In her first encounter with the old woman who runs the kisaeng house after her rape, she is already a ghostly and terrifying figure. As she attempts to inflict harm upon herself in this scene, we also get the impression that it is the old woman, rather than Yŏngch'ae, who is most threatened by the violence inflicted on Yŏngch'ae's body. When Yŏngch'ae screams, "My blood is tainted blood," it sounds as much like a threat to disseminate her blood, now weaponized, as it does a statement of guilt or regret for her lost virginity (no. 42).

Despite never witnessing this moment, Hyŏngsik sees a similar vision of a blood-spraying Yŏngch'ae in a dream involving his other love interest, Sŏnhyŏng.

> He could see Sŏnhyŏng and Yŏngch'ae side by side. At first they were both dressed in garments white as snow, and each held a flower in one hand, and held one hand open towards Hyŏngsik, as though asking him to clasp their hands. 'Take my hand, Hyŏngsik! Please!,' they said, smiling and holding their head slightly to one

> side coquettishly. Shall I take this hand, or that one? Hyŏngsik thought, and reached both of his hands into the air, then hesitated. Then Yŏngch'ae's appearance began to change. The white, snowlike dress gave way to a bloody, torn skirt of some nameless kind of silk, and her bloodied legs showed through the torn skirt. Tears fell from her eyes, and her lip was bleeding. The flower in her hand disappeared, and she held instead a fistful of soil. He shook his head and opened his eyes. Sŏnhyŏng still stood before him, dressed in white, and smiling. 'Please take my hand, Hyŏngsik!,' she said, reaching her hand out to him, and bowing her head. When Hyŏngsik reached for Sŏnhyŏng's hand in a daze, Yŏngch'ae's face as she stood beside Sŏnhyŏng was hideously transformed like that of a ghost. She bit her lip and sprayed blood over Hyŏngsik. Hyŏngsik started with terror (no. 45).

Hyŏngsik's dream links Yŏngch'ae's radical and violent transformation more explicitly to the injustice of her situation. Not only does Hyŏngsik have all the power in the fantasy he sets up, choosing between two women who beg to be with him, but he compounds the violence of Yŏngch'ae's rape by chasing her out of the fantasy as soon as the marks of this violence become visible. In the end, however, he is unable to keep her away, apparently not even by opening his eyes. It is when he rejects her this way and makes a move toward accepting the still ostensibly pure Sŏnhyŏng that Yŏngch'ae becomes monstrous and sprays him with blood as she does the old woman. Yŏngch'ae's "ghost"—both alive and dead, real and imagined—is a queer presence; her defiled blood, even if it lacks substance, has a radical power to trouble the very attitudes that view her body as defiled in the first place.

Perhaps it is not surprising, then, that Hyŏngsik argues shortly thereafter that it is wrong for Yŏngch'ae to choose to die, disallowing the power she obtains as a queer ghostly figure. His case is presented in episode 53, a strange installment that breaks from the plot of the story and takes a form more like that of an essay. Episode 53 also represents a stark shift in the style of the novel, its text containing a sudden burst of sinographs. The installment is structured to contrast the views of Usŏn and Hyŏngsik on Yŏngch'ae's responsibilities after being raped, with the narrative ruling in favor of Hyŏngsik's ostensibly more compassionate view that Yŏngch'ae should not commit suicide simply because her virginity is lost. It begins by presenting a logical fallacy in Usŏn's view of the situation, which sees suicide as the proper course of action for Yŏngch'ae as a "good woman" who has lost her virginity, even though he would have had no problem with Yŏngch'ae as a kisaeng going on living without her virginity. The narrator points out that "if one followed the implications of this line of thought, one could say that Usŏn believed that it was a sin for a 'virtuous woman' to be unchaste, but not a sin for a woman who was not a 'virtuous woman' to be unchaste. This was a reversal of premise and conclusion. In actuality one did not remain chaste because one was a virtuous woman; one was a virtuous woman because one was chaste" (no. 53). If Usŏn's logic is unfair, however, then so is the narrator's counterpoint, which implies that Yŏngch'ae, having been raped, is no longer a "virtuous woman."

Indeed, Hyŏngsik's opinion on the matter struggles with this same contradiction. He recognizes that Yŏngch'ae's failure to remain chaste was not intentional, but rather than absolve her of blame, he concludes that she has responsibilities beyond those of remaining chaste and loyal to her parents (the only moral imperatives guiding Usŏn's view, it would seem) and must remain alive to carry out these further responsibilities.

> Even if she had failed to carry out these two responsibilities, she still had countless other responsibilities in her life. There was the responsibility of loyalty, and her responsibility to the world, and to animals, and to the mountains and streams, and stars, [and to God,] and to Buddha. It was wrong for her to end a life with so many responsibilities, just for the sake of two duties (even if those two duties were important, and even if she had not succeeded in fulfilling those duties as she wished). It was nevertheless one of life's glories when a person who was passionate, and pure of mind and body, made their most important responsibilities their very life (no. 53).

Not only does this position further burden Yŏngch'ae with "responsibilities" beyond chastity and filial piety (which were impossible for her to fulfill in the first place), it also hedges in the final line, allowing that Usŏn's position—that Yŏngch'ae's virginity was equivalent to her entire life's value—could also be "one of life's glories." In the end, Hyŏngsik's view is no less confused than Usŏn's, though the narrative leaves the inconsistencies in the former implicit. In the end, Yŏngch'ae is faced once again with competing normative systems, both endorsed by the narrative and both internally contradictory, eradicating all possibility for her to meet their demands.

However, it is at this point that the queer language of episode 53 intervenes to make this paradox visible, just as Yŏngch'ae's queer sexuality does earlier in the novel. At the moment the narrating voice fails to call out the incoherence of those normative demands, a sort of translating presence appears, rendering the narrative voice itself incoherent. This highly visible critique is enacted through the breakdown of the vernacular prose of the installment, which contains multiple sinographic glosses in most lines, each gloss placed in parentheses after the hangŭl word to which it corresponds. Thus the vernacular quality of the text is dismantled, as the pronounceable hangŭl is constantly interrupted by hanja, which must be pronounced either as silence or as repetition.

The overly glossed text of this installment is particularly jarring in comparison with the mixed-script pieces surrounding it on the pages of the *Maeil sinbo*, which do not create this sense of unnecessary repetition and were likely much easier for contemporary readers to process smoothly. Nor are the glosses present to clarify the meanings of ambiguous hangŭl words, as most of them are repeated again and again, long after the connection between a given hangŭl word and its corresponding hanja should be clear. What at first presents itself as a clarifying hanja translation of a potentially confusing hangŭl text becomes a confusing nuisance in itself.

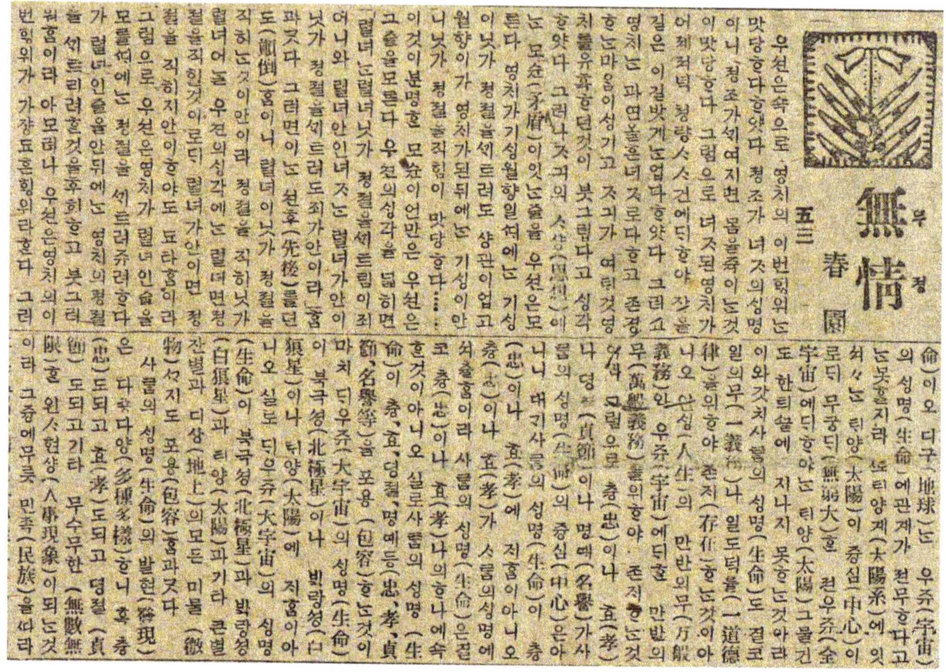
無情 무정

五三

春園

FIGURE 1. 53rd Installment of *Mujŏng* (*Maeil Sinbo*, 1917).

The translating presence begins to distance itself from or even do battle with the narrating voice, creating its own story at the visual level of the text.

By interrupting the flow of the hangŭl-only prose, these sinographic glosses do not simply hybridize the text but actually expose the inherent hybridity of the ostensibly simple hangŭl text itself. This process is clearest with reference to the final line of the installment, which compares Hyŏngsik's line of thinking with Usŏn's, characterizing them as follows: "One man was English-style and the other was Chinese-style" [하나는 영문식 (英文式) 이요, 하나는 한문식 (漢文式) 이다] (no. 53). To reiterate, even though the "English-style" thought of Hyŏngsik is presumably favored, the narrative endorses both as bases for judging Yŏngch'ae's actions. What is highlighted by the particular textual representation of "English-style" and "Chinese-style"—written in hangŭl as 영문식 and 한문식, respectively, and then repeated in the corresponding sinographs (英文式, 漢文式)—is that at the linguistic level, neither can be separated from the other. Hyŏngsik's "English-style" thought can appear only in the hanja-derived language of translated English mediated by Japanese. In fact, we could just as easily assume these sinographic glosses are Japanese kanji as Korean hanja. The point is that the language to which they belong is undecidable—they represent translations of English and other Western languages as well as Japanese and Chinese in a way that makes the languages impossible to disentangle. This admixture is violently drawn out into the queer space of the parentheses, just as Yŏngch'ae's blood is drawn out from inside her body. This linguistic queering exposes the impossibility of the demands on the language of the text just as it points toward the contradictions and overlaps between "English-style" and "Chinese-style" demands on Yŏngch'ae's sexuality.

Furthermore, the 文 or 문 (mun) in *Yŏngmunsik* and *Hanmunsik*, which I have been translating as "English-style" and "Chinese-style" respectively, implies that the two philosophical "styles" in question are rooted in English and Chinese *writing* in particular. This installment, as essentially an essay on the ethical conundrum facing Yŏngch'ae in this moment, suggests that Yi saw experiments in written style as potentially enabling of not only new thought, but also new ethics. Something about the ethical quandary specifically made him or his editors decide it could not be expressed in pure vernacular style. This breakdown in the coherence of the language through the doubling of so many words makes this passage impossible to read as "pure" anything. The incoherence, the disruption, the deviance are what enables the ethical orientation it allows, or perhaps forces, its reader to feel.

In both cases, the unruly translator of the episode 53 interlude and Yŏngch'ae's furious blood-spraying specter, as queer figures, unravel the impossibilities and contradictions in the demands made by competing and overlapping normative systems. Both the language of the novel and the sexualities it describes are overdetermined by this network of norms, but the queer or incoherent presences that "come out" within them begin to move toward positionalities that reconfigure these structures.

MISRECOGNITION, CODE-SWITCHING, AND THE PERFORMATIVITY OF LITERARY STYLE

In addition to the breakdown and overt incoherence of the prose in episode 53, *Mujŏng* anticipates one of the hallmarks of texts more straightforwardly included within the framework of Zainichi literature, in that it attempts to represent in text the multilingual world its characters inhabit. These characters occasionally code-switch, necessitating the mixture of Japanese and English in various forms into the already experimental (and sometimes unstable) Korean text. The transliteration and translation that occur in these moments can also be read as having a queering function, especially in juxtaposition with the novel's frequent depictions of characters performing or embodying other identities. These transitions and their resultant misrecognitions once again draw our attention to the ethical and relational nature of recognition in the first place.

For instance, on her way to Pyongyang to commit suicide, Yŏngch'ae dresses and styles her hair in the manner of a student, a disguise she uses throughout the novel to avoid the shame and often violence associated with being recognized as a kisaeng. On the train, she meets Pyŏng'uk, a Korean woman on break from studying in Tokyo. Kwŏn Podŭrae discusses this meeting in terms of their mutual "misrecognition": Pyŏng'uk assumes that Yŏngch'ae is a student and asks her if she is also on break, whereas Yŏngch'ae wonders to herself "how a Japanese woman could speak Korean so well" (no. 88). According to Kwŏn, this misrecognition occurs because "Yŏngch'ae and Pyŏng'uk meet when both of their outfits are functioning as false signs [*chal mot toen kiho*]."[26] Moreover, the "misrecognition" that Kwŏn describes is an indication of their successful passing, whereas Yŏngch'ae's previous attempts to pass have met with suspicion and ultimately recognition.

In this case, Yŏngch'ae reveals of her own accord that she is not a student without Pyŏng'uk ever suspecting as much. On the other hand, Yŏngch'ae immediately corrects her own misrecognition of Pyŏng'uk as Japanese without any hint from the latter: "[Pyŏng'uk] spoke Korean so well that Yŏngch'ae realized she must be a Korean woman studying in Japan" (no. 88). Yŏngch'ae's initial misapprehension and immediate correction is consistent with other examples of ethnic coding on clothing in the novel. As Kwŏn points out, readers are trained to recognize the *hisashigami* hairstyle as code for student in the case of Sŏnhyŏng, only to see that code garbled when Yŏngch'ae (decidedly not a student) appears with the same hairstyle.[27] In the same way, readers are taught prior to encountering Pyŏng'uk in Japanese clothing that different ethnic styles of dress can be read as codes for the ethnic identities of their wearers.

As a result, Pyŏng'uk is misidentified when she engages in ethnic crossdressing, but as noted above, the confusion is quickly cleared up, and her Korean identity reaffirmed. Notably, it is spoken language that reveals Pyŏng'uk's true ethnic identity. Still, the connection of Pyŏng'uk's identity to the language she uses takes on a similar structure to that configuring the relationship of gender identity to its presentation in the form of clothing and hairstyle. That is, the text establishes language use as a more or less unquestioned sign that indicates to Yŏngch'ae that Pyŏng'uk is not Japanese but in fact Korean, but at the same time it allows the misrecognition to occur despite Pyŏng'uk's use of the Korean language from the outset.

This contradiction presents itself in *Mujŏng* not only in terms of language use but also in terms of naming. Characters adopt names in order to take on different roles, identities, and positions. In Pyŏng'uk's case, her choice of name is linked explicitly to perceived masculinity versus femininity. Here is the first mention of Pyŏng'uk's name, appearing after she has already comforted Yŏngch'ae on the train and insisted on taking her to her parents' home:

> The woman student's name was Pyŏng'uk. According to Pyŏng'uk, her name had been Pyŏng'ok at first, but she had changed it to Pyŏngmok because she thought

> Pyŏng'ok seemed too soft and feminine. 'Pyŏngmok,' though, was a bit too strong and masculine, so she made her name Pyŏng'uk instead, which seemed to be somewhere in between the other two names.
>
> 'Pyŏng'uk is a lonely name, isn't it?' she said to Yŏngch'ae once. 'I don't want to have to be quiet and soft as required of women by traditional thought. Nor do I want to be quite as strong and stiff as a man either. I think somewhere in between is just right.'
>
> 'Yŏngch'ae,' she said smiling. 'Yŏngch'ae. That is a pretty name.' At home, though, she was called Pyŏng'ok, not Pyŏng'uk. She would still answer when they called her by the name Pyŏng'ok (no. 91).

This passage provides an excellent illustration of how gender norms function in general. It is especially clear in English translation, for a reader without any knowledge of the underlying Korean or the sinographs from which these names are derived, that there cannot possibly be anything masculine or feminine about these sets of sounds. "Pyŏng'ok" and "Pyŏngmok" can only become feminine and masculine, respectively, within an already extant system of signs and values. Of course, in the time and place of *Mujŏng*'s initial publication, the femininity and masculinity of the names would have seemed more obvious or even natural, but the character *ok* (玉) is no more immutably tied to the notion of femininity than the sound "ok." Both signs can only be interpreted within an existing code of gender norms or language—they are literally just discourse.

Furthermore, in the translation of the novel's text—which represents the name in hangŭl, which in turn represents a set of sinographs (imagined in the minds of readers with sinographic literacy and likely written down by Yi in his original mixed-script draft of the novel)—as well as in Pyŏng'uk's multiple name substitutions, we can see the same kind of queer layering of dissonant signs. These layers of representation with no fixed core may serve as a functional metaphor for the ethics of identification. Pyŏng'uk is free in some sense to choose her name, and she switches among several options before landing on Pyŏng'uk, which she seems to feel best represents her identity. Nevertheless, she cannot escape her original name (deadname?), which was chosen for her by others. When she is at home, her relatives still insist on the name they gave her rather than the one she has given herself. Hence, the success of Pyŏng'uk's renaming depends on the spaces she occupies and the others with whom she interacts. The difference between her successful passing as Pyŏng'uk—or becoming Pyŏng'uk—outside the home and the restriction of her name choice inside her home has less to do with any potential gap between the label "Pyŏng'uk" and the characteristics of the real person it represents (which, again, is mediated by never-ending layers of signs) than with the willingness of those around her to accept the identity she presents.

With this queering of identity in mind, I would like to return to the issue of style in *Mujŏng*, particularly the project of representing the novel in hangŭl. Just as the novel's project of (re)presenting heteronormative identities is disrupted by transitions in those identities, its project of pioneering a hangŭl style as normative modern vernacular is disrupted by code-switching. The character Sin Usŏn is especially prone to mixing Japanese into his speech, which, when represented in hangŭl, queers the language of the text as a whole, not simply the linguistically hybrid lines spoken by Usŏn and other bilingual characters. That is, just as in Judith Butler's reading of drag as queering gender norms by exposing the lack of substance beneath the performance of such norms, the transliteration of foreign words into hangŭl has the potential to expose the foreignness of even the Korean words the hangŭl is supposed to represent unproblematically.[28]

For a concrete example, we need read no further than the first installment of *Mujŏng*, in which Usŏn mixes both English and Japanese into his speech as he converses with Hyŏngsik. These instances of code-switching are punctuated with dots that emphasize them for the reader in the manner of boldface or italics in English print matter. In the first such instance, Usŏn addresses Hyŏngsik as "Mister Yi" (Misŭtŏ Ri, 미스터 리).[29] This, like many of the moments when Usŏn code-switches in conversation with Hyŏngsik, instantly places the two of them in a shared space. It establishes the two characters as sharing a certain background, with enough education to have been exposed to English and Japanese—in this case, almost certainly an experience of studying abroad in Japan. The attachment of this kind of language to Hyŏngsik as a term of address even *identifies* him as belonging to this particular social space, in the way that Pyŏng'uk's names place her into specific spaces.

Later in the installment, Usŏn starts to mix Japanese words into his speech. First, when Hyŏngsik announces that he is on his way to meet a girl, Usŏn responds with the Japanese "omedetō," transliterated into hangŭl as "omedettoo" (오메데또오) and without a gloss explaining the meaning of the term (congratulations). In this moment, the reader too is brought into the space that Usŏn and Hyŏngsik occupy through their shared knowledge of Japanese, assuming that the reader also has this knowledge. Usŏn follows this congratulatory remark by commenting that the girl must be Hyŏngsik's betrothed, employing the Japanese term "iinazuke," represented in hangŭl as "iinajŭk'e" (이이나즈케). In this case, however, "iinajŭk'e" is followed by a parenthetical explanation of its meaning: "yakhonhan saram" (약혼한 사람), "person to whom one is engaged." As we observed with episode 53, these parentheses mark off a queer space that intervenes in the main text, disrupting the vernacular representation with extra information not necessarily generated by the narrating voice. "Iinajŭk'e" (이이나즈케) represents the sounds of a Japanese word (許嫁/いいなづけ), pronounced orally in the world of the story, whereas "yakhonhan saram" (약혼한 사람) glosses these sounds with semantic information in Korean. However, even as the parentheses attempt to separate the two into different spheres of labor—one phonetic, one semantic—they still share the same presentation in hangŭl signs, which carry both semantic and phonetic information at once.

In other words, the Japanese characters that would typically represent Japanese words are covered over by hangŭl in the process of transliteration: a kind of linguistic drag. A word that is ostensibly Japanese beneath the surface is presented as Korean, at least in its textual appearance. As with other cases of misrecognition in the novel, what is beneath the surface is at once concealed and readily apparent—in some cases even marked for emphasis. The hangŭl characters here are presented in the same fashion as Korean words, while never denying their non-Korean identity. However, queering the oral/phonetic/Japanese versus textual/semantic/Korean dichotomy allows us to view the hangŭl within the parentheses as likewise misrecognized insofar as it is presented as strictly Korean. The *yakhon* in the explanation of the meaning is derived from a sinographic word, its foreign origins no less apparent to the presumably educated reader. Of course, this kind of borrowed vocabulary, the two-character sinographic compound, has been so thoroughly domesticated as to become a part of the fabric of the Korean language itself. The point is that this fabric is always already multilingual, even if the hangŭl-only style of Yi's text masks its inherent hybridity.

In fact, in this installment we see native Korean, Sino-Korean, Japanese, and English words all represented in hangŭl. Their origins are apparent to certain readers in certain knowledge spaces, and yet it is impossible to schematize their differences without prior knowledge independent of the text at hand and the strictly visual signs it has to offer. The normative logic that sorts words into Japanese or Korean provenance presumes a particular national-linguistic essence prior to its visual representation within the hangŭl text, and yet that essence can never present itself without such a visual sign. In terms of gender, this is performativity. The dressing of "other" signs in hangŭl transliteration parodically ruptures the link between presentation and identity, exposing the incoherence embedded in normative style.

• • •

The novel ends with all of the central characters coincidentally convening on the same train. The train's terminal station is ambiguous but also irrelevant: for all of the characters, their ultimate destination (education in Tokyo or the United States) cannot be reached via train. Better yet, the destination is not a place but rather a time—their own personal futures as well as the Korea of the future that they will help build as its most privileged and educated subjects. At both the personal and national levels, that future is reached via the West (in this case the United States), which is in turn reached via Japan. The train's journey from rural Korea to Seoul and then on to even more civilized destinations reflects a journey through an imperial timeline, revealing the recursive structure of violence and colonization that renders each stop in the journey temporally behind the stop that follows.[30]

As Ellie Choi writes, this journey is useful "as a spatial framework to understand how the traumatic experience of modernity for colonized Korea necessitated the reinvention of tradition and history towards a stabilizing 'ethnic national' identity."[31] In other words, the construction of an ethnonation is inseparable from the situation of Korea within a spatiotemporal framework set up by imperialism—or rather, multiple intersecting imperialisms. In the final installments of *Mujŏng*, this "traumatic experience of modernity" and the burgeoning ethnocentrism it induces are not only highly visible but also tangled up with heteronormative romance, as travel becomes the setting for resolving the romantic triangle(s) central to the plot. In the end, everyone involved settles neatly into normative gender roles and relationships, and is simultaneously integrated into a global capitalist teleology, committed to pursuing progress for the Korean nation.

In the same way that its unruly characters are eventually disciplined into proper (gendered) national subjects, *Mujŏng* has been embraced by the standard historiography of modern Korean literature, despite whatever queerness it embodies.[32] That the queer elements of the novel could be explained away or even co-opted by normative narratives of Korean literary modernity is indicative of just how difficult it is to resist such a working alliance of norms, even when (or especially because) it is internally contradictory. At the same time, the accommodation of *Mujŏng*'s queer elements within the canon of modern Korean literature also points to the possibility of reconfiguring incoherence into coherence, and perhaps even vice versa.

3

The Power to Know

Kim Saryang and the World as Addressee

Kim Saryang's "Haha e no tegami" ("Letter to Mother"), published in the April 1940 issue of *Bungei shuto*, is an enigmatic piece of writing.[1] It takes the public form of an open letter—at least, public enough to be published in a coterie journal. Yet it does not address a public figure. Rather, Kim writes to his unnamed mother, repeating the refrain "Dear Mother" (Ai suru hahaue-sama) as he recounts in an intimate, confessional mode his experience of being nominated for the prestigious Akutagawa Prize. The nomination of Kim's short story "Hikari no naka ni" ("Into the Light," 1939) for the prize—and its publication in *Bungei shunjū* as a result—marks Kim's entry into the elite literary circles of the Japanese (language) bundan, and, arguably, the inauguration of Zainichi Korean literature as a subgenre thereof. Despite the piece's epistolary form, then, it is clearly written for the bundan itself as much as it is for Kim's mother.

I will return to the question of the audience for Kim's letter in a moment. But beyond the undecidability of its addressee, the content of the piece is also less than straightforward. In it, Kim recounts the by turns awkward and exhilarating experience of receiving word of his nomination at his mother's home in Pyongyang, traveling from there to Tokyo, and ultimately attending the awards banquet as runner-up for the prize. Among the most frequently cited passages of the letter is Kim's initial reaction to the advertising copy for the publication of "Hikari no naka ni," a blurb in which author Satō Haruo calls the story "a work that thoroughly weaves the tragic fate of a nation [*minzoku*] into an I-novel."[2] In response, Kim says in the letter, "I asked myself, 'Is this right? Is this right?'"[3] He goes on:

> Dear Mother, I wondered. Had I really written the kind of thing Satō Haruo said I had? I felt a sort of tightness in my chest, as if I had been thrust into an enormous commotion,

> something much bigger than writing a simple story. At least in that moment, I made too much of it. Even though it's my own story, I've always felt that there's something not quite right (*sukkiri dekinai*) about 'Hikari no naka ni.' It's a lie, you're still writing lies, I said to myself, even as I was writing it. Since then I've received many comments from friends and mentors about this issue. But all I could do was remain silent.[4]

Critics have wrestled with the meaning of this "lie" that Kim alludes to here, offering any number of interpretations of the something "not quite right" that Kim mentions but refuses to identify.[5] One wonders whether contemporary readers of *Bungei shuto*, or the "friends and mentors" to whom Kim refers, or indeed, Kim's mother herself, knew what Kim meant here when he spoke of this "lie," of his feelings of doubt and dissatisfaction. The presentation of the letter as intimate communication between close relations suggests that if the referent of the "lie" is not spelled out, it may have been clear with the proper extratextual context. If the reader of the letter fails to grasp the meaning of this "lie," is it due to Kim's circumspection, or simply because this was not the reader he intended to address?

This returns us to the question of which reader(s) Kim *was* intending to address. If the staging of Kim's letter to his mother in a magazine already invites skepticism of its authenticity as personal correspondence, then the final lines of the letter essentially remove all doubt. "I believe my younger sister should be home from Keijō [Seoul] on spring break. Please have her translate this letter from *naichigo* [Japanese] and read it to you," the letter ends.[6] This final reminder that Kim's writing here is ostensibly addressed to his mother throws into relief the fact that he is writing in Japanese, which his mother cannot understand.

The first question this raises, of course, is why Kim would write to his mother in a language she could not read. One possibility, as I have already suggested, is that the letter was never actually intended for her eyes, but rather for those of the Japanese (*naichi*) bundan. But if the intended audience is the readers of the magazine, then why present a piece of writing that is otherwise indistinguishable from an essay as a letter, repeatedly inserting "Dear Mother" as a conspicuous reminder that the addressee is not, in fact, the addressee? And how is this question of addressee mediated by the practice of translation, to which Kim alludes at the end of his "letter," and in which he was deeply invested throughout his career?

This chapter takes up these questions in order to shed light on the ways that audience is situated and implicated within the politics of representation. These questions take on particular urgency in the context of a body of work such as that of Kim Saryang, whose texts have been read through lenses of minor literature, postcolonial and subaltern studies, the Japanophone, and of course, Zainichi literature. What I want to argue here is that each of these potential frameworks through which Kim's texts are read are fairly explicitly concerned with questions of who, how, and in what language Kim is *speaking for*, without necessarily interrogating the implicit audience *to whom* he is speaking. Through an exploration of Kim's critical and fictional texts, I aim to unpack the multifarious impacts of the addressee on the act of speech—particularly its textual forms or representations in text.

Specifically, I read Kim's "Kusa fukashi" ("Deep in the Grass," 1940) alongside the discourse on World Literature—both in the historical moment in which Kim was writing, and in its contemporary iteration. In both cases, the viability of World Literature hinges on the politics of translatability, placing a burden on the marginal writer to produce legible representation for consumption by the always implicit audience demanding such "windows on the world": the Euro-American hegemonic center.[7] Kim's position as a colonial subject of a non-Western empire complicates his relationship to this implicit audience, which required a second layer of translation to reach. Even if Kim is optimistic with regard to the possibility of translation across these multiple layers of power and hegemony, his fiction betrays a lack of confidence in even intralingual communication. In "Kusa fukashi," Kim attempts to translate the lived experience of the least worldly Korean subjects—those furthest removed from the "civilizing" influence of the imperial center—for a metropolitan audience. The failure of this attempt is suggestive of the possibilities engendered by miscommunication and illegibility, as well as an alternative ethics of translation and representation.

ZAINICHI LITERATURE AS READERSHIP: KIM SARYANG'S CANONIZATION

Kim Saryang's biography is a story of traversal, not only of the metropolitan and peripheral spaces of the Japanese empire, but also across languages and literary audiences.[8] He was born Kim Sich'ang in 1914 to a wealthy family in Pyongyang. Though little is known about his parents, the scant evidence available suggests his father held traditional Confucian views—Kim writes that his father objected to sending his older sister to school—whereas his mother was a Western-educated Christian.[9] He first came to Japan in 1931, attending Saga High School near Fukuoka, then Tokyo Imperial University (now University of Tokyo), where he studied German literature and wrote a thesis on Heinrich Heine. It was during his university days that Kim began to publish stories and essays.

The year he graduated, 1939, was a breakthrough in his career. He was involved in editing a special issue on Korea for the magazine *Modan Nippon*, to which he contributed a translation of Yi Kwangsu's latest short story, "Mumyŏng." At the same time, he was publishing criticism in both Korean and Japanese. But perhaps most impactful was his introduction by Chang Hyŏkju, a Korean writer who had already achieved success in the Japanese bundan, to Yasutaka Tokuzō, the publisher of *Bungei shuto*. Yasutaka became a fast friend and a champion of Kim's work, and the publication of "Hikari no naka ni" in *Bungei shuto* led to its nomination for the Akutagawa Prize.

Kim continued to travel back and forth between the Korean peninsula and metropolitan Japan, writing for both Japanese and Korean publications, until the

Pacific War broke out in late 1941. The day after the attack on Pearl Harbor, Kim was arrested and detained for six weeks upon his refusal to serve as propagandist for the war effort. He was released in January 1942 and returned immediately to Korea. There he continued to publish in the few Korean-language venues that remained in the early 1940s, in addition to the Japanese-language journal *Kokumin bungaku*. Japan's August 1945 defeat found Kim in Korea's government-in-exile in China, and he spent the postwar years writing mostly plays and reportage, eventually as an embedded writer with the North Korean army following the outbreak of the Korean War. He fell ill in 1950 shortly after the Incheon Landing, and is presumed to have died sometime that year.

Despite Kim's colonial-period success in both Japanese- and Korean-language publishing, he quickly fell into obscurity in both postwar Japan and the Koreas. The one space in which Kim's work was read and celebrated in the aftermath of the empire was within the nascent Zainichi literary establishment. At least according to standard narratives, Zainichi literature as a genre was emerging, if not yet fully formed, in the late 1940s and 1950s, primarily in the pages of *Minshu Chōsen* under the editorship of Kim Talsu, the so-called "father" of Zainichi literature. Kim Talsu and Kim Saryang were personally acquainted in the early 1940s when the two moved in the same publishing circles, and Kim Talsu himself translated Kim Saryang's postwar writings from North Korea that appeared in *Minshu Chōsen* in the 1950s. Kim Talsu also headed the editorial board that anthologized Kim Saryang's complete works, which were released in 1973 and included many Korean-language works presented for the first time in Japanese translation.[10] It would not be an exaggeration to say the editorial team that published Kim Saryang's complete works comprised the very founders of Zainichi Korean literature and criticism: Kim Talsu, Kim Sŏkpŏm, Ri Kaisei, An Usik, and Im Chŏnhye.

Within the context of Kim Saryang's broad disavowal in Korean and Japanese national literary spheres, it is worth pausing over the question of why he became so canonical to the emerging genre of Zainichi literature, precisely at the moment of its emergence *as* a genre. Shortly before Kim's complete works were published, one of the editors of the collection, Ri Kaisei, was awarded the Akutagawa Prize in 1972. Another of the editors, Kim Sŏkpŏm, had been nominated for the prize in 1970. Kim Talsu had been a favorite of the Japanese bundan since the late 1940s, but the attention of the Akutagawa Prize committee in this moment signaled the indisputable entry of Zainichi writers into the Japanese-language literary mainstream. Ironically, in a way that mirrors the mutual anxieties of colonial Korean writers like Kim Saryang and the metropolitan Japanese bundan of his time, this moment of acceptance brought about a greater need to codify and distinguish Zainichi from Japanese literature.[11]

Possibly due to these anxieties, the incipient Zainichi bundan sought for itself a grounding in colonial (literary) history, a goal fulfilled by identifying Kim Saryang as a forebear—better yet, a patriarch. Why Kim Saryang? One could point to his personal and professional connections to the editors themselves, or to his literary and critical success in the Japanese-language milieu, or to his stated mission of representing Korea to a Japanese audience. Of course, all the above could also be said of Chang Hyŏkju, Kim Saryang's contemporary. And yet it was not until much later that Chang received any serious attention.[12] As Kim Sŏkpŏm spells out quite explicitly, it was Chang's collaboration with the imperial regime and eventual decision to "cease to be Korean" that disqualified him from canonization.[13] In other words, Zainichi literature as coherent genre was constructed via disavowal.[14]

Precisely because of these disavowals—including disavowals of collaboration, Korean-language writing, and intersectional difference that echo the exclusionary logics that marginalized these writers from national literatures in the first place—Zainichi literature in the early 1970s was as tightly-knit and coherent as the genre would ever be.[15] It was produced by an elite, male-dominated cohort of writers ideologically committed to a narrow and exclusive Zainichi canon, several of whom coincided with the editors of Kim Saryang's complete works. I invoke this history not to argue that Kim Saryang or anyone else rightly belongs within the boundaries of Zainichi literature. Rather, I wish to reiterate that those boundaries themselves, insofar as they have any semblance of coherence, are the result of the active suppression of internal heterogeneity. Kim Saryang's position vis-à-vis Zainichi literature is emblematic of the political nature of literary frameworks and their formation.

Yet Kim's case also points to the actual impact such frameworks have, regardless of their instability and incoherence. Kim Saryang's works found a material audience of Japanese-language readers via their reprinting (and in some cases translation) under the auspices of the Zainichi bundan. I would also like to suggest that insofar as these works were presented in connection with Zainichi literature, they also found an *imagined* audience: the audience for Zainichi literature, an audience that overlaps with, but could not possibly be equivalent to, the audience Kim imagined for himself. Moreover, both the material circulation and the conceptual grouping of Kim Saryang with Zainichi literature achieved through the publication of his collected works are direct causes of my own encounter with these texts.[16] In the end, this is what literary frameworks do. They cause encounters between texts and their imagined and eventually material audiences.

THE WORLD AS READING SUBJECT

Kim Saryang, perhaps more than his Zainichi interlocutors in the 1970s, understood his own work and its audience in this sense. He wrote self-consciously on how the possibility or impossibility of reaching certain audiences shaped the direction of his own career. For Kim, the key factor in thinking through the question of audience was language. As outlined above, Kim was a bilingual writer who navigated the challenges of writing for multiple readerships distinguished by language. In the late 1930s and early 1940s, he published with near equal frequency in Korean and Japanese. Kim's commitment to bilingualism is particularly notable given that he debuted at a moment of palpable "crisis" in the Korean language.[17]

As Christina Yi details, by the late 1930s, a generation of educated Koreans had come through the colonial school system, many pursuing higher education in metropolitan Japan.[18] Particularly after the outbreak of the Second Sino-Japanese War in 1937, the Japanese colonial government in Korea ramped up its efforts toward imperialization (*kōminka*), which Yi argues convincingly were centered around language policy. This meant that the late 1930s and early 1940s saw the "suppression of Korean, through educational measures restricting and then finally abolishing the teaching of the Korean language in public schools in 1938 and 1941, respectively, and the forced shutdown of a number of Korean-language presses starting in the late 1930s."[19] This curtailing of the Korean-language media landscape occurred on top of heightened censorship during wartime that affected both Korean- and Japanese-language publications.

Given these limitations on what could be published at the time, Kim criticized imperial suppression of the Korean language surprisingly directly in his 1939 essay "Chōsen bungaku fūgetsuroku" ("Record of Second-Hand Knowledge of Korean Literature"). This was the first of several essays Kim would write that situate him specifically as an intermediary, there to transmit—perhaps even translate—knowledge of the Korean *mundan* to the Japanese bundan. Kim begins the essay by noting the widespread sense of crisis in Korean-language literary circles: "Based on the language problem, it is said that now is a moment of crisis for Korean literature."[20] The most direct cause of the "language problem," according to Kim, is in fact a crisis of readership. He states that the Korean public is even now largely illiterate (citing a figure of 80 percent illiteracy) and points out the shortsightedness of Japanese education policy that attempts to jump straight from the current situation to literacy in Japanese rather than first educating the population in more approachable hangŭl. If it is necessary to prohibit the Korean language from schools, Kim wonders, "shouldn't we just move all schools to the Tokyo area?"[21]

Kim's sarcasm is hard to miss here, as is his denunciation of colonial policy. However, he couches his critique in terms that demonstrate his internalization of many of the tenets of *kōminka* ideology. First, his ironic proposal to send all schoolchildren to Tokyo, presumably because the standard Tokyo dialect (*hyōjungo*) is the only acceptable form of the national language, would seem to place Korea in the same category as other regions of imperial Japan, both *naichi* and *gaichi*, with non-standard dialects. Korea as one "region" (*chihō*) of the Japanese imperial nation-state (rather than having its own national identity) and Korean literature as "regional literature" (*chihō bungaku*) were both crucial for the articulation of Korean subjects' simultaneous difference from and oneness with the metropole under *kōminka*.[22] Second, in focusing on the Korean reading public—more specifically, the lack thereof—as the central cause of the crisis in Korean literature, Kim perhaps inadvertently lends credence to the notion of Korean deficiency. Ironically,

Kim points to widespread Korean illiteracy as the key to maintaining a particular language and culture through "centuries under the yoke of Chinese learning."[23] As he explains, because only the most elite fraction of the population could read and write, the rest of Korea was never exposed to this hegemonic foreign influence. Similarly, Kim remarks on the failure of Narodnik-style literacy programs in Korea in class-based terms: "[These movements] had their heyday, but how many illiterates were they really able to enlighten? The people [*minshū*] always desire that which can fill their most immediate needs."[24] Much as the Japanese empire placed the burden to assimilate on Korean and other colonial subjects, Kim seems to place the burden to "desire" literacy—and by extension, Korean literature—on the uneducated masses.

Both the problem of the internal heterogeneity of the purportedly unified Japanese empire and the yawning gulf of class inequality in colonial Korea demand intersectional analysis of Kim Saryang's career. Fundamentally, these intersecting power differentials have less to do with who is represented, and more to do with who can listen, read, or interpret that which is represented—in other words, who has the power to *know*. Indeed, the issue of knowledge privilege is woven through Kim's critical and fictional work. Knowledge privilege also provides a lens through which to read the contemporary discourse on World Literature as well as the ways that Kim himself participated in a much earlier discourse on the same. Kim's own academic work on German literature from the era of Goethe and the coining of *Weltliteratur*, combined with his status as the darling of English-language critics (myself included) who comprise the implicit audience for World Literature, makes him a valuable case study on the development of the concept across historical contexts and readerships.

Within this context, I would like to draw attention to the shakiness of the ground on which Kim is standing as a purported communicator of knowledge about the Korean peninsula to the Japanese audience. His own elite position prevents him from knowing or even communicating with the Korean people, a limitation to be explored further in the context of "Kusa fukashi." I raise this issue here because questions of knowledge transmission and communication are, to my mind, at the center of debates on World Literature today, which are often framed in terms of the theoretical and practical problems of translation (yet another discourse in which Kim Saryang took an active part).

Perhaps the most direct and forceful takedown to date of the proposals of World Literature is Emily Apter's *Against World Literature: On the Politics of Untranslatability*, framed explicitly as an argument on translation. Apter articulates a skepticism toward the assumptions of commensurability that underlie World Literature and comparative studies more broadly. In her words, the reemergence of World Literature in conjunction with a revitalized translation studies in the early twenty-first century "ignored problems more internal to their theoretical premises. With translation assumed to be a good thing *en soi*—under the assumption that it is a critical praxis enabling communication across languages, cultures, time periods and disciplines—the right to the Untranslatable was blindsided."[25] Following Apter, I would like to explore the possibility of translation as something more ethically complex than an inherent "good," precisely by calling into question the inherent goodness of "communication across languages, cultures, time periods and disciplines."

However, what Apter shares with the proponents of World Literature is a positive evaluation of the field's "deprovincialization of the canon and the way in which, at its best, it draws on translation to deliver surprising cognitive landscapes hailing from inaccessible linguistic folds."[26] Her reference to a deprovincialized canon here refers to interventions toward a less Eurocentric curriculum in comparative literary studies, and yet the cited ability of translation to bring the previously "inaccessible" into greater visibility raises the question, inaccessible to whom? The implicit audience for World Literature—whether in translation or marked as untranslatable—is the same Western reader. Apter refers to untranslatability as a "right" and describes it in religious terms throughout the book, yet seems to view representation in the canon as its own ethical imperative, a contradiction that proves difficult to resolve. To frame the question of who owns a discourse, literary or otherwise, as a problem of whose speech or writing is represented within is to elide the material and imaginary pathways by which literatures are commodified and consumed—in other words, who has the power to *read*.

Kim Saryang and the postwar founders of Zainichi Korean literature responsible for canonizing him were well aware of the transnational politics of readership. Kim frequently pointed to the necessity of representing Korea to the *world*. In fact, this imperative constituted his contemporary and retrospective justification for writing in Japanese despite the Korean-language "crisis" that informed his career. In the same essay in which he laments the lack of Korean-language readers and publication venues, Kim offers such a justification:

> Should we write in Japanese? Of course, it is fine for those who are able to write in Japanese to write in Japanese. However, in the case of making all kinds of sacrifices to go out of one's way to write in Japanese, I think one must have a powerful affirmative motivation for doing so. Such as the motivation to convey the culture, everyday life, and humanity of Koreans to the larger Japanese readership. Or to say it in a more humble sense, the motivation to take on the role of an intermediary in order to spread Korean culture *to the East or the world.*[27]

Here I would like to highlight once again Kim's self-perception as an intermediary between the Korean people and "the world," a position enabled by his fluency in the Japanese language. This statement comes within the broader argument Kim is making that Korean writers should in fact write for a Korean audience, situating himself and his Japanese bundan predecessor Chang Hyŏkju as exceptional cases. Chang himself described his role as a Japanese-language writer in very similar terms:

> There are few nations (*minzoku*) in the world as tragic as Korea. I desperately want to convey this reality to the world. For that purpose the scope of the Korean language is too limited. On this point, I thought I needed to enter the Japanese bundan somehow, since it would also provide more opportunities for translation into foreign languages.[28]

Chang, much more explicitly than Kim, sees his intercessory role as one of expanding the audience—particularly the foreign-language audience via translation—for representations of the Korean *minzoku*.[29]

Yet even as Kim Saryang advocated for continued writing in Korean in order to serve the developing Korean-language reading public (outside exceptional cases like Chang and himself), he also pushed for systematic translation of classical and contemporary Korean literature into Japanese as a means of transmitting it to the world at large. Kim's championing of translation as a means to broader representation comes back to the ethical issues at play in contemporary debates on World Literature and translatability, but it also makes Kim's own interest in German literature noteworthy. In addition to writing a graduate thesis on Heinrich Heine and critiquing the ethnocentrism of Nazi literature in essays published in Korean, Kim frequently invoked Goethe in his essays on the state of literature in the Korean language.

Kim studied German literature in Japan at a time when the latter already considered itself culturally synchronous with, rather than "behind," Western Europe, including Germany. Fascist intellectuals in both spaces were simultaneously trying to reconcile a nationalist emphasis on "blood and soil" with the project of imperial expansion, albeit in very different ways.[30] But in Kim's essays on Korean literature in the late 1930s and early 1940s, Germany becomes a point of comparison as a *peripheral* literature with respect to the Francocentrism of European literature and culture around the turn of the nineteenth century.[31] The marginal position of German-language literature with respect to "the world" during Goethe's career takes on a particular valence when invoked in comparison to colonial Korea. Kim had no choice but to understand his position with respect to *multiple* hegemonic centers. From this perspective, studying German literature for him could never be reduced to understanding a monolithic West against which a monolithic East was defined, but rather as a set of interconnected center-periphery relations.[32]

As Chang Munsŏk points out, when Kim analogized contemporary Korean literature to German literature in the time of Goethe, it was not a matter of the European representing the "universal" and the Korean the "particular," but rather about the potential for radical creative leaps forward in literary language from the precise moment that language is under greatest threat.[33] This is how Kim was able to summon optimism about Korean literature while acknowledging the crisis that threatened its very future. Perhaps Kim drew this sense of optimism in part from Goethe's notion that "national literature is now a rather unmeaning term; the epoch of world literature is at hand, and everyone must strive to hasten its approach."[34] World Literature promised the possibility of literature without nation to writers who had lost their nation. Much of what Kim argues in his critical essays boils down to the notion that a literature's worldliness is *found in translation*.

By the same token, the problems with contemporary World Literature and Goetheian *Weltliteratur* apply to Kim's optimistic outlook on translation, foreign influence, and worldliness. All three rest on an elite, patriarchal, Eurocentric definition of the world—not the world as that to which World Literature might provide a "window," but rather the world as the reading subject looking *through* this proverbial window.[35] Indeed, Kim's proposal for unidirectional translation, from Korean *to* Japanese as vehicular language and ultimately *to* the world (i.e., the West) is evidence of his conception of the worldly reading subject.[36] The same is true of his view of himself as intermediary, representing Korean culture and everyday life to the world—a view shared by his Zainichi literary progeny. Ethical problems arise not only at the site of the native informant's packaging of Korea for Japanese or worldly consumption, but also at the moment we ask how the native informant obtained his information in the first place. Communication among colonized Koreans, with enormous differences in class, gender, lifestyle, education, and even language, can hardly be assumed to be smooth and transparent. Thus, what appears unilateral and unimpeded in Kim's notion of translation as the path out of the nation and to the world, is in fact built on layers of multidirectional translation, misrepresentation, and misinterpretation.

"KUSA FUKASHI": FAILED ETHNOGRAPHY AND THE FAILURE OF ETHNOGRAPHY

If the internal incoherence of colonial Korea is somewhat elided in Kim's critical work, his fiction brings it to the fore. I turn now to "Kusa fukashi," a short story penned in 1940, and loosely based on Kim's trip the same year to the Hongch'ŏn region of Kangwŏn Province, an almost ethnographic mission to observe the slash-and-burn farmers who resided in the area's mountain ranges.[37] Like many others in Kim's oeuvre, the story is the product of a process of translation and adaptation across not only languages but also genres, as it incorporates elements of travelogues Kim wrote in both Korean and Japanese around the same time he published "Kusa fukashi."[38] Thus, Kim's fictional and non-fictional work on rural slash-and-burn farmers positioned him as a reporter, mediator, and sometimes literally a translator. While "Kusa fukashi" is not necessarily autobiographical, it does explore these questions of positionality and representation through the figure of the Korean intellectual speaking *to* the metropole *for* the periphery.

The protagonist of the story, Pak Insik, is a *naichi*-educated medical student who has come to a mountainous region in Korea as part of a Narodnik program sending educated young people to remote areas of the peninsula to offer literacy training, medical care, and other services. There he encounters his former Korean teacher, nicknamed "Hanakami-sensei" (Mr. Noseblower) due to his constant nervous nose-blowing. His teacher is serving as an interpreter for Insik's uncle, the local magistrate. Insik recalls his school days, when he and his fellow students demanded Hanakami-sensei's ouster due to his obsequious behavior toward the ethnically Japanese teachers who outranked him despite his seniority. In the story's present day, Hanakami-sensei is providing Korean-language interpretation for a speech Insik's uncle is giving in Japanese. The speech urges the local people to comply with the Japanese imperial policy encouraging Korean subjects to wear dyed clothing rather than their traditional white. Later, Insik sees Hanakami-sensei painting symbols in ink on people's clothing in order to mark (and simultaneously carry out) their compliance with the policy. Insik witnesses this scene after his uncle's initial speech, then later at the local market, and even at Hanakami-sensei's home, where the latter's wife is enraged because he has soiled her white clothing with ink.

In the second half of the story, Insik travels from the village into the mountains, where the indigenous people still practice slash-and-burn agriculture. He has trouble finding anyone to whom to offer his services, though he does come across some abandoned huts with strange incantations posted on their walls. He also encounters two small children who fear him too much to take the gifts he offers. Finally, he arrives at an abandoned temple. After arranging to spend the night there, Insik learns that the two men there have attracted many of the local people to their religious sect, one of whose tenets is that the Korean people must continue to wear white clothing as a sign of their faith. Awakened from a fitful sleep, Insik overhears the mountain dwellers gathered at the temple chanting the strange incantations he found in the huts. He flees the temple, at which point the narrative jumps forward several years to Insik's reflection on this experience. He wonders whether Hanakami-sensei, who disappeared shortly after the events of the story, fell victim to this religious sect—which has now been revealed to have committed hundreds of murders—while attempting to promote dyed clothing in the mountains. Here the story refers to an actual cult-like religious organization, the Paekbaekkyo (White-White sect). The leaders of the group made headlines in 1937 for the mass murder of over three hundred people, most of them in rural areas of Korea.[39] Thus, in many ways, "Kusa fukashi," with its references to peninsular current events and Kim's own ethnographic travel writing, carries out precisely the kind of mission Kim, Chang, and their postwar Zainichi successors described as motivation for their writing: raising awareness of the plight of Korea, particularly its poor and rural populations.

However, the story also questions the possibility of such seamless communication across not only the Japan-Korea divide, but also class, gender, educational, and regional lines. The opening scene of "Kusa fukashi" explores the multifaceted forms of translation that occur—or, more precisely, fail to occur—across all such boundaries. In fact, this scene poses a situation not unlike that in

"Haha e no tegami." A message is being delivered in a language its audience cannot understand (Japanese), by a speaker who could just as easily have delivered the message in a language the audience could understand (Korean). And the whole strange configuration of speaker and listener is enabled by the presence of a translator, who can bridge the linguistic gap that is intentionally opened up, creating the possibility of communication where it was purposely foreclosed. Both "Haha e no tegami" and the opening scene of "Kusa fukashi" draw attention to the importance of the Japanese language in its mundane material form, not as vehicular language enabling a broader (imagined) audience, but in this case as a language that deliberately excludes. Japanese becomes a mechanism for demonstrating a gap in power between those who use it and those who cannot.

In the case of "Kusa fukashi," this gap in power, created via language, is central to the overall setup of the story. In the scene in question, Insik's uncle, the regional magistrate, has gathered the local people together to hear his speech on the merits of dyed rather than bleached clothing. Despite the complete lack of Japanese fluency among the audience, Insik's uncle delivers his speech in *naichigo* (the language of Japan-proper—the term Kim uses to refer to the Japanese language throughout the story). The narrative wastes no time expositing the language politics in play here, particularly that Insik's uncle believes that it is "beneath his station to use Korean."[40] The text goes on to explain that he makes a habit of maintaining this sense of station through exactly the kind of non-communicative language use happening here:

> Since coming to the village, Insik had seen his uncle drone on and on so proudly in atrocious Japanese [*naichigo*] many times, even to his young mistress who didn't know a word of Japanese. So he was not particularly surprised at the fact that his uncle had gone out of his way to bring an interpreter along so he could give a speech in his pathetically awkward Japanese to a group of mountain dwellers, not one of whom could have understood Japanese (169).

Of particular note here is the way Insik's uncle's practice moves from the domestic to the public sphere. At home the dominance is specifically gendered, with the use of Japanese confirming the magistrate's place within the hierarchy of the house, just as it will confirm his dominance in public before his subjects. In both cases, the presence of the audience is important, even if their comprehension is not. It is important that the speech come via the medium of Japanese, albeit not for the purpose of transmitting the content to the ostensibly primary audience. Instead, that primary audience hears a different, though equally important message: those with power use Japanese, and those without do not.

However, much like Kim's "Haha e no tegami," the opening of "Kusa fukashi" raises the possibility of secondary and tertiary audiences for the content. At one level, of course, the audience for the magistrate's speech is the mountain dwellers gathered at the meeting hall, those physically present and literally hearing his awkward Japanese. Moreover, due to the presence of an interpreter, it is also clear that the speech is not purely performative: it is delivered with the actual intention of influencing the behavior of the local people. And yet, because the message is delivered in a medium that makes it completely inaccessible to this intended audience, there is an implicit second audience for the speech: those who are in a position to assign and respond to the prestige afforded by facility with the Japanese language.

Whereas Kim's secondary (though in all likelihood primary) audience is the readers of *Bungei shuto*, for the magistrate in "Kusa fukashi" that role is filled in part by Insik himself. However, in this case the performance does not have its intended effect. Instead Insik, whose *naichi* education affords him an even higher position in the status hierarchy his uncle is trying to climb, finds his Japanese fluency wanting. But beyond Insik's reaction within the confines of the story, Kim seems to induce a similar reaction among his Japanese-language readers by emphasizing the imperfections in the Japanese speech.

> 「ええと、ちゅまり吾人は白い着物を廃止して、色を染めだ着物を着用（つあく）せねばならんのである」と叔父は胸を張って泰然と後手をし御自慢の弁舌をふるっている。「朝鮮人が貧乏（びん）になったのは白い着物を着用したがらである。経済（げえ）的にも時間（がん）的にも不経済なのである。即ち白い着物は早（す）ぐ汚れるから金が要り、洗うのに時間ががるのである」
>
> 'Err, zat is to say, we must quit using white clozing and use dyed clozing,' said his uncle, puffing out his chest and clasping his hands firmly behind his back. His arrogant speech continued: 'It is white clozing zat has made Koreans poor. It is uneconomical in terms of bos money and time. Zat is, white clozing is quick to get dirty and costs money to replace, and takes time to wash' (169).

Each of the underlined words above contains a stereotyped mispronunciation of the Japanese. The Korean-language rules governing the use of voiced and unvoiced consonants make certain Japanese words difficult for Korean speakers to pronounce, and not two decades before the publication of "Kusa fukashi," Koreans had been outed by pronunciation tests given by vigilantes in the aftermath of the Great Kantō Earthquake in 1923. Failure of such language tests had lethal consequences, with thousands of Koreans massacred as rumors swirled blaming them for the chaos in the wake of the disaster.[41] The magistrate's imperfect Japanese here is perhaps not a direct reference to this history, but much like the language tests given in the violent fallout from the earthquake, these marked mispronunciations serve as proof of his failure to perfect the process of assimilation, his failure to become a consummate Japanese imperial subject. Even if he has risen above the Korean-speaking masses he is addressing, his imperfect Japanese nevertheless relegates him to the middle rungs of the social ladder.

Moreover, particularly in the instances where the error is represented in ruby characters attached to sinographs (typically used to clarify the reading, an example of which is present here in the case of 早（す）ぐ), it becomes conspicuous beyond the level necessary to establish the imperfection of the magistrate's Japanese language skills. Without these pronunciation (mis)guides, the reader would still be aware of the magistrate's identity and position from the second word of the quote from the speech, ちゅまり (chumari) rather than つまり (tsumari). The rubies serve only to exaggerate, to the tertiary audience of the short story's readers, the degree of inaccuracy in the speaker's pronunciation. The sheer number of pronunciation errors represented in the text is perhaps meant to bolster the narrator's description of the magistrate's Japanese as "pathetically awkward," but it also seems to suggest that Insik is painfully aware of each and every mistake, emphasizing his knowledge privilege with regard to the Japanese language.

In many ways, the notion of knowledge privilege is a central thread running through "Kusa fukashi." The story is essentially structured around a series of moments in which Insik is in a position to know more than the people he is observing. He is often positioned as an eavesdropping figure, observing locals who do not know that they are being observed. In some cases, he is literally looking out through a window. Insik first witnesses the marking of the villagers' clothing through a window from inside his uncle's house, then sees the same scene repeated at the local market, this time through the window of the car that will take him into the mountains. He inadvertently sees and overhears Hanakami-sensei's wife's furious reaction to his marking of her white clothing. Later, during his journey in the mountains, he observes the homes of the mountain villages in their absence, including the inscrutable incantations posted on their walls. Throughout the narrative, he hears and knows, but rarely communicates or interacts. Ironically, it is precisely this knowledge privilege, compounding Insik's overall social privilege, that makes communication impossible in many of these cases.

This dynamic is particularly clear in the moment of translation within the story's opening scene. As Serk-Bae Suh has detailed, in the context of colonial Korea, an irony emerged at the site of translation, wherein Japanese settlers and government officials in power tended to be monolingual and therefore reliant on translation, whereas the colonized, who inevitably performed the labor of translation, were often bilingual. This created moments in which the power politics of the empire were inverted, even if the mutual belief in translation as an equal and equivalent exchange performed an assimilating function.[42] But here I wish to highlight the audience for the speech, in this case also monolingual, and marginalized to a point where even translation cannot bridge the gap.

More specifically, at least in Insik's judgment, in terms of the practical goal of promoting dyed clothing, the Korean translation of the speech is just as useless as the inscrutable Japanese. He notes the material realities that prevent the speech from having any meaning for the villagers:

> Insik was repulsed, thinking how stupid the whole thing was—did the people gathered here really care one way or the other if their clothes were white or black?

> Of course, from an economic perspective, and from the standpoint of hygiene as well, it wasn't that he necessarily disagreed with the promotion of dyed clothing. But at a glance, he couldn't see a single person clad in white clothing. Weren't all their clothes just the ashen color of prisoners' garments, as if they had been wearing the same shabby clothing for years on end? As a matter of fact, the only conspicuously white clothing to speak of in the meeting hall was the white linen suit of the internal affairs official seated primly next to the dais (170).

Here there is a palpable sense of Kim's attempt to turn a critical eye toward Japanese colonial policy while writing around the constraints of censorship. His critique is not rooted in a nationalist defense of the tradition of white clothing, of the sort that is commonly articulated in retrospective denunciations of Japanese colonial suppression of Korean culture. Rather, it attends to the problem of class, which was certainly no less salient at the time. As Insik points out here, the rhetoric around the economy of dyed rather than white clothing rings hollow for an audience whose poverty does not allow for any meaningful choice in what they wear. The contrast of the worn, dingy clothing of the mountain dwellers with the white Western clothing of the *naichi* government official serves to underscore the hypocrisy of the decree.

However, as Piao Yinji has argued, the problem with Insik's exclusively class-based analysis of the problems with promoting dyed clothing is that it denies the poor the agency to care about ethnic or cultural tradition.[43] Kim may have been reacting to a tendency among colonial intellectuals to elide questions of class in favor of the ethnonation, as defined and represented by its cultural elites. However, even within Kim's story, working-class Koreans are no less likely to cling to markers of ethnic identity than their more privileged counterparts. As is clear in the case of Hanakami-sensei's wife, a lack of resources or social standing can make the symbolic value of an article of white clothing that much more precious. The doubly or multiply marginalized positions of Hanakami-sensei's wife and the other rural villagers do not relegate them to the passivity of victimhood that Insik subtly ascribes to them. Ironically, it is Insik's membership in the relatively elite strata of colonized intellectuals that causes him to miss the possibility for agency here. To him, ethnic and class marginalization may seem to be opposing forces, but for those subject to both at once, they cannot be disentangled. The intersectional nature of their position makes it difficult to articulate in the language available to someone like Insik or, indeed, Kim Saryang.

The intersectional language politics in play here are further shaded in as Insik flashes back to his participation in a student strike at the middle school where Hanakami-sensei was employed as the Korean-language instructor. He recalls the overt discrimination Hanakami-sensei experienced, paid less than his Japanese peers and denied promotion. He is even reduced to the demeaning role of taking his colleagues' lunch orders and cleaning up after them. We should note here that within the all-male space of the school, it is this feminized domestic labor that marks Hanakami-sensei as lower status than his Japanese colleagues. This feminization is also interpreted as subservience by his students, who come to view him as an ethnic traitor. Moreover, given his position as a Korean-language instructor, in the context of increased emphasis on the Japanese language (as *kokugo*, national language) and devaluation of the Korean language in colonial education policy, a large part of what the students at the school learn from Hanakami-sensei is an internalization of the notion that Korean itself is inferior to Japanese. As we have already seen, Insik's uncle has learned this lesson well, and gained some measure of power within the colonial state as a result.

In Insik's recollection of his school days, however, he notes his and his fellow students' resistance to the language hierarchy presented to them. Here "Kusa fukashi" once again explores the affective capacities of opaque language outside the function of transparent communication. The question of addressee can be helpful in unpacking these alternative functions of language, which become particularly salient in a passage describing Hanakami-sensei's reaction to a statement scrawled on the chalkboard in his classroom:

> One time a certain student wrote 'We are not ××' in Korean on the blackboard. Hanakami-sensei spotted it as he entered the classroom, and his arms and legs were shaking when he finally managed to climb atop the dais, where he just stood there looking embarrassed and mopping up sweat for a while. Eventually he regained his composure and opened the textbook. He took the chalk in his hand and turned to face the blackboard, his raised hand trembling as if he were trying with all his might to remember a certain character. But for some reason, he ended up writing those same characters, ××, from the graffiti (172–73).

Perhaps the first question to ask is to whom the graffiti is addressed. Given the subservient teacher's panicked reaction to the message, it is likely safe to assume that it is subversive, perhaps a declaration that "we are not [Japanese]," in direct opposition to official rhetoric. But if the writer meant to deliver this message primarily to those insisting that the students become Japanese (or otherwise submit to colonial authority), then the Japanese language might have been the better medium for making the sentiment understood. Instead, the use of the Korean language itself is the source of the subversiveness; in this case, the medium is literally the message.

At the same time, the (Korean-language) medium suggests alternative addressees. The author of the graffiti may have intended it for his fellow students' eyes, as a rallying cry to resistance, rather than as a direct message to the powers that be. Perhaps more suggestively, the story also leaves open the possibility that the message is intended for Hanakami-sensei himself, who is positioned awkwardly between the students and their mostly Japanese instructors (just as he occupies this mediating position in the translation scene with which the story opens). His nervous response further suggests that regardless of intention, he himself reads the text as a sort of threat, perhaps because of his ambiguous position potentially within but more likely outside the "we" (*wareware*) of the declaration.

But the censorship of the statement, its core content presented as ×× rather than the "original" taboo phrasing, constitutes an even more striking level of opacity. Kim Saryang may have placed these × characters here himself, anticipating that an actual censor might object to the content, exposing the text to more heavy-handed censorship than the excision of a single word. In this way, the text also draws attention to the censorship apparatus as an inevitable component of its audience. In fact, much like the use of Korean in the graffiti itself, the use of the censor's mark, despite acting as an obstacle to transparent communication, is perhaps more effective than an overt statement at conveying the subversive quality of the unintelligible content. The ××, repeated twice in the passage above and soon after, may draw even greater attention to itself than the "original" characters might have done.

In fact, this censored or pseudo-censored content is only one of many instances in "Kusa fukashi" in which non-meaning text, whether as an opaque representation of a concealed semantic message or simply in its raw material form, drives the events of the story. The flashback sequence in which the ×× first appears concludes with a demonstration carried out by the students, in which they are chanting, "Down with ××" (173). In such close proximity to their previous appearance, one wonders if the ×× here refers to the same antecedent as the ×× Hanakami-sensei trembled to see on the blackboard. In either case, the unseen characters translate directly to the action of the student strike.

Similarly, the story soon introduces the non-meaning characters ×, ○, and △ in its description of the forcible act of marking the villagers' white clothing. While it is never explained precisely why a villager might receive the character × versus ○ or △, regardless of the meaning, the painting of the character itself renders the clothing "dyed" rather than white in the eyes of the bureaucracy carrying out the policy. The writing itself has a material and symbolic impact, even stripped of any underlying meaning. Moreover, the question of audience lends further clarity to the violence being enacted on the bodies of the villagers. That is, the audience for these symbols is certainly not the villagers themselves, who bear the marks upon their backs. As it turns out, Insik's uncle states quite clearly whose eyes the symbols are meant for. Just before Insik first witnesses the writing on the clothes, his uncle explains:

> They were really impressed with my speech just now. So the number of people switching to dyed clothing went up again, see? And actually that means my rating goes up too. If I don't get the numbers up, I won't be a magistrate for long, will I? A college boy like you wouldn't understand, but in government, it's all about numbers, numbers! And my county's rating will get even higher. 'Cause tomorrow's market day, so we're going out to the market to bring the campaign straight to the people (177).

At this point the magistrate starts laughing maniacally, and drags Insik to the window, where he sees that bringing the campaign for dyed clothing "straight to the people" means painting directly on their clothing. In one sense, Insik is once again the audience for this spectacle, with readers of the text experiencing it through his mediation. But within the Japanese colonial bureaucracy, the primary audience is the magistrate's superiors, who will rate his performance based on the number of residents wearing dyed clothing. In other words, the violence being done to the villagers here is not simply a textual recapitulation of the magistrate's speech, which they can neither comprehend nor counter. Rather, they become a text to be read by others.

Thus, the first half of the story highlights the complicity of Insik's uncle and Hanakami-sensei as mediators (and translators) of colonial policy, both delivering the colonizer's message to the masses and rendering the masses themselves a text for imperial consumption. The farcical opening scene featuring a completely superfluous translation, followed by the linguistic and material violence done to the local people through the marking of their clothing, suggests that the violence of the imperial state lies in the unidirectional flow of speech and text. Translation here facilitates this unilateral dictation, rather than acting as means of communication and equal exchange. Insik himself serves as a mediating figure for the readers of the text, his sense of indignation at this violence making it impossible to miss. However, as the story moves in the second half to Insik's own failures to communicate with the mountain-dwelling masses, it becomes clear that even his attempts to become the audience for rather than the dictator of knowledge, or to communicate for the purpose of empathy and mutual understanding rather than dominance, are doomed to fail nonetheless.

The first problem he encounters is the difficulty of locating the people he is looking for. In the first half of the story, Insik's uncle brings up bureaucratic statistics multiple times—not only his county's ratings for the adoption of dyed clothing, but also the relative number of slash-and-burn farmers still present in his jurisdiction. Just as he is boasting that he has made them all into "proper farmers," a fire breaks out on a nearby ridge (185). As Insik and his uncle gaze at the fire out the window, the magistrate is concerned less with the potential damage than with whether it is occurring across county lines, bolstering his claims to successful assimilation of the slash-and-burn farmers within his jurisdiction. Though it is already clear in this scene, it becomes all the more obvious as Insik ventures into the mountains that the county boundaries have no meaning there. The farmers move around frequently, and have no permanent settlements. The people who live in these spaces are a problem for the colonial bureaucracy precisely because they are so difficult to locate, survey, observe, and control. Insik himself recognizes the intractability of this problem, albeit through a shared sense of the superiority of "civilized" ways of life: "If the magistrate tried to stop them again from living within his jurisdiction, he could chase the slash-and-burn farmers around from every which way, but they would inevitably flee to still more uncharted depths of the mountains, just like savages [*banzoku*] under aboriginal assimilation policies" (195).

Nevertheless, Insik's explicit goal in traveling to the region is to empathize with the indigenous people, acting as a savior figure by offering food, medicine, and basic education. Everywhere he looks, then, he sees a problem in need of solving. When Insik finally reaches the slopes where the slash-and-burn farmers live, he comes upon a single small hut hidden among the trees and surrounded by verdant fields. Despite the evident success of the absent farmers who work the surrounding land, the description of their living space itself focuses on its impoverished and dilapidated state. His initial encounter with the dwelling is described as follows:

> The hut, which looked like it could be blown away at any moment, was deserted. Insik tried calling out but there was no answer. Peering through at the dirt floor, he could see broken pottery and a few dirty-looking bowls strewn around, and there was an a-frame pack [*chige*] propped up next to a small hearth. Upon examining the dimly lit room, he could find no further trace of household belongings. There were flies buzzing around in the fetid air, and the earthen walls were plastered with eerie-looking paper amulets [*jufu*] lettered in ink (193).

This is also the reader's first introduction to the cult-like religious practices that have taken hold among the mountain dwellers.

In this first encounter, the space is overwhelmed by a sense of absence and silence. Insik finds no one to answer his calls, and nothing in the house that will tell him anything about its absent residents. Ironically, the only thing here for him to "read" is a physical text, the *jufu*, strips of paper bearing stylized characters, used to ward off calamity. But the actual words on the *jufu* are excised from the text of "Kusa fukashi." In contrast to the distinct visibility of non-meaning characters in the first half of the story, the characters Insik sees here are not reproduced, merely described as *bokuji* (characters written in ink). This may also imply that the incantations are calligraphed, important more for their visual impact and physical presence rather than as a medium for linguistic content. After all, not all texts are supposed to be legible.

The silence of the scene does not last long, however, as Insik suddenly hears the sobs of two small children hiding in the corner of the hut. His immediate instinct is to try to speak to them.

> 'Oh, I didn't see you kids there,' Insik broke the silence, choking on the words. 'No need to be scared. Where have your mommy and daddy gone?' Far from coaxing them out of hiding, this just made the children cry all the more desperately. . . . As he started to take the bundle of sweets from his pack, he may have just imagined it, but his hands seemed to be shaking violently. 'There you go, I'll give you something tasty,' he thought, but the words wouldn't come out. He had suddenly remembered hearing that if you gave these mountain children toys, they wouldn't even know that they were for playing, and if you gave them treats, they wouldn't even know they were food (193–94).

Here Insik is forced to reckon with the nigh unbridgeable gulf between the mountain-dwelling children and himself. It is unclear if the language he uses is even intelligible to them. But even assuming they can understand each other's Korean despite their significant regional and educational differences, Insik's message is clearly not getting through. He appears and likely sounds so similar to the colonial operatives destroying their way of life that the content of his speech no longer matters—all the children can glean from their interactions with him is a sense of fear. Notably, this problem seems to have plagued Insik's peers who have traveled to the mountains before him. They have already warned him that even the basic act of gift-giving results in failure to communicate. Faced with the impossibility of mutual understanding, Insik himself begins to tremble, possibly in fear of the radical otherness of the children to whom he cannot speak.

Eventually the children also flee, leaving Insik alone to continue his journey in search of someone to save. Instead, he finds a different kind of "savior." When Insik reaches the secluded temple, he finds that the elderly priest ostensibly in charge has ceded the ground to a younger man whom he regards as a sage with supernatural powers. When Insik asks this younger man what he hopes to do here, he responds that he is here "to save the wretched masses" (198). He relies on the *Chŏnggamnok*, a cryptic prophetic text from the Chosŏn period that predicts the downfall of the current dynasty and the subsequent establishment of a new utopian order, to argue that the Korean people must continue to wear white in order to be saved.[44]

> 'We Koreans, who wear white clothing, must follow the *Chŏnggamnok* in order to be saved. The fate of the white-wearing race and the path they must follow are all revealed within its pages.'
>
> 'The *Chŏnggamnok?*' Insik asked.
>
> 'Heh heh heh . . . it's nothing difficult. It is written in the *Chŏnggamnok*, that if we wear white clothes and chant ××××××××× we will be saved. Heh heh heh. . .'" (199).

As with the earlier × marks, it is hard to be sure whether there was text censored here, or whether Kim himself chose not to reproduce the content of the chant. With the story's overt references to the Korean news media's reporting on the Paekbaekkyo murders in 1940, it is possible the author or the censors did not wish to print the violent sect's mantra. Another possibility is that the chant's actual words are so cryptic that the ×s represent the meaning, such as it is, just as well as the "original" characters could. In either case, the text once again opens up a radical gap between the reader and the subject matter, which cannot or will not be bridged by Insik (or indeed, Kim Saryang).

The story's climax coincides with the height of this refusal to communicate. Insik awakens in the temple in the middle of the night to the sound of chanting coming from the courtyard. Once again, he peers out through a gap in the sliding doors of the temple. He sees that the local people have gathered in the courtyard of the temple, and have brought gifts of food for the religious leader. One of the key ironies of the story is that Insik—bilingual, knowledgeable, and approaching in a spirit of empathy and charity—is unable to reach the mountain people, whereas the guru figure, with his cryptic text and material demands, is the "savior" they accept. In the end, as readers aware of contemporary current events would know, their trust will be violently betrayed.

But in addition to the abject position of the slash-and-burn farmers, condemned whether they assimilate or resist, this scene highlights once again the failure of communication. As the chants continue, still left unrepresented in the text, a sudden gust of wind blows open the sliding door, exposing Insik to the gaze of those outside. At the moment Insik becomes vulnerable to bilateral knowledge rather than eavesdropping from a position of knowledge privilege, he runs. The final image before the story flashes forward in time is another fire in the mountains. Having earlier described the sight of the mountain fire as "cursed" (呪われた) (189), the imagery of the fire is linked through a common character to the unrepresentable incantations of the sect, present on the paper amulets in the hut (呪符) and in the sound of the chants (呪文). In the final moments of the story, even Insik himself is carried away by the non-meaning power of these overlapping symbols: "Burn! Turn everything to ash. . . . Yes, turn everything to smoke," he exclaims as he flees the temple (202). Even devoid of representable meaning, the material presence of the language of the incantation—much like that of the fire, the Japanese language in the opening scene of the story, the non-meaning characters scrawled on the backs of the villagers, the marks of the censor—wields enormous power.

• • •

The power of the non-meaning and the unrepresentable highlighted at the end of "Kusa fukashi" stands in stark contrast to the various failures of translation, communication, and mediation that occur throughout the text. The ultimate example of this comes in the final retrospective passage in the story, which finds Insik safely reintegrated into the colonial order, serving as a doctor in a rural village. His uncle has lost his job in a bribery scandal and is now working as a land broker. But the fate of Hanakami-sensei is left ambiguous. He is known to have gone into the mountains to promote dyed clothing shortly after the events of the story, and was never heard from again. Connecting his own experience in the mountains with reports of the Paekbaekkyo's grisly murders, Insik surmises that his former teacher may have been murdered by the very man he met at the temple. This final act of bureaucratic mediation leads to his death.

Hanakami-sensei, like Insik himself, acts as an ambivalent intermediary or translator of colonial policy to the hinterlands. Insik is charged with performing a kind of ethnography on the mountain people and communicating the knowledge he finds to the authorities. Hanakami-sensei, on the other hand, brings the message of the authorities in the other direction. In both cases, the demand for a mediating translator figure rests on the assumption that communication is possible in the first place. But even among the Korean characters in the story, the differences often prove unbridgeable. As soon as intersectional differences—particularly differences of class and indigeneity, in this case—are introduced, it becomes clear that the translators fail not simply because Korea is incommensurable to the Japanese audience, but because the translators themselves are radically alienated from portions of the ostensibly monolithic population they are supposed to "represent."

This is how I read the "lie," the feeling of something "not quite right" (*sukkiri dekinai*) Kim Saryang identifies in "Hikari no naka ni," which lends itself to interpretation by metropolitan critics as representative of the struggles of the colonized Korean subject. The fundamental untruth here is the very notion that this subject can be known in the first place, whether by the Japanese readers of Kim's fiction, or even by Kim himself. For a reader like myself, approaching these texts decades after they were written and from an English-language background, the possibility of such representation is even more obviously foreclosed.

And yet, Kim is read as representative within a variety of frameworks. As noted earlier in the chapter, for decades Kim's only significant audience was the canonical writers and critics of Zainichi literature. Thus, Zainichi literature was the only framework through which he was read. More recently, Kim has become the subject of anglophonic scholarship on the literature of the Japanese empire, opening his work up to readings through a much wider range of critical lenses. However, neither postcolonial theory nor minor literature nor the emerging framework of the Japanophone can produce a reading of Kim's work that is anything other than *sukkiri dekinai*—they all leave us with a feeling of something "not quite right." This, I would argue, is precisely because Kim was writing about those figures who resist the domesticating and assimilating functions of translation and hermeneutics. And as long as our scholarship sets out to perform these same functions, we fall into the same traps that Kim himself could never quite escape. Perhaps we tell the same "lie" as well.

4

Representing Radical Difference

Kim Sŏkpŏm's Korea(n) in Japan(ese)

Kim Sŏkpŏm, one of the central figures of postwar Zainichi literature, describes the experience of writing in Japanese as a Korean author in the following way:

> It is said that in Korea there is a strange-looking imaginary creature called a 'pulgasari,' which can dissolve iron and swallow it down, and I wonder, could 'Japanese' [Nihongo] be about to dissolve me, to swallow me completely into its stomach, 'Japaneseness'? Or rather, I wonder, say I were eaten by 'Japanese,' is there some way I could, as the 'pulgasari' does, chew my way through its iron stomach and break free? Could there be a way, somehow?[1]

Aside from the visceral nature of the analogy, what is striking about this passage is the immense power ascribed to the Japanese language. It is an all-consuming force, relentlessly eroding the writer's Korean identity and pushing toward an inexorable "Japaneseness." Kim's goal is to "break free" from inside the mechanism of Japanese, but part of what complicates this process is that, unlike the "pulgasari" creature in his analogy, the Japanese language exists within Kim even as he exists within the Japanese language. As Japanese destroys him from the inside out, how can he do the same to it?

This is the central question of Kim's essay, "Gengo to jiyū: Nihongo de kaku to iu koto" ("Language and Liberty: The Act of Writing in Japanese," 1970), penned at a turning point in the history of Koreans in Japan. At the time of its publication, the past decade had seen the sharp decline of large-scale repatriation of Koreans in Japan to North Korea, normalization of diplomatic relations between Japan and South Korea, and a general shift toward the assumption of long-term residence in Japan. In short, the Zainichi population was increasingly assimilating into mainstream Japanese society, a throwback to the violent assimilation project of the Japanese empire. In this context, Kim's questions take on a tone of crisis. How can he maintain an empowering sense of difference in a (post)colonial assimilation regime? How can he effectively take on a Korean identity without reproducing the ethnonational hierarchies of difference that subjugated him in the first place? And how might he do this with only the language of the colonizer at his disposal, as a consciousness that cannot exist apart from Japanese?

These questions around postcolonial difference and representation echo one of the central tensions in the ongoing critical discussion, now in its fourth decade, of Fredric Jameson's essay, "Third-World Literature in the Era of Multinational Capitalism," and its claim that "all third-world texts are necessarily . . . allegorical, and in a very specific way: they are to be read as . . . *national allegories*."[2] Aijaz Ahmad identifies a number of problems with this idea in his famous response to the piece, not least among them that the framework Jameson employs in his essay reifies the categories of "first-" and "third-world."[3] However, as Jameson then responded, deconstructing these categories is not necessarily the more productive move.[4] If his "othering" of the colonized world is problematic, then so too would be the collapse of its distinction from its former colonizers.

Though the critical discourse on national allegory is now itself an object of nostalgia, it continues to resurface even in much later works of criticism. This is perhaps especially true in Korean studies, where, as I discuss below, the lack of a clear referent for the "nation" of national allegory keeps the debate alive.[5] But even in a much broader set of fields, rereadings of Jameson and Ahmad's debate continue to be produced.[6] These various attempts to construct or deconstruct the nation, or to maintain or eradicate the distinction between first- and third-world literatures, reflect ongoing anxieties surrounding the coherence of disciplinary units and area boundaries. It is a debate fundamentally about the ethical configuration of knowledge-producers with respect to the knowledge they produce. As such, critics find themselves in the same double bind as the writers they examine. As in Kim's essay, the question becomes, what to do with difference?

In this chapter, I look to Kim Sŏkpŏm's fiction and criticism for possible answers to this question. Kim's stories offer potential for "lines of escape"[7] from this double bind—that is, the impulse to avoid an essentialist difference on the one hand, while resisting assimilation into bland and violent "sameness" on the other. While Kim's works of criticism directly confront this problem at a theoretical level, his fiction provides a glimpse of what one potential resolution might look like in practice. His writing is thus a productive site at which to consider some of the issues Jameson and his critics raise: not only the politics of difference, but also the more central issue of national allegory itself.

As it happens, Kim's work has frequently been read as allegory.[8] However, his position as a Korean writer in Japan complicates any attempt to read his work through a first- versus third-world frame. As a legacy of Japan's colonization of the

Korean peninsula, Zainichi literature may occupy the position of "third-world" with respect to Japan, even as Japanese literature is in many ways itself a "third-world" literature with its own corpus of national allegories. Within this recursive structure, it is unclear what exactly a Zainichi allegory would allegorize. Whereas most allegorical readings of Kim and other Zainichi writers see them as thematizing hybrid or in-between identities, it is an open question whether that theme and its centrality are inherent in the texts or produced after the fact through their very framing as "Zainichi literature." At least in the case of Kim Sŏkpŏm, this kind of reading is somewhat counterintuitive in the context of the author's explicit goal of maintaining a specifically Korean identity wholly apart from Japan.

For this reason, my approach is not so much to resist allegorical reading of Kim's stories as it is to probe the historicity of the collective entity they are supposed to allegorize. In other words, my focus is on the nature of the "national" in Kim's stories rather than the allegory. Over just the first half of Kim's long career (now over sixty years), his relationship to "Korea" changed profoundly, and concomitantly so did his ways of imagining it in his texts. I argue that Kim manipulates the language available—ironically, the Japanese he so vividly describes as ravenous "pulgasari"—to create spaces to be particularly "Korean" in a way that may or may not be national, but is productively different.

KOTOBA NO JUBAKU AND THE NON-ESSENTIALIZED NATION

I will not rehearse at length the details of Jameson and Ahmad's debate, which is by now familiar.[9] Instead, I want to focus on the frequently reappearing question of what is meant by "nation," and, by the same token, what constitutes a specifically "national" allegory. This question is a central pillar of Ahmad's critique. He points out that although Jameson repeatedly and explicitly posits national allegory as the specific form of allegory inevitably produced by third-world writers, at the same time he fails to separate the category of nation from other possibilities for allegorical representation. More specifically:

> Jameson insists over and over again that the *national* experience is central to the cognitive formation of the third-world intellectual and that the narrativity of that experience takes the form exclusively of a 'national allegory,' but this emphatic insistence on the category 'nation' itself keeps slipping into a much wider, far less demarcated vocabulary of 'culture,' 'society,' 'collectivity' and so on. Are 'nation' and 'collectivity' the same thing?[10]

Ahmad seems to suggest here that "nation" should be distinguished from collectivities in general, though he too does not specify precisely how. If Jameson's usage of "nation" is fundamentally ambiguous, then in the end, so is Ahmad's. Moreover, a similar slippage with regard to collectivities is still present in more recent entries into the national allegory discussion, which are often much less focused on the "national."[11]

Even if the only kind of allegory up for consideration is specifically national, the kind of collectivity that might fall under the rubric of "national" is open to many possibilities. Of course, in its common usage today, the specificity of "nation" often arises from an implied connection with a state. But the case of Korea—and especially Koreans in Japan—shows that a nation is not simply shorthand for a nation-state. It is worth noting in the first place that the overlaps of terminology are especially difficult to sort out in Korean- and Japanese-language discourse, where the Korean word *minjok* or the Japanese *minzoku* (民族) serve as equivalent for both the English words "nation" and "ethnicity." The words *kungmin/kokumin* (国民, the nation, the people) and *kukka/kokka* (国家, country, nation, state) also frequently stand in for "nation," but only in contexts where a state is assumed, as they include the sinograph 国/國 (*koku/kuk*), implying sovereignty. For this reason, uses of these terms were censored during the Japanese empire's colonization of Korea, leading to widespread use of *minjok* to refer to the colonized Korean "nation." Even after decolonization, there is no such nation-state as "Korea," only the two states on the divided peninsula, both laying claim to a larger Korean nation that exceeds the boundaries of their respective sovereignties.[12] If "Korea" is a nation, it is not in the *kukka* sense but only as a *minjok*.[13]

In fact, the concept of a Korean nation has been so thoroughly ethnicized that little or no effort is made to distinguish between the two, which is readily apparent in the rhetoric of Korea as ethnically homogenous (*tan'il minjok*). Meanwhile, the same belabored rhetoric is applied to Japan, where *tan'il minjok* becomes *tan'itsu minzoku* (単一民族), and the presence of the Korean minority is often one of the first points raised in its refutation. For Zainichi Koreans, "Korea" as nation or *minzoku* is that much more removed from statehood, especially for those, like Kim Sŏkpŏm, who maintain a defunct "Chōsen" nationality rather than adopting South Korean citizenship, thus remaining effectively stateless. At the same time, clinging to Korean ethnicity is not the empowering political move that it might be in a supposedly homogenous Korea, but instead serves to minoritize and oppress in the context of a supposedly homogenous Japan. In this way, if Zainichi writers like Kim wish to deploy the Korean "nation" in their work, there are obstacles to defining that nation in terms of either political sovereignty or ethnic heritage. On top of this, they may not have access to the Korean language, another commonly cited basis for the nation. This is exactly the problem that Kim grapples with in his critical endeavors.

In the late 1960s and early 1970s, a moment of transition for the field of Zainichi literature as second-generation writers like Ri Kaisei, Kin Kakuei, and Kim Sŏkpŏm started to come to the fore, Zainichi intellectuals debated the political implications of writing in Japanese.[14] At present it may seem inevitable that

Zainichi literature should be written in Japanese. However, the language debate in the early decades of the postwar, itself a reiteration of the colonial-period debate in which Kim Saryang took part (as discussed in the previous chapter), reveals that this was not always the case, nor was the Zainichi community's framing as an ethnic minority of Japan. Both debates, then, were concerned with the specific nature of Korean difference in moments when that difference was subject to violent erasure via assimilation. Kim Sŏkpŏm was particularly active in the postwar iteration. From 1970 to 1972, he published many essays on the topic, which were eventually compiled into book form and published as *Kotoba no jubaku: "Zainichi Chōsenjin bungaku" to Nihongo* (*The Spellbinding of Language: "Zainichi Korean Literature" and the Japanese Language*, 1972).

In the main essay of this collection, "Gengo to jiyū," Kim starts by laying out the elements of the peculiar relationship that Zainichi Koreans have with language: namely, that while they experience Japanese as a foreign language, since it is the language of a foreign country formerly positioned as colonizing power, they also have no linguistic space outside of Japanese from which to be conscious of a distance from the Japanese language.[15] These strange language politics, he argues, cannot help but affect the creative process of Zainichi writers, causing (at least in his case) no small amount of agony. He expresses a desire to have his work, which is inevitably positioned vis-à-vis Japanese(-language) literature and read by a Japanese-language audience, maintain a sort of particularity or strangeness within what he experiences as an oppressive Japanese-language frame. Kim emphasizes that this linguistic positioning of Zainichi Koreans, forced to be conscious of a "lack" of their so-called ethnic language, cannot be cut off from the history of colonialism, under which Koreans were forcefully robbed of their language and culture. Thus, he argues, the issue of language for them can never be entirely a personal one, but inevitably involves the ethnonation (*minzoku*).[16]

Importantly, even if this naturalized tie between language and ethnic identity is contrived, it still has the power to cause real suffering. Kim describes an intense emotional pain or even "self-hatred" at his own inability to write in Korean at a satisfactory level, or even to avoid the process of assimilation or "Japanization" of Zainichi Korean culture and literature.[17] He calls this process "the spellbinding of language" (*kotoba no jubaku*),[18] describing a double bind akin to the one Jameson raises in his response to Ahmad, that is, the impossibility of maintaining difference without reducing it to "otherness" when the only language available is already overdetermined by imperial history.

The key to undoing this spellbinding is what Kim describes as a process of transcending the particularity of the colonial history and postcolonial circumstances in which Zainichi Koreans are embedded and accessing the "universal" (*fuhensei*). Kim quickly stresses that this "transcending" is not tantamount to escaping or negating such particularities, and argues that in fact the experience of particularity or difference is itself a universal experience.[19] It is for this reason that

Kim claims that a complete subjective consciousness is only possible for Zainichi Koreans through the becoming of a specifically Korean national subject, and it is the embrace of this national identity—not the rejection of it—that allows for a will toward the universal. Moreover, the transcendence of particularity (nationality) is not necessary for the achievement of autonomy; rather, the possibility of a turn toward the universal is, in and of itself, subjective autonomy.[20] In other words, rather than the universal itself, which Kim leaves vague and unproblematized in his essay, it is this orientation toward the universal that constitutes the possibility of radical Zainichi difference. As he searches for a space to occupy that escapes both the pressures of assimilation and the parochialism of national identity, the goal always remains slightly beyond his reach, just like the elusive universal. What matters is the will toward this deferred, alternative space rather than the actualization of the "universal."

In the final section of his essay, Kim looks at the interface between the particular and the universal in the context of literary production. He makes reference to structural linguistics, and the arbitrary relationship between signifier and signified in the creation of meaning. While recognizing that Korean and Japanese words differ not only at the level of signifier (particularly in terms of sound) but also at the level of signified, as even "equivalent" words will conjure up images, memories, and experiences that vary depending on the listener's specific background, Kim draws on the translatability of languages to posit a space that is truly universal. In this universally commensurable space, the Zainichi author attains the freedom to create a specifically Korean world that exists within the boundaries of the Japanese language, while simultaneously exploding those very linguistic bounds. It is at this unreachable "universal" level, rather than the surface level of material words, that Kim calls for Koreans writing in Japanese to inscribe a "Korean flavor" (*Chōsenteki na taishū*; literally "Korean bodily odor") into their writing to avoid being too "Japanized" by writing in Japanese.[21]

At first glance, this may appear to be an assertion of essential difference and a desire to maintain a pure and complete Korean ethnic identity. To be sure, Kim's essay leaves the reader demanding to know what, exactly, constitutes a "Korean" flavor or the danger of a literary work being "Japanized." Ōe Kenzaburō and Ri Kaisei mention having these questions in a roundtable discussion with Kim printed in *Kotoba no jubaku*, but the latter refuses to answer them over and over.[22] Therein lies the key to understanding Kim's conceptualization of the Korean nation: it is not a reified entity with a set of cultural or other characteristics that can be defined and stereotyped. Rather, it is an imagined construct, deployed for the purpose of creating a space in which to articulate a specifically *non-reified* difference as an act of postcolonial resistance. In this sense, Kim Sŏkpŏm's project could be productively compared to Spivak's strategic essentialism, in that his nation is merely a tool for resisting postcolonial hegemonies.[23] Where he departs from such a strategy is in his unwillingness to actually essentialize his nation, ascribing to it no homogenizing power. Kim's Korea is never immanent, but always elsewhere, and this gap enables the possibility of representing difference.

TRANSNATIONAL IDENTITIES AND THE POLITICS OF READING DIFFERENCE

In this way, Kim's grappling with language politics illuminates the underlying question in the discourse on Jameson's statement on national allegory: what can be written (or read) into a text, and by whom? Jameson's essay is less about the relative merits of national allegory than the question of what is possible for third-world authors to write in the first place. Where Jameson concludes that a first-world libidinal narrative is an impossibility for the third-world writer, Kim's question is, predictably, even more desperate: is even the national narrative Jameson describes a possibility for the Zainichi writer? In other words, is it even possible for Kim to articulate a Korean identity in any language—in language itself—much less in Japanese?

These questions highlight the specificity of Kim Sŏkpŏm's position within Zainichi literature and the status of Zainichi literature as "third-world" without necessarily having access to a "nation" to allegorize. Kim is acknowledged as a kind of exception within the genre of Zainichi literature for writing mainly about the events of the 4.3 Incident (in which thousands of residents of Cheju-do, an island off the southern coast of the Korean peninsula, were massacred following an armed uprising to protest the 1948 elections that set up two divided Korean states) rather than about Korean characters in Japan.[24] The 4.3 Incident is the setting of the two major works from the early part of Kim's career, *Karasu no shi* (*Death of a Crow*, 1957) and *Mandogi yūrei kitan* (*The Curious Tale of Mandogi's Ghost*, 1970). *Karasu no shi* tells the story of Kijun, who is employed as an interpreter for the military police, but acts as a double agent, passing secrets to rebels hiding in the mountains. Meanwhile, he is in love with their leader's sister, Yangsun. The story reaches its climax when, in order to maintain his cover as a spy, Kijun must watch in silence as Yangsun and her elderly parents are killed in a mass execution. *Mandogi yūrei kitan*, on the other hand, chronicles the life of Mandogi, a "dimwitted" temple boy who unwittingly becomes involved in the uprising and is arrested by the police. He, too, is to be shot in a mass execution, but the bullet fails to kill him, and he returns as a "ghost" to wreak havoc on the authorities. Eventually, he burns down the temple he has served for so long and is seen going into the hills, presumably to join the guerrillas there in their fight.

Both novels have been read as allegories for the Zainichi experience. These readings attempt to domesticate Kim's work—to locate in his writings on Cheju-do an underlying concern with Japan or its Korean minority. Elise Foxworth, for instance, suggests that Kijun in *Karasu no shi* is representative of Koreans in Japan, who are similarly caught in a marginal or intermediary position, and have the option of "passing" for Japanese just as the spy character must "pass" before his American employers.[25] Christopher Scott makes a similar argument, viewing *Mandogi yūrei kitan* as a rewriting of the 4.3 Incident into the history of Japan, rather than as a novel of Korea to be dismissed as "foreign" by its Japanese-language readership. Scott further relates the novel to Japan by once again reading Mandogi as an allegory or stand-in for resident Koreans, "focusing on the narrative representation of Mandogi's 'ghost' (i.e., ghost writing) as an allegory about the identity and agency of the Zainichi Korean writer (i.e., ghostwriting)."[26] He summarizes his own position as follows:

> *Mandogi* is first and foremost an allegory about the 4.3 Incident. . . . Kim has been writing about the incident in Japanese for nearly fifty years, but Japanese critics often see his work as far removed from Japan or Japanese literature. *Mandogi*, in particular, has been read as a foreign text. I, however, see *Mandogi* more in terms of its hybridity, its double-ness, or what one critic has called its "zainichi-ness." . . . The mystery of Mandogi also haunts the narrator, who is unable—or, as I will contend, reluctant—to retell Mandogi's story accurately or faithfully. This unreliable narrator embodies the dilemma of the zainichi Korean writer, who often feels fake or inauthentic because of living in Japan and writing in Japanese.[27]

Through his incisive analysis, Scott is able to see the allegory operating at a higher level: not only is Mandogi's ambiguous identity a comment on Zainichi identity, the narrator, too, stands for the Zainichi writer and his fraught position within Japanese or Japanese-language literature. In either case, the novel is rescued from its status as a "foreign text" and its "Zainichi-ness" is reasserted.

While such allegorical readings of Kim's work are certainly productive, revealing a depth in the texts that is not readily apparent, they may run the risk of reproducing the structures of power and privilege critiqued in the context of Jameson's original deployment of national allegory. What is especially visible in these readings of Kim is what Shu-mei Shih calls the "time lag" or "nostalgia" of allegory:

> Allegory is only one kind of meaning-producing form, and it is also but one of the hermeneutical codes we can bring to the reading of texts. Clever readers can, I would suggest, interpret any text as an allegory, as long as they labor to do so. The temporal gap between the literal and the allegorical meaning of a text is then the designated field of interpretive labor. In the end, it is in the politics of allegorical interpretation as a value-producing labor—who has the privilege of doing it, who is forced to do it, who has the luxury not to do it—that the nostalgia of the First World theorist becomes legible and can be fruitfully critiqued. The time lag of allegorical meaning production in the movement from the literal to the figural evokes the belated temporality of Third World culture in modernity.[28]

To be sure, this "interpretive labor" is highly visible in attempts to read Kim Sŏkpŏm's Cheju-do fiction as Zainichi allegory, even where such a figurative meaning is not obviously present. As readers labor to interpret Kim's stories in this particular way, they reproduce a narrow conception of what Zainichi literature categorically is: representative of the Zainichi experience. They participate in a circular process, in which the very coherence of the genre of "Zainichi literature" is constituted by a specifically ethnic experience, and the framework of "Zainichi literature" inscribes that same coherence of "Zainichi-ness" onto the texts within its purview.

Where these readings depart from the national allegory framework is in the entity that is ostensibly allegorized. Rather than allegories of the broader Korean nation—whatever that might entail—the collectivity that Kim cannot but represent in his stories is specifically the Korean minority in Japan. However, it is clear from his essays that Kim is not interested in espousing this kind of hybrid identity. As soon as Japan becomes part of the equation, Kim already feels a loss, able only to view his existence in Japan as a painful legacy of colonial injustices that created the Zainichi situation in the first place. Moreover, for Kim, accepting Zainichi identity is tantamount to accepting the permanent division of the Korean peninsula and the impossibility of a whole and complete Korean nation. Although Kim's position on this issue is not mainstream in the Zainichi community, it offers one potential scenario in which a minority or ethnic identity may be expressly at odds with the nation. While adopting a hybrid identity like Zainichi may be a liberatory or empowering stance in many situations, in this case at least it also runs the risk of foreclosing other potential options for identification, such as the Korean nation of Kim's imagination.

This is not to suggest that the category of Zainichi be dropped in favor of reinforcing normative national or nation-state boundaries. The Korean nation-states established on the peninsula in the wake of the Korean War have provided ample evidence that such a model is more than capable of producing oppression. In the first place, Zainichi identity is a perfectly valid option, which members of the community choose to perform in any number of diverse and empowering ways. But a non-reified nation like the one Kim sets out to create in his fiction has its own liberating potential. In fact, the thorough ethnicization of the Korean nation(s) and the Zainichi community can reproduce the same imperialist rhetoric that these groups set out to refute. The nation, carefully deployed, may offer more potential to be explicitly imaginary, to wear its unreality on its sleeve.[29]

Thus it becomes crucial to unravel the Zainichi community's contingent transformation from displaced or exiled members of a Korean nation at large to a minoritized ethnic group, defined always within and with respect to Japan. This brings us back to one more potential problem with reading *Karasu no shi* and *Mandogi yūrei kitan* through the same lens of Zainichi allegory: its ahistoricity. That is to say, "Korea" (not to mention "Zainichi") simply did not mean the same thing to Kim when he debuted with *Karasu no shi* in the late 1950s that it did during his re-entry into the Japanese-language literary scene with *Mandogi yūrei kitan* in the early 1970s. Over this decade-plus, during which Kim Sŏkpŏm attempted and abandoned a writing career in the Korean language, the "Korea" that acted as the binding force for the coherence of the Zainichi community underwent a shift from nation to ethnicity, and in a parallel process, the collective itself shifted from one of exile to one of minority—where "exile" is understood as emphasizing physical displacement from the real or imagined space of a nation, and "minority" as emphasizing the hereditary difference of ethnicity. These shifts took place due to a range of Cold War political factors and in parallel with postwar struggles to disavow the colonial past in both Koreas and Japan,[30] but most illuminating for our purposes here is the shifting politics of language.

Kim Sŏkpŏm's early career in particular demonstrates that authors like himself, who would eventually be called Zainichi, were not always so isolated, linguistically and otherwise, from the Korean peninsula, especially in the first decades following the end of World War II and the collapse of the Japanese empire. It was only later, toward the 1970s, that Zainichi literature became codified as a minority literature of Japan. Kim's fiction and essays reveal the situation to be more fluid and complex in the early postwar years, and they shift in response to political changes and new understandings of the position of Koreans in Japan. In Kim's novels, we can see the manifold ways that the politics of language are intertwined in Kim's struggle to enunciate a liberating Korean identity in response to what he sees as a deepening crisis of assimilation.

BEING AS RESISTANCE: KOREA(N) IN THE SPACE OF JAPAN(ESE)

This deepening sense of crisis, as Kim Sŏkpŏm perceived his choices as Zainichi Korean narrowing to assimilation and minoritized difference, manifests itself in the struggles encountered by the characters in *Karasu no shi* and *Mandogi yūrei kitan*. The ethnicization of Zainichi Koreans is readily apparent in the gap between the positions of Kijun and Mandogi, the protagonists of the two novels. As noted above, both men occupy a tenuous or ambiguous position that can be likened to that of the Zainichi community in general (with the above caveats about allegory in mind). However, the specific circumstances in which these characters find themselves differ significantly in a way that corresponds to differences in the political conditions of the novels' respective historical moments.

In *Karasu no shi*, Kijun's lack of power arises, counterintuitively, from his role as a spy. In fact, much of the drama in the novel turns on this irony: even as Kijun's spying places him in a dynamic position, allowing him movement across languages and spaces, its pressures in turn impose restrictions on his speech and actions. His indispensability as a double agent forces him to place the needs of the party before his own, and results over and over in his inability to say or do what he wishes. Though he is loyal to the cause of the partisans, led by his dear friend

Chang Yongsŏk, Kijun at one point grumbles to himself, "Ah, I want to be freed from this mute-like existence, and I too want to pick up a gun and fight with all my heart like him,"[31] emphasizing his "mute-like" silence as the symbol of his lack of freedom as a spy. The novel follows Kijun through increasingly difficult moments of forced silence, culminating when he must watch, without revealing his inner anguish or compassion, as Chang's family is massacred by his employers.

The novel brings home the tragic irony of Kijun's position in a scene in which he is confronted by Yi Sanggŭn, the dissipated son of a wealthy islander, who suspects that Kijun is a spy. Sanggŭn taunts Kijun by mentioning that he is thinking of becoming a spy and elaborating on how liberated and powerful spies must be. Being aligned with neither side of the conflict, he says, is real power: "My actions have nothing to do with either of them, and in that way, I'm free. It must be the same way for a spy" (90). Kijun's only option is to respond vaguely lest he reveal too much, but his inner monologue is narrated as follows:

> Yi Sanggŭn could know nothing of the nebulous world of the spy. He could know nothing of that dark part of your mind . . . where you struggled with an unseen tension, constantly wracked with horror by a sense of yourself as a tiny hero and then a demon. Kijun was barely able to suppress his voice, rising sickly sweet in his throat to say, 'You know, real spying isn't like that at all' (91).

Again, Kijun finds himself unable to speak his mind, reprising the very powerlessness he faces as a spy. However, at every turn, including this climactic scene, Kijun's silence is ultimately voluntary. The powerlessness, silencing, and marginalization that he experiences are, in the end, the result of a political position he has chosen for himself, whereas in *Mandogi yūrei kitan*, Mandogi's very birth is seized upon to subject him to ridicule and exclusion.

In the first place, Mandogi is intellectually disabled, frequently addressed by characters in the novel simply as "dimwit" (*usunoro*) or "stupid" (*baka*). If Kijun suffers from an excess of linguistic ability, doomed to spying by his knowledge of English, Korean, and presumably Japanese, then Mandogi certainly lies at the opposite end of the spectrum. The narrative specifies more than once that Mandogi does not "understand a word of Japanese,"[32] and his Korean (uncannily represented in Japanese) seems somewhat limited, with Mother Seoul, his abusive mother figure at the temple, once exclaiming that she thought he was mute (32). Mandogi's biological mother is also described as "nearly mute" (15), suggesting that Mandogi's own impairment is hereditary. This word "mute" (唖, *oshi*) is the same that Kijun uses to lament his obligatory silence in *Karasu no shi*, but in the case of Mandogi, that silence is embodied. The linguistic impossibilities faced by Mandogi are no longer a matter of choice or even the illusion of choice, but instead are inscribed on his body and obliquely attributed to heritage. If Mandogi is to be read as an allegorical Zainichi figure, he is a thoroughly ethnicized one.

Mandogi is also marginalized in other ways by the circumstances of his birth, namely his lack of official parentage or place of origin. As the novel explains in its very first pages, Mandogi was dropped off at a temple as a small child by his mother. Mandogi's father is given no name, ethnicity, or other identifying markers, and is described only as having appeared one day at the Osaka temple where his mother was employed, eventually raping her in a closet. Mandogi's "identity," then, at least in terms of ethnic or social origins, is completely ambiguous. This alienates Mandogi not only at the affective level, but also at an official level, as it excludes him from the *koseki* family register system. Nonetheless, just as Kijun's "power" as a spy turns against him, Mandogi's marginalization is flipped around, becoming a disruption for the systems of power he encounters. For instance, the novel opens with a discussion of Mandogi's namelessness and mysterious origins, but quickly hints that this may be more of a problem for the police than for Mandogi himself.

> He had been nameless since birth, with no family register, so when he was asked for his name, age, parents' names, and permanent residence, he didn't have a good answer. This kind of person, the kind without any distinguishing data, became a nuisance for the draft officials making the lists. The vagabonds with no addresses were no problem, as they could be arrested and sent straight to the work camps, but those without definite birth dates, and especially those without definite names, were even difficult to put on the draft list (11).

Whenever Mandogi encounters bureaucracy, on the occasion of his conscription into forced labor at a Hokkaido mine or his arrest in the middle of the 4.3 Incident, his lack of "data" up to and including his name becomes a kind of guerrilla tactic. Later, after Mandogi's botched execution, his continued actions after his disappearance from all records create an even graver problem for the police. As a "ghost," Mandogi's marginal status is *disembodied*, which renders him impossible to control. Eventually, Mandogi burns down the temple headquarters and goes up the mountain to join the resistance, all made possible by his reduction (elevation?) to a non-entity. Even as Mandogi is thrown into greater crisis, he is able to maneuver into a position of resistance.

The same type of reaction to crisis can be seen at the stylistic level in the bilingual play that Kim includes in both novels. The hybrid nature of the language in these texts could itself be seen as a representation of sorts of the Zainichi experience, the caught-between positionality that is so often supposed to define what it is to be Zainichi and to write Zainichi literature. Indeed, the insertion of Korean words into the Japanese text, the non-standard glosses of Japanese words, and other moments of heteroglossia in Kim's texts locate them within a genealogy of linguistically hybrid literature going back to the Japanese empire.[33] However, the uncanniness of the language in Kim's texts goes beyond a simple admixture of Korean and Japanese, and instead radically challenges the spatial consistency of those languages. Kim fights in the texts against the "spellbinding of language," and works to destroy the Japanese language, along with its ethnic logic, from the inside out. Although this labor is evident in both *Karasu no shi* and *Mandogi yūrei kitan*, a closer examination reveals different strategies in play between the two novels according to the language politics of the moment.

The complicated language that Kim employs in *Karasu no shi* reflects the ongoing complexity of the linguistic environment into which it was published in 1957. On one hand, the work is clearly intended for a Japanese audience, and it includes explanatory notes for Korean concepts and objects that may be unfamiliar. For instance, Kim uses the word *paji* for traditional Korean trousers, and includes a note explaining that they resemble Japanese *monpe* pants (45). On the other hand, he peppers his Japanese with Korean place and personal names, all glossed with katakana, a practice that serves as a constant reminder that the story is somewhat removed from Japan and assumes a certain knowledge of the Korean peninsula. In other cases, he glosses a known character with a phonetic representation of a Korean word. For example, in dialogue, Kim uses the character for "red" to indicate the communists, but he glosses it with the katakana *barugan'i* for the Korean *ppalgaeng'i* (commie): 赤 (バルガンイ) (40). This device adds little to the understanding of readers who do not already know the Korean word in question, beyond the simple reminder that the speech is taking place in Korean. In the most extreme case, it may even slow down a monolingual reader, who must supply the meaning for the gloss. For the bilingual reader, however, it points to a more colorful term than the "red" of the main text. At some level, then, the novel is intended for or at least offers a richer textual experience to bilingual readers.

One of the most interesting examples of this kind of playful or disruptive linguistic practice comes from a work published just months before *Karasu no shi*, Kim's earliest attempt to fictionalize the history of the 4.3 Incident: "Kansha Paku-soban" ("Pak-sŏbang, Jailer," 1957).[34] A prisoner insults the title character's pock-marked face by calling him *nassumikan*, referring to a citrus fruit with a rough, lumpy rind. In Japanese, the fruit is called *natsu mikan*, the closest Korean phonetic approximation of which is *nassŭ mik'an*. What appears in the story, *nassumikan* in Japanese katakana, is a Japanese approximation of the Korean approximation of the original Japanese. Kim draws extra attention to these layered contortions within the plot of the story, as Pak is initially confused by the word and consults an acquaintance about its meaning and origins, suspecting it to be a word from the Cheju dialect. He tells his friend, Chin, that he has heard people saying that Chin's face looks like a *nassumikan*, distancing himself from the insult, and asks if he has any clue what it means. This leads to a humorous scene in which the two puzzle over the meaning of the word with similar *mikan* fruit literally right in front of their noses. Eventually one of the local government officials who was educated in Japan stops by and solves the mystery, explains that a *nassumikan* is a Japanese word, and adding that "oddly enough, Pak-sŏbang's face looks just like one" (13). Again, the linguistic play in this scene is certainly not confusing enough to leave readers with only the Japanese language out of the joke, but those who can hear the Korean pronunciation behind the Japanese representation of the word spot right away the source of Pak's confusion, and get to enjoy an additional layer of ironic humor. Though this kind of bilingual text may seem inscrutable decades later in the absence of a substantial Korean-Japanese bilingual readership, at the time there were plenty of readers who would have fully appreciated it.

In *Mandogi yūrei kitan*, however, rather than assuming a bilingual audience, Kim writes largely for readers, both Korean and Japanese, who have little or no familiarity with the Korean language. This is not to say that *Mandogi yūrei kitan* contains none of the linguistic complexity and playfulness of earlier works like *Karasu no shi* and "Kansha Paku-soban." Kim still includes many Korean words in the text, but rather than inserting Korean by glossing standard Japanese words or compounds with phonetic Korean readings, Kim uses unfamiliar compounds of Chinese characters that stretch the boundaries of Japanese. For example, Kim repeatedly refers to Mandogi's fate using a four-character compound (四柱八字 [サジュパルジャ]) found in Korean but not Japanese, sometimes glossed in katakana as *saju parucha* for the Korean *saju p'alja*, and elsewhere glossed in hiragana as the Japanese word *unmei* (fate) (12–13).

If the insertion of Korean into earlier works seems almost like a game, simply providing additional layers of meaning and humor for an assumed audience of bilingual readers, then the device at work here betrays a greater sense of crisis. Whereas before both reader and writer could be comfortable in the existence of a linguistic space outside the range of either Korean or Japanese ideological monolingualism, now Kim seems to be desperately trying to create such a space, to push back against the bounds of a language that suddenly feels oppressively Japanese. He is attempting to teach a Korean word to his readership, in a way; and indeed, on numerous other occasions in the novel, he goes out of his way to provide extensive definitions and notes on Korean words that appear in his text, sometimes in long, awkward parentheticals, and other times digressing for paragraphs at a time in the narrative itself. Now one senses the author in battle with the Japanese language. Kim's greatest weapon in this battle with Nihongo is the potential of these linguistic acrobatics to create the new, imaginary space that he seeks as other potential spaces of identity close off around him. He plays with the visual and oral elements of text in a way that violates the boundaries of the Japanese and Korean languages, occupying the always particular "universal" space of literature that Kim refers to in "Gengo to jiyū."

If we return to *Karasu no shi* with this line of thinking in mind, we can see how Kim creates a "Korea" in his work that is liberated from claims to authenticity or truth. This freedom arises as the text draws attention to its own uncanniness by never allowing the reader to forget that what is being represented in Japanese is Korean speech in a Korean setting. Nearly all of the character and place names in the work are glossed with katakana representing the Korean pronunciations of the names, such that the sense of place in the novel is tightly tied to the sounds of the Korean language. But the more interesting device is the insertion of Korean glosses into the spoken lines of the characters themselves.

For instance, in one scene in *Karasu no shi*, two minor characters have the following brief exchange:

> 「へへへっ、おてんとさんもちと情(じょう)がねえな、たまにあおらでも洋煙草(ヤンタムベー)をふかすんでさあ. . . いっひひひ」
> 「ははっ、令監(ヨンガム)（爺い）」

> 'Heh heh heh. The sun, he's a bit of bastard, eh? Sometimes even I smoke the *yangdambae* [Western cigarettes], y'know. Ee hee hee hee.'
> 'Ha ha, *yŏnggam* (*jijii*) [old man].' (54)

This brief dialogue embodies the many facets of the language play present in the novel. First, the *furigana* Japanese gloss of the word *jō* (情(じょう)), the contractions and elisions of sounds ("tama ni wa" pronounced as "tama ni a," for example), and the phonetic representations of laughter lend an overall oral quality to the lines, causing the reader to hear them rather than just reading or seeing them, even as the parenthetical gloss of *jijii* (爺い, old man) indicating the meaning of the Korean word *yŏnggam* (令監(ヨンガム)) interferes with this mode of reading by adding untransmittable, strictly visual or semantic information. But then, the Korean *furigana* glosses have the potential to cause the reader not just to hear the words of this conversation, but to hear them in Korean. If the creation of a Korean space within a Japanese-language work of fiction is the definition of "Korean flavor," then *Karasu no shi* can clearly be seen as a successful implementation of this "flavor."

In the end, however, we are forced to remember that the Korean space and Korean sounds created in the novel are nothing more than fiction. Even if the Japanese text of the novel represents in reality an audible Korean language, ultimately that "reality" is not actually real. But what is crucial here is not that these Korean sounds do not exist, but that even in their utter emptiness they have the power to destabilize the imposing presence of the Japanese language and to open up new possibilities within it. In the same way, it is precisely the fundamental incoherence and unreality of the Korean "nation" of Kim's imagination that allows it to become a weapon against assimilation and the erosion of productive difference. The "Korea" that Kim posits in the tension between the orality and visuality of the words on the page has radical potential as a space of escape from the "spellbinding of language."

Kim pushes this space further in *Mandogi yūrei kitan*. Its narrator has a much more oral storyteller quality; the long, sometimes rambling paragraphs, rhetorical questions, and speculative sentence endings create a character within the narrating voice itself, and its indirect style of quotation that foregoes quotation marks blends characters' voices directly into the narrative. This style makes it difficult to parse whether characters have actually "said" their quoted lines, adding another layer of ambiguity to that arising from the translated nature of the dialogue, which, as in *Karasu no shi*, must have occurred initially in "Korean." Even in the absence of quotation marks, however, the dialogue retains a direct quality due to its marked orality. Or, interpreted another way, the dialogue is indirect, but reported with a high degree of oral flavor by the narrator—either way, it goes out of its way to report sound, not just meaning, to the reader.

As in *Karasu no shi*, this "oral" Japanese paradoxically creates the imaginary space in which the reader can "hear" the Korean sound of the dialogue even as it stands in for and covers over that "original" Korean in its position as pseudo-translation. At certain moments in *Mandogi yūrei kitan*, however, the two languages seem to come into competition with each other for primacy. In one such moment, Mandogi is calling out for Mother Seoul as he chases her down the mountain: "ソウルぼさつさまァ！ (*Souru bosatsu samaa*)" (30). The lengthened vowel at the end of his exclamation emphasizes that this is spoken language, directly quoted even if not punctuated as such. Mandogi then discovers that at some point he has switched to shouting for his mother: "おっ母さん (*Okkasan/Ŏmŏni*)" (30). If Kim is assuming a generally monolingual Japanese-language reader, the "ŏmŏni" (omoni) gloss can only be there to offer the Korean word as a potential or prescriptive phonetic reading of the characters "おっ母さん." However, this puts the original (?) Japanese word in a peculiar position, because "okkasan" depends on its own orality to distinguish it from the more neutral "okaasan" for "mother." That is, if we assume a sort of division of labor between the "Japanese" and "Korean" words in the dialogue, wherein the Japanese represents the translated meaning of the characters' speech and the Korean sounds reflect the actual linguistic environment of the story's reality, then that logic necessarily breaks down here. The Japanese "okkasan" clearly takes on a phonetic role in addition to its primarily semantic role, just as the Korean "omoni" gloss influences the reading at the level of the meaning in addition to sound. Not only does this situation exemplify the inseparability of sound from meaning—signifier from signified—in a linguistic sign, it also locks the Japanese main text in dialectic with its Korean rubies, an unresolvable conflict over which is the "original" and which is "translated."

The most enticing example of this kind of device, however, is Mandogi's name itself. Kim invites a careful consideration of the function and composition of Mandogi's name by discussing it frequently and at length, including the very opening of the novel, which explains that Mandogi is simultaneously "nameless" and has many not-quite-names, including "dimwit," "temple boy," and "Keiton" (Korean "kaettong," glossed as 犬糞 "dog shit" in the text). At one time the narrator notes that the main utility of Mandogi's name is as an audible signal (*oto no shirushi*) to come when he is called (10), and the pronunciation of his name is very much at issue when his name is changed in a reference to *sōshi kaimei*, the imperial policy under which many Koreans were forced to adopt Japanese names:

> そのとき「一郎」という日本式の名を「万徳」という名の下にくっつけて、つまり名である「万徳」を姓に変えて当局は、万徳一郎という妙な名前を付けた。ところが万徳はまるっきり日本語を解さない。わっしは万徳一郎ではない。それは自分の名前ではない。自分の名前はマントクではなく、法名といってマンドギの「万徳」なんだと、漢字のその二文字を、わざわざ紙を置いて、鉛筆を舐め舐め、ていねいに書いて見せる。

> At the time, the officials attached the Japanese given name 'Ichirō' to the name 'Mandogi,' making his given name 'Mandogi' into his surname, and they gave him the strange name 'Mantoku Ichirō.' But Mandogi couldn't understand a word of Japanese. 'I ain't Mantoku Ichirō. That's not my name. My name's not Mantoku, but the priest's name, "Man . . . dogi."' Licking the pencil, he painstakingly wrote down the two Chinese characters and showed the page to the official (11).

Invoking the memory of *sōshi kaimei*, Kim is able to show how essential the pronunciation of a name is to someone like Mandogi. Even if the characters remain the same between "Mantoku" and "Mandogi," they are, in both political and affective senses, completely different names—different identities, perhaps. At the same time, because it exists in a written medium, strictly speaking, Mandogi's name is represented (or exists) only as a visual sign. Though it occasionally appears in katakana, in almost every instance it appears only in sinographs, which, as is demonstrated in this very early scene, contain the potential for "misreading." Indeed, Kim plays with this potential by very selectively glossing the name. It is glossed in its first appearance in the text, but thereafter almost exclusively in instances where it is spoken aloud. Considering the fact that Kim glosses frequently-used Korean words like "kongyangju" and "Halla-san" in nearly every single appearance, it is possible that he leaves the characters in Mandogi's name without gloss specifically to emphasize the multifarious possibilities for its reading.

To further complicate the matter, it should be pointed out that "Mandogi" is not a possible Korean reading for the characters 万徳, which would be read "Mandŏk." "Mandogi" is the product of the addition of a diminutive suffix "i," which can be added to names ending in consonants, in this case causing the preceding consonant to be voiced. In Korean hangŭl, this looks like: 만덕 (Mandŏk) + 이 (i), 만덕이 (Mandŏgi). In katakana, on the other hand, the final consonant of the Korean reading of the Chinese characters gets attached to the vowel sound in the diminutive suffix and represented in a single character: マンドギ (ma-n-do-gi). The katakana gloss is not simply representative of the Korean pronunciation of Mandogi's characters, then. Not only does the gloss overload the characters with more than their reading would produce in Korean, it creates a wholly new name in the process, one that would not be possible in normative Korean or Japanese.

Whereas *Karasu no shi* posits an imaginary Korean space that manages to escape the pressures of assimilation, *Mandogi yūrei kitan* offers not only the space but the possibility of a being or non-being that occupies that space. Mandogi, even before he takes on his "ghostly" form, is never quite present in the text. There is always an element of Mandogi that is deferred to another plane, but never wholly absent either. In a sense, this is the source of Mandogi's marginalization: just as his lack of proper name, birth, heritage, and *koseki* prevent him from enjoying complete "existence," disenfranchising him with respect to the various systems in which he is embedded, the uncanny representation of his name, which can never be fully accommodated by the system of language in which it is embedded, makes it a non-name—yet one more way in which Mandogi, with his surplus of names, is nameless. Nevertheless, just as Mandogi's "ghost" lives, and through his very existence as a non-entity comes to disrupt the political system that seeks to kill him in the first place, Mandogi's name, as a non-name, haunts the Japanese language without retreating to an equally "spellbinding" Korean. What begins as marginality, in the unique space created by the text, can become empowerment: a radical mode of being or becoming *in* a space of non-existence.

. . .

I return now to Kim Sŏkpŏm's utilization of the pulgasari in his illustration of the problem of the "spellbinding of language." The image of an otherworldly ravenous beast allows Kim to vividly describe the sense of crisis imposed by the Japanese language and the colonial and postcolonial conditions that made Japanese the only linguistic space available to Kim as a writer. However, from this position of vulnerability, Kim himself sets out to be the pulgasari, to somehow take back the upper hand despite having already been completely devoured. As with Mandogi, who can pick up a weapon and fight back only after he is "killed," it is from the moment of greatest crisis that Kim qua pulgasari can explode the system from within.

Yet the passage quoted at the outset also offers a more subtle clue as to how that escape might take place. Within the first mention of the pulgasari is a strangeness that hints at the radical space of difference that Mandogi comes to occupy. "In Chosŏn there is a strange-looking imaginary creature called a 'pulgasari.'" In other words, a creature that explicitly does not exist still manages to be "in" Korea without ever being at all. It is in this imaginary but still particularly Korean "space" that a radical, productive difference—ever elusive—may be located.

This radical difference is the key to unraveling the double binds that trouble both the aftermath of Jameson's thesis on third-world literature and the discourse surrounding Zainichi literature. The debate over national allegory struggles to treat the "first" and "third" worlds as at once commensurable and historically different, whereas Zainichi writers struggle to maintain an unassimilated particularity within the Japanese language and culture without embodying the essentialized difference that created Korea as ethnic other in the first place. What is needed in both cases is an empowering sense of difference that operates outside the bounds of the (post)imperial hierarchies that simultaneously subsume particularities while maintaining inequity. The imaginary space produced in literary text offers the ground on which to build this unruly sense of difference.

What makes Kim Sŏkpŏm's literary project particularly radical is that the Korean space he produces ironically depends on the Japanese language in order to come into existence. With only the language of the colonizer available, the violent reification and exclusion of difference has already been carried out. Nevertheless, Kim is able to create imagined, non-reified difference in the moments of unresolvable dissonance—incoherence, perhaps—embedded in his hybrid text. By radically representing Korea(n) in Japan(ese), Kim suggests a path outside the overdetermined mode of national allegory and a potential escape from the incoherent constraints that bind the third-world writer.

5

Speaking Intersectionally

Disability, Ethnicity, and (Non-)Representation in Kin Kakuei's Kogoeru kuchi

As I have argued up to this point, Zainichi and colonial Korean writers faced a set of representational impossibilities as a result of the intersectional nature of colonization by a non-Western empire and the imbrications of Japanese and American imperialisms. Yi Kwangsu's innovations toward a modern Korean literature, Kim Saryang's attempts to bring Korean literature to the world, and Kim Sŏkpŏm's project of carving out space for Korean-language fiction in Japan all arise out of the contradictions inherent in this intersection. However, the writers examined thus far ultimately did little to problematize the internal coherence of the literary categories within which they were writing—colonial, Korean, or Zainichi.

By contrast, the writers I take up in the second half of the book worked within a more obviously fraught relationship to the genre of Zainichi literature and the Zainichi community itself. One of the earliest writers to turn a critical eye toward the political project of Zainichi literature after its emergence in postwar Japan was Kin Kakuei.[1] As with Yi Yangji and Yū Miri, the subjects of the following chapters, the tension between Kin and the Zainichi literary establishment arises from his marginalized position *within* the Zainichi community. Both Yi and Yū have been accused of subordinating ethnic concerns to issues of gender, but in Kin's case it is the disabled rather than the gendered body that undermines the Zainichi nationalist narrative of a cohesive minority community.[2] In this chapter, I explore the representational conundrums arising at the intersection of disability and ethnicity through a reading of Kin Kakuei's *Kogoeru kuchi* (*Frozen Mouth*, 1966).

The rise to prominence of writers like Kin, who foregrounded axes of identity aside from Zainichi ethnicity, coincided with a broader contestation over political representation of the Zainichi community. Kin's career began in the late 1960s, on the heels of the normalization of diplomatic relations between Japan and South Korea that was brokered by the United States. The mass demonstrations opposing the terms of the treaty were at the time the largest since the Anpo protests in 1960.[3] The movement brought together a diverse coalition: Japanese leftists and progressives opposed the talks on the grounds of its further entrenchment of US Cold War interests in the region (with the escalating war in Vietnam in the background) and viewed the mobilization as a practice run for the renewal of Anpo approaching in 1970, while Zainichi Koreans on both sides of the ideological thirty-eighth parallel decried their lack of representation in the negotiation process itself.

Members of the North Korean–aligned General Association of Korean Residents in Japan (Ch'ongryŏn) naturally objected to the recognition of South Korea as the only legitimate state on the peninsula. Meanwhile, dissidents within the South Korean–aligned Korean Residents Union in Japan (Mindan) faulted the Park Chung Hee regime's overly accommodating bargaining posture, which capitulated on issues of war responsibility and reparations in exchange for economic aid from Japan. South Korean negotiators also excluded Zainichi representatives from the process and failed to prioritize their demands. Nevertheless, the normalization treaty, signed in 1965, did allow Zainichi Koreans to obtain passports by applying for South Korean citizenship. As this option provided more stability and freedom than the travel documents issued by Ch'ongryŏn, the late 1960s saw a massive shift from *Chōsen-seki* status to *Kankoku-seki*, and an accompanying influx of membership from Ch'ongryŏn to Mindan, which became the consular apparatus for South Korean nationals in Japan. At the same time, Japan's acknowledgment of only the southern regime further entrenched the division of the peninsula and dimmed hopes for timely reunification—the condition for a happy return from exile, which was originally the ultimate goal of both Ch'ongryŏn and Mindan. Thus, not only was the organizational structure of Zainichi politics fracturing and shifting, the peninsular orientation of both organizations was becoming increasingly obsolete as the younger generation demanded representation that acknowledged the overwhelming likelihood of continued division and an ongoing Korean presence in Japan. With generational, political, and intersectional fault lines forming across the Zainichi community, the 1960s witnessed a bitter fight over who could claim the legitimate right to speak for the Zainichi.

Kin Kakuei's fiction-writing career sits atop all these fault lines. Born in 1938 in Gunma Prefecture and educated at the University of Tokyo, he is situated solidly within the "second generation" and frequently mentioned alongside Kim Sŏkpŏm and Ri Kaisei as one of a trifecta of canonical Zainichi writers from this transitional era. However, whereas Kim and Ri were embraced by the Zainichi intellectual establishment due to their commitment to Korean ethnonationalism in diaspora—what John Lie calls "Zainichi ideology"—Kin's reputation would have to be rehabilitated by later critics taking issue with Zainichi nationalism.[4]

Rather than focusing on the ethnonationalist politics of the Zainichi collective, Kin's work is largely concerned with the issue of stuttering, which the author himself struggled with until he took his own life in 1985.

In fact, the specific accusation lobbed at Kin (and many of the similarly anti-nationalist writers who followed him) was that his writing failed to transcend the personal and achieve an "ethnic consciousness" (*minzoku ishiki*). One contemporary critic compared Kin unfavorably to Ri Kaisei precisely by arguing that the main difference between the two lies in their attention to the personal versus the collective. Whereas Ri is ostensibly concerned with both the personal and the political, Kin's work is concerned first and foremost with "whatever is inside himself, in his case the stutter, but in the same way that if someone were born with a toothache that went on for twenty years, he could never face an external problem without first dealing with the toothache."[5] Even more favorable assessments of Kin's work see his contribution to Zainichi literature as a reassertion of the personal, as opposed to the collective.[6]

In *Kogoeru kuchi*, his best-known work, Kin engages directly with the dichotomy of personal versus political in the context of the normalization talks. In the words of the story's protagonist, Sai, a stutterer like the author himself:[7]

> To tell the truth, the South Korea–Japan talks are a secondary problem to me. It's the stutter that I have to deal with first and foremost, the stutter that is the most pressing problem holding me back. Compared to that, the South Korea–Japan talks, and not only that but all political problems—no, not just political problems but any problems besides the stutter—barely feel like problems at all.[8]

Here Kin (or at least his fictional alter ego) would seem to agree with both his critics and his champions: that he is not a political figure if the only possible subject of politics is the nation-state.

This fissuring of personal from political (qua national) is ironic when read in juxtaposition with the national allegory discussion in the previous chapter. The question of whether Kin's narratives can even be reduced to the personal in the first place—rather than being inevitably co-opted by the collective—has interesting implications for the framing of Zainichi literature as "third-world," "minor," or even "ethnic." The uneasiness with Kin from the standpoint of Zainichi ideology dovetails neatly with the supposed inevitability of national allegory by being the exception that proves the rule. That is, thinly veiled behind every critique of Kin's work as overly "personal" is the implication that his fiction is *too Japanese*, too assimilated, insufficiently Zainichi. If Kin's work is decidedly not allegorical of a collective, then it is no longer a Zainichi narrative, but instead belongs to the colonizer.

However, in Kin's case, the personal is shorthand for disability, which can hardly be divorced from politics. Kin's narratives of stuttering are, if not dismissed as merely personal, read as allegories for ethnic subjugation and the obstacles to "speaking" from a minority position.[9] In this way, a circular logic emerges whereby any personal narrative written within the rubric of Zainichi literature is inevitably read as transcending the personal and becoming representative of the collective, even as attempts to represent collectives other than the Zainichi (as ethnonation) are *depoliticized* and reduced to the personal, ergo trivial. This incoherence embedded in the hermeneutics of representation forecloses the possibility of an intersectional narrative.

As such, I argue in this chapter that Kin's response to this structural incoherence is to take a pessimistic outlook toward representation itself as a path to solidarity and personal or political liberation. Instead, he looks to the body. By focusing on the embodied nature of speech, we can see how the disruption of normative speech might actually enable alternative, non-representational modes of articulating difference and building relationality. Crucially, these radical alternatives, as well as the representational impossibilities from which they emerge, are only visible through an intersectional lens, acknowledging the politics of disability as they interact with ethnic and language politics at the site of the speaking—or especially the silent—body.

THE IMMATERIAL BODY

Kin's *Kogoeru kuchi* exemplifies intersectional incoherence by weaving a complex web of human connections mediated not only by ethnicity and disability, but also gender and sexuality. The novel begins by introducing Sai, a graduate student in chemistry. This biographical detail, like his stuttering, overlaps with that of the author.[10] The day the novel takes place, Sai has to give a research presentation, which ends in failure when he loses control of his stutter. Feeling depressed, Sai reminisces about his Japanese friend Isogai, also a stutterer, who has died by suicide. The narrative then flashes back to Sai's first meeting with Isogai and recounts their friendship, up until Sai receives Isogai's suicide letter. The letter then takes over the narrative, flashing back yet again to Isogai's turbulent childhood, when his battered mother found comfort in the arms of a Korean paramour, coincidentally also named Sai. When the affair is discovered, Isogai's mother throws herself on the train tracks. In his depression, Isogai begins to visit a prostitute, and develops a sexually transmitted infection as well as tuberculosis. Before the illness can claim his life, he chooses to end it himself. Isogai concludes his personal confession by asking Sai to look after his sister, Michiko. The narrative then shifts back to Sai's perspective in the present day, where he heads from the lab to Michiko's apartment, and it is revealed that they are now dating. The novel ends as Sai and Michiko finally have sex.

One of the most conspicuous aspects of the novel, aside from this complex nested structure, is its constant references to the physical body. The word *shintai* (身体, body) occurs repeatedly throughout the text, not to mention the abundance of references to parts of the body, particularly those involved in producing speech: the chest (*mune*), the throat (*nodo*), and of course the mouth (*kuchi*) of the title. While many of these references describe bodily sensations related to the central character's emotional state, the most conspicuous of these phrases are the ones describing the physiological aspects of his stutter as part of the main thread of the narrative. Much of the novel's treatment of stuttering hinges on whether the stutter is an impairment of the body or the mind, and to what extent its physical and mental aspects can be disentangled from each other.

On the one hand, the narrator makes it clear that his stutter is not only a psychological problem, but that there are physical properties to it as well. In the opening chapter he describes his disability as follows: "My thoughts don't translate smoothly into words. I can't say anything easily. I'm not saying I can't psychologically, it's that I physically can't" (13). Hence, perhaps, the emphasis on the body throughout the text. Whatever traits of personality, social position, or mental state might create obstacles to Sai's speaking, he emphasizes that these are not what ultimately create the impediment. It is not, in other words, in his head. The stutter is grounded in the material reality of the body.

This is not to say that Sai's stutter, or stuttering in general (according to him), does not have non-physical causes. He explains:

> In certain atmospheres, I have trouble—stutterers have trouble saying anything at all. When we try to voice our thoughts, no sound comes out. Even the stutterer himself doesn't understand why this happens. In such an atmosphere, the mind and body (*shinshin*, 心身) grow tense. This tension exerts a sort of influence over the diaphragm, the vocal chords, the throat, the tongue, the lips, and other organs related to breathing and speaking, causing a kind of cramping, and that is most likely what blocks the voice from coming out (14).

It is worth noting here that Sai conflates his own experience of stuttering with that of stutterers (*kitsuonsha*) in general. He starts the first sentence making himself the subject (*boku wa*), then immediately stops and expands the subject to be categorical (*kitsuonsha wa*). With this move, he creates a collectivity based on shared bodily experience, with himself as its representative. What follows sounds scientific, like a description of stuttering in medical terms. Nevertheless, it remains unclear whether this description is actually generalizable or merely extrapolated from Sai's personal experience. Ironically, whereas this medical explanation of stuttering lends it a kind of authority to apply generally to all stutterers, its emphasis on the body makes the process described impenetrably personal. It happens within Sai's body and is thus inaccessible to anyone outside. The body is at once the grounds for universalization and for irreducible differentiation. From the outset, then, Kin's emphasis on the body is a way of exposing the contradictions at the heart of broader Zainichi debates over the personal and the political, the individual and the collective, and the irreconcilable representational tensions between the two.

Tobin Siebers outlines a similar problem in one of the foundational texts of disability studies, "Tender Organs, Narcissism, and Identity Politics." In this essay, Siebers advocates for the recognition of disability as a basis for social identity. In doing so, he notes the difficulty of mobilizing a disabled collective when the discourse surrounding disability remains focused on medical solutions to individualized problems rather than the struggle for rights of disabled people as a coalition, largely because disability is so thoroughly bound up with narcissism in cultural narratives.[11] In other words, the popular stereotypical perception of people with disabilities sees them as overwhelmingly and exclusively concerned with the self—once again reducing disability to mere personal (as opposed to political) matter. According to Siebers, it is this perceived link between disability and narcissism that renders an identity politics of disability so difficult to form:

> The association between narcissism and disability makes it almost impossible to view people with disabilities as anything other than absolutely different from each other. Physical and mental disability are more difficult to overcome than prejudices against race and sex not only because people are less likely to identify with a blind person, for example, but because the perception of the individual with a disability is antithetical to the formation of political identity—which is to say that individuality itself is disabled for political use in the case of people with disabilities.[12]

While I am not certain disability is "more difficult to overcome" than racism or sexism—all three are intersectionally constituted—the idea that disability is difficult to collectivize when viewed as an experience of the individualized body certainly resonates with Kin's writing and its reception. Rather than as its own form of political identification, disability in Kin's life and work is viewed as something that can only differentiate his granular individual experience from Zainichi politics. Only the ethnic aspects of identity can be connected to such a politics. However, this difficulty in reconciling individual and collective concerns is not limited to disability. In fact, it calls to mind one of the central tenets of intersectional analysis of race and gender: not only are both categories internally heterogeneous, but any deviance in experience from the imagined normative representative of such a category is dismissed as a personal matter, not relevant to the collective.[13] Even outside the realm of disability politics, a model that grounds itself in the body and examines the impacts of intersecting identity hierarchies thereupon exposes the violence of single-axis frameworks.

On the other hand, returning to the novel, after thoroughly situating Sai's stutter in the body at the outset, *Kogoeru kuchi* goes on to exhibit a slippage, attributing the stutter to mental or often atmospheric factors rather than portraying it in terms of the body. This slippage arises in part because of a slippage in Sai's actual stutter, which disappears and reappears depending on the context. In the stressful environment of Sai's research presentation, he is able to speak without stuttering at all until about halfway through the talk, when his concentration is broken by a single difficult word. Despite having read pages of complicated scientific material (several paragraphs of which are reproduced in the text), Sai finds the word "tetrahydrofuran" (*tetorahidorofuran*) almost impossible to pronounce without stuttering. (Many readers, I imagine, can sympathize.) Once that barrier is broken, Sai enters a vicious cycle in which his stuttering makes him more nervous, and his nervousness makes him stutter all the more. In this scene, the only lengthy mimetic reproduction of Sai's speech in the text, the physical aspects of his stutter are barely mentioned. The focus is squarely on his emotional state and its effect on the quality of his speech. In other words, the stutter originates from a nervous energy in Sai's mind which then manifests itself on the body, rather than the other way around. This dynamic seems to be confirmed by the fact that Sai never stutters in front of Isogai, with whom he feels at ease: in the absence of the fear of stuttering, Sai's stutter ceases to exist.

In this way, the actual functioning of Sai's stutter over the course of the text conforms less to his initial physiologically grounded description of his impairment, and more to the qualified version of that description that follows shortly thereafter: "If a word feels difficult to say, it's fair to say I almost always stutter. Or perhaps I stutter *because* a word feels difficult to say. Perhaps it is this feeling that a word is difficult to say that manipulates my organs into hindering my speech" (16). He continues, "In my case, the stutter was not just a stutter anymore, but had become a neurosis" (16). Here the narrator particularizes his own stutter, as opposed to earlier descriptions generalizing it to represent all cases of stuttering. Rather than a strictly physiological process observable across any number of equivalent stuttering bodies, the narrator's stutter is now a product of his unique psyche, which, according to the conceits of the novel, is never fully transmittable to the outside world. Kin quickly establishes the experience of stuttering as something incommensurable itself, even as the stutter is, if not the cause for, then at least a metaphor for incommensurability in general.

Indeed, the trope of disability is often interpreted metaphorically. In "Impaired Body as Colonial Trope," Kyeong-Hee Choi notes the proliferation of images of disabled bodies within colonial-period Korean literature, particularly in the 1920s and 1930s.[14] Choi interprets these bodies in texts from this period as a trope standing for the incomplete text and the silenced author within a disabling colonial censorship regime:

> I view the trope of disability as a metaphor linking the character, the writer, and the text: the character, the literally 'ill-formed,' who is hampered by an environment that imposes material and conceptual limits; the writer, as disabled as his or her main character by the constraint of censorship imposed from without and internalized within; and finally, the censored literary work that is impaired, like both its creator and its protagonist, as a textual body.[15]

While this schema offers a productive mode for reading colonial Korean texts written under the eye of the censor, it follows a trend in criticism of narratives of impairment wherein disability is seen as a mode of narrating every marginal identity other than itself. This tends to elide any serious discussion of *disability* as a social category that intersects with colonialism.

Even outside (post)colonial contexts, David Mitchell and Sharon Snyder have theorized a similar interpretive trap with respect to disability, which they call "narrative prosthesis."[16] Narrative prosthesis refers to the notion that literary narratives constantly depend on disability as a means of representing difference. According to Mitchell, this is the necessary condition for the telling of all stories, which "operate out of a desire to compensate for a limitation or to reign in excessiveness. This narrative approach to difference identifies the literary object par excellence as that which has somehow become out of the ordinary—a deviation from a widely accepted cultural norm."[17] However, even as disability functions as a metaphor for any number of modes of social difference, it is almost never recognized as disability itself.

> Literature borrows the potency of the lure of difference that a socially stigmatized condition provides. Yet the reliance on disability in narrative rarely develops into a means of identifying people with disabilities as a disenfranchised cultural constituency. The ascription of absolute singularity to disability performs a contradictory operation: a character stands out as a result of an attributed blemish, but this exceptionality disqualifies the character from possessing a shared social identity.[18]

That is to say, the specificity of disability is erased as the disabled body is put into the service of representing every other type of difference.

Here intersectionality acts as an important check on the temptation to read a disabled Korean body as standing in for a colonially "disabled" Korea. To the extent that we read such a body in text *as* a body, then it is necessarily both disabled and Korean. Or, as Paula-Irene Villa writes, "Embodiment is *per se* intersectional in its form . . . it exceeds any categorical frame."[19] The body is the site at which the impacts of Japanese and Western imperialisms, as well as social hierarchies within the Zainichi community itself, are felt. As such, the allegorized disabled body is inherently intersectional: it stands for some other form of difference, but cannot escape the reality of disability. A reading grounded in the body is thus more equipped to navigate around the homogenizing logic of identity categories, including disability.

Reading Sai's stutter as a metaphor for ethnic disempowerment, then, is not only an oversimplification of the novel's complex intertwined modes of difference and belonging, but also contributes to the erasure of disability itself as one such mode. If the stuttering body is meant to "represent" the repressed state of being Zainichi, then it necessarily imagines Zainichi as a collective to which many *metaphorically* disabled members can comfortably belong. But ironically, it is Sai's *actual* disability that prevents his ethnic belonging. Only by attending to the intersection of ethnicity, disability, and other modes of identification is it possible to stage a critique of "Zainichi-ness" as the putative norm from which bodies can deviate. This, in turn, allows for a foregrounding of the fundamentally unstable and relational location of center and margin, revealing the inevitable reduction of any single-axis narrative of marginality to a retrenchment of the center it orbits.

At the same time, focusing on the body both brings intersectionality to the fore and reveals the particular representational conundrums of disability. For instance, the erasure of disability as a category of social difference is only one part of the problem with narrative prosthesis. As Mitchell explains, once a physical impairment has set a narrative in motion, the actual limitations imposed by the disability in question can be largely ignored: "The identification of deficiency inaugurates the need for a story but then is quickly forgotten once the difference is established."[20] *Kogoeru kuchi* adheres to this pattern. In its prosthetic function, the stutter marks Isogai and Sai with an aberrance that necessitates the story's telling—not only for the reader of Kin Kakuei's text, but also for Sai, the reader of Isogai's text within the text. Sai meets Isogai for the first time during self-introductions in one of his university classes, and states that "it was because he stuttered [that I noticed him]. If he hadn't stuttered, I probably would have forgotten his name, would never have given it a second thought, just as I could have cared less about the rest of my classmates' names" (45–46). Notably, in Isogai's confession, he singles out the same moment, recalling that he remembered Sai's name in particular because it was a Korean name, and because he had known another man named Sai (65). Here we see ethnicity acting as the marker of difference that prosthetically enables the narrative in direct parallel with Isogai's stuttering.

Nevertheless, once Isogai's difference is established, his stutter plays no role at all in propelling his story forward. He mentions that he has always struggled with the stutter at the beginning of his letter to Sai, but afterward continues with the story of his family's dysfunction and eventual shattering, and on to his own mental and physical breakdown, leading to his suicide, without ever mentioning his speech again. In fact, even outside the letter, it is easy to forget Isogai's stutter exists, as it is never mimetically represented in the text. Whereas Sai's speech is occasionally marked with the use of extra punctuation, such as commas and ellipses occupying the space of the pauses, Isogai's stutter is mentioned only at the diegetic level. Readers never learn what, if any, effect Isogai's stuttering has on his day-to-day life or relationships. Once Isogai is presented as an object of interest, his stutter becomes a non-factor in the development of his character and the plot of the story in general. His disability starts the narrative, but then plays no part in it—another sense in which disability in the novel is able to represent anything but itself.

But in a perhaps overly literal sense, how could disability ever represent itself in text? Insofar as impairment is a physical reality of the body, it will always remain somewhat uncaptured by textual representation, as with actual speech. In fact, because the textual body is not a body at all, a textual disability never actually disables the body. This slippage is visible in *Kogoeru kuchi*, wherein Isogai's stuttering voice is translated into text that is completely stripped of the mark of difference. As noted above, Sai's "voice" is sometimes punctuated in a way that reproduces the stutter, but the very inconsistency of this mechanic reinforces the inconsistency of Sai's stutter itself. Both stutters seem to vanish any time it is convenient for the narrative. Ironically, within the narrow bounds of Kin's text, the stutter as disability serves in almost all instances to *enable* the stuttering character to speak. That is, it allows them to form the human connections that they repeatedly lament their inability to achieve. Although the disability is deployed to conjure the mark of difference, it never produces actual disability—and indeed, never could.

Reading *Kogoeru kuchi* in this light has the potential, in turn, to complicate Mitchell and Snyder's schema of narrative prosthesis. In discussing disability as the central metaphor that allows for the expression of difference, Mitchell states that "the corporeal metaphor offers narrative the one thing it cannot possess—an anchor in materiality. Such a process embodies what I term the materiality of metaphor."[21] However, it must be emphasized here that this materiality is an oxymoron, as it is to the end a strictly imagined materiality. The textual body can have no disability that is not strictly discursive. While the text can create an illusion of grounding in the material body, the actual body is always displaced, existing in a space the text can only posit. Its paradoxically immaterial substance supplies a medium for radical non-representation. The very inaccessibility of the body in text offers an alternative to speech, a rejection of its representational burdens.

CONFESSION AS IDENTIFICATION

Perhaps the quintessential representational burden in the canon of modern Japanese literature is the task of writing the self, a project no less impossible on its face than reproducing the body in text. Nevertheless, *Kogoeru kuchi*, like many works of canonical Japanese fiction, revolves around acts of confession and self-revelation.[22] In fact, Kin's novel is structured around at least two extended confessions: Isogai's letter to Sai revealing his backstory and the reasons for his suicide, and the narrator's revelation (to the reader) of his internal struggle with stuttering. A third confession—the confession that Sai wants to make to Isogai but never actually carries out—also haunts the narrative, its possibility foreclosed from the outset. This contradictory desire to confess but inability to do so exists alongside a paradox of identification. That is, how can Sai identify himself to Isogai as a stutterer when he never actually stutters in his presence? Is he a stutterer at all, to Isogai? And if not, was there any concealed identity to confess in the first place? There is an inherently relational and intersectional quality to the process of identification that can be glimpsed by unpacking the various ways in which *Kogoeru kuchi* identifies characters specifically as "stutterers" (*kitsuonsha*).

In the first instance of such an identification, the narrator, addressing the reader, declares that he is a stutterer. Because the text is our only window into the reality of its world, his statements do not simply reveal a reality of which he has privileged knowledge; they create that reality in the very moment he reveals it. In other words, the narrator's confessions of identity are the only mode through which his identity comes into being. For a substantial portion of the novel, his statement that he is a stutterer is the reader's only way of identifying the narrator at all, since he does not "confess" to being Korean until the second chapter, and never even reveals his name until the third. In this way, Sai is literally stutterer first, Korean second—and both before he is "Sai."

Notably, however, he does not state directly "I am a stutterer" (*Boku wa kitsuonsha*), but rather makes the revelation in the following context: "When [Isogai] died by suicide, I felt as if a part of myself had died rather than someone else. Maybe it was because he was a stutterer like me (*boku to onaji yō ni kitsuonsha datta*). So perhaps I saw myself in him" (8). In other words, the narrator's first announcement to the reader of his stuttering—his initial confession—serves to establish his connection with Isogai rather than his alienation from others. From the beginning, then, stuttering offers the possibility of a social bond. In fact, all the acts of confession performed in the novel, and even the one Sai fails to carry out, are involved in the formation and maintenance of this bond between Isogai and Sai.

However, there is an important difference between the narrator's self-identification versus his recognition of Isogai as a stutterer. Returning to the scene in which Sai and Isogai first meet, Sai hears Isogai stuttering, and through this recognition identifies him as a fellow stutterer. If the narrator becomes a stutterer by confessing such an identity to the reader, then Isogai has neither the opportunity nor the need to make such a confession, because he is readily recognizable as such. His identity is audible, allowing for his *identification* as stutterer, and thus preempting his possible agency in *identifying* as stutterer. This is certainly not to suggest that identification, as disabled or otherwise, is either an active or passive process with no overlap. On the contrary, I wish to point out that *Kogoeru kuchi* plays cannily with the complex relationship between the embodied performance of a given identity (in this case that of the stutterer) and the discursive enunciation of identity (Isogai *is* a stutterer).

Stuart Hall theorizes this interaction of ostensibly interior psychological factors with the external ideological aspects of identity in the process of subject formation itself, in what he calls a process of "articulation." Using the by now familiar metaphor of speech as political agency, Hall writes:

> Identity is the meeting point, or the point of future, between, on the one hand, the ideological discourses which attempt to interpellate or speak us as social subjects, and, on the other, the psychological or psychical processes which produces us as subjects which can be spoken. So I certainly don't want to restore the notion of identity as unified essence, something continuous with the self, an inner truth that can be discovered. On the contrary, I understand identities as points of suture, positions of *temporary* attachment, as a way of understanding the constant transformations of who one is or as Foucault put it, 'who one is to become.'[23]

Not only is the malleable nature of the connection between self and subject position obscured by the rhetoric of confession, the particular subject position of disability further complicates the picture by introducing the body (and the embodied nature of speech) into the equation. If, in Hall's formulation, subjects articulate subject positions or identities in order to attain the autonomy to speak, then what happens when the subject position articulated is one that is ideologically interpellated as disabled from speaking?

On the other hand, disability highlights the intersections of discursive and performative modes of identification. In the case of speech disability, a stutter is only recognizable in the context of a speech act, meaning that a subject can both enunciate and embody an identity in a single action. In other words, Sai could simultaneously claim a disabled identity by saying "I am a stutterer" and, if he stuttered as he said it, *perform* the identity he was claiming in the same speech act. In this hypothetical speech act, the two ostensible modes of identification are collapsed into the same utterance. More provocative, however, is the hypothetical speech act whose possibility the novel forecloses: Sai's confession to Isogai that he, too, is a stutterer. Since Sai does not stutter in the presence of Isogai, a tension arises between the two means of becoming stutterer: declaring oneself a stutterer versus performing the physical act itself.

In more concrete terms, *Kogoeru kuchi* portrays Sai's stutter as almost completely a matter of social context. The severity of the impediment varies based on Sai's moods, his interlocutors, and, in an admittedly circular logic, whether he is already stuttering. Crucially, he admits that in Isogai's presence, he never stuttered at all.

> Any time I spoke to Isogai, I didn't stutter at all. Even I found it strange. Could it have been because of the relief that came from knowing he was a stutterer too, and in fact a more severe stutterer than I? Listening to his broken and faltering speech, I felt as if my awareness of myself as a stutterer was absorbed by his stutter, and the stutter that usually inundated my whole self was drained away into nothing. To tell the truth, with Isogai, I should have been free to stutter without embarrassment. But whenever I'm free to stutter, for whatever reason I don't. And whenever I can't bear to stutter, that's when I stutter the worst. And so, I had never once stuttered in front of Isogai (51).

The fact that Sai never performs the act of stuttering in Isogai's presence raises the question of what it would mean for Sai to confess to being a stutterer when, as far as Isogai is concerned, he is demonstrably not.

This foreclosed confession can be productively analyzed through Lacan's formulation of the subject's appearance in language. In Lacan's well-known example of the statement, "I am lying," the paradox of the utterance is resolved by teasing apart the subject of the enunciated (the pronominal "I") and the subject of enunciation (the unconscious, the subject that comes into being through discursive contact with the other).[24] If the "I" in this sentence transparently represents a stable enunciating subject, then the statement is nonsense. However, by acknowledging the instability of the pairing, it becomes possible to interpret the statement as referring to another subject at a different moment, who could be lying even as the subject of the enunciated tells the truth about the lie. If Sai were to utter "I am a stutterer" in the presence of Isogai without stuttering, he would create the same kind of paradox, which could again be resolved by acknowledging the temporal disjuncture of the enunciation and the instability of the self across time. In this way, his confession could never reveal a hidden, fixed identity, and could only reveal the ambivalence of such an identity. If, on the other hand, he did stutter while saying "I am a stutterer," then there would be no apparent contradiction, but there would also be no need for the enunciation in the first place. In fact, it is the very failure to produce normative, communicative speech that brings the subject as stutterer into being. This is not to say that the subject as stutterer is a stable entity, but rather to suggest that such a subject cannot be accessed via speech. If, in Hall's sense of identity as articulation, subject positions are required in order to say anything at all, then the stuttered confession or non-confession suggests the power of *not* saying.

To sum up, Sai's desire to confess to being a stutterer without ever actually becoming a stutterer emphasizes the instability of the constructed category of "stutterer" by disrupting the smooth interaction of modes of identification. In other words, in a context in which Sai the stutterer does not stutter, it becomes clear that his identification as stutterer, whether through his own claim to such a Self or his recognition as such by an Other, occurs independently of his actually *embodying* a stutterer. Whatever material, biological, or essential elements of stuttering are involved in the process of Sai's identification vanish the moment he engages with Isogai. As a result, if enunciation, recognition, and embodiment work together to shape a sense of identity, then here this mechanism is shattered into its constituent parts, and a coherent identity fails to take shape.

And yet, despite this incoherence, the bond between Sai and Isogai is able to form. Even as Sai fails to embody a stutterer, Isogai is still able, somehow, to recognize in Sai an affinity that readers are led to believe arises from their shared identity. While the narrator emphasizes that the basis for Sai and Isogai's friendship is their common impairment, we receive no real insight into Isogai's perspective until his suicide letter to Sai. There Isogai suggests that his affinity for Sai is related to his being Korean—perhaps an indication that he sees their mutual marginalization as their basis for camaraderie—but also subtly hints that Sai was uniquely able to understand the experience of stuttering. After insisting that Sai knows nothing about him, Isogai confesses to being a stutterer, while admitting that this confession is not necessary, as Sai must already be aware. He continues, "You know that I have a stutter (*domori*), a quite severe stutter even. You know, and yet you never mentioned it. I know it was out of compassion and sympathy for me that you didn't" (64). Isogai's claim that Sai is the one who knows nothing about him (rather than the other way around) flips on its head the structure of knowledge privilege erected by Sai's unconfessed secret. Not only that, his invocation of "sympathy" (*dōjō*) suggests that their emotional bond is independent of the mutual *knowledge* either confession would create. Isogai's solidarity with Sai is founded on recognition without recognition, or identification without identification.

This uncanniness gives rise to the possibility of confession even as it forecloses that same possibility. In other words, in order for Sai's confession to be possible, his identity must be hidden from Isogai, which can only happen because Sai never stutters in front of Isogai. At the same time, Isogai's recognition without recognition defies the whole logic of confession. Once the two are placed into this ambiguously sympathetic relationship, Sai's hypothetical confession to Isogai that "I am a stutterer (too)" could only result in confusion. Isogai's recognition, such as it is, would evaporate in the face of this claim, which would appear false precisely because Sai is not recognizable as a stutterer, having never embodied a stutterer before his eyes (or, more literally, his ears).

Nevertheless, even though Sai's confession never occurs, his desire to confess in itself allows him to take ownership of the stuttering subject position without also having to own its disabling elements, neither the material stuttering nor the breakdown in solidarity between him and Isogai. Ironically, this sense of community can continue only so long as the confession of common identity is not carried through. As a result, when Isogai ultimately dies and Sai's confession to him is deferred in perpetuity, the unstable relationship among the enunciation, embodiment, and recognition of his identity, as well as all of the possibility that emerges from this flux, can extend indefinitely into the horizon. The impossibility of confession—or, if you prefer, the impossibility of speech—need not preclude solidarity, and may in fact enable it.

AURAL-VISUAL DOPPELGÄNGERS AND THE MEDIUM OF TEXT

In *Kogoeru kuchi*, the impossibility of confession and the impossibility of narratively representing the body come together in the rupture of embodied speech from text. Speech, like the disabled body, is of course never literally present in text, but like the disabled body it is easy to imagine speech as that which the text sets out to represent, the authentic or original material that text can only mimic.[25] Yet even if the text does not mimic embodied speech, it may conjure it within the reader's sonic imagination. Similarly, Sai's confession is perpetually deferred to a temporality outside that of the text, just as Isogai's stutter is displaced. Neither is materially represented in the text. The material and discursive aspects of the body explored in Kin's novel prompt readers to attend to the question of sensory medium—that is, the question of how the visual medium of text (imperfectly) represents the sounds of spoken language. With its focus on speech disability, *Kogoeru kuchi* is of course concerned with this specific representational problem, but also more generally with speech as stand-in for political expression.

This figurative understanding of speech as subjectivity or political agency is used in countless metaphors, from "voicing the voiceless" to "freedom of speech," and perhaps most relevantly in Gayatri Chakravorty Spivak's rhetorical query, "Can the Subaltern Speak?"[26] As is well known, Spivak's answer to this question is no, within a language whose terms are always already dictated by masculinist imperialism, the subaltern cannot speak. Her key intervention is essentially an intersectional reading of the Western theoretical project of decentering the subject, whose failure Spivak locates "precisely through Deleuze's and Foucault's double incapacity to recognize, on the one hand, the nonuniversality of the Western position and, on the other, the constitutive place of gender in the formation of the subject—as the subject of language not only in the grammatical sense but in the sense of having a voice that can access power."[27] Within such a structure of subject formation, the third-world woman is relegated to a place that is inevitably misread or illegible.

By way of illustration, Spivak ends her essay with the enigmatic image of an Indian woman, Bhuvaneswari Bhaduri, who hanged herself while menstruating. She had been tasked with a political assassination and committed suicide when she lost the nerve to carry it out. Spivak reads her choice to die specifically while menstruating as a defense against any *misinterpretation* of her act as being caused by the shame of an illicit pregnancy.[28] Spivak's use of Bhuvaneswari's suicide has been criticized as a rather literal example of subaltern "muteness,"[29] but I want to suggest the slippage her essay exhibits between speech, text, and representation—without regard for the corporeal specificity of each mode—runs the risk of reducing subjectivity to speech. Once again, the actually mute body is co-opted into a project of critiquing a strictly figurative muteness.[30]

This is not to suggest that such a conflation undermines Spivak's conclusion that speech is impossible from subaltern positions, since she is not in the business of recovering lost voices or texts, but rather of critiquing the ideological constraints that render them unrecoverable in the first place. Instead, I wish to note the irony of mounting such a critique while engaging in what we might call critical (rather than narrative) prosthesis: the opening up of a representational aporia into which the disabled subject slips, in much the same way as the subaltern. More importantly, the Bhuvaneswari Bhaduri story also suggests that greater sensitivity to the irreducibility of speech, text, and body can reveal that there is in fact a kind of corporeal agency that exists even in silence—outside language, outside the possibility of being understood.[31]

Indeed, Kin's text utilizes this dynamic to develop the overarching theme of the novel: the alienation of all embodied subjects, not only those who stutter. However, it is not as simple as reading the stutterer as universally representative of the human condition, trapped within the narrow confines of the self by what Sai describes as an inability "to be understood by others just as I am" (14). This alienation is a result of a metaphorical rather than literal inability to speak. Thus, the stutterer is situated as a particular rather than universal subject as the novel goes on to draw attention to the gap between written and spoken language. Isogai, who ostensibly stutters so severely that he is essentially unable to communicate orally, makes use of written language in the single instance in which he claims to "want to be understood by another" (*tanin ni rikai shite moraitai*) (64), that is, his suicide letter to Sai. If Isogai's speech disability (or Sai's for that matter) is meant to serve as a metaphor for his inability to make himself understood, then the ease with which he writes undermines the utility of that metaphor. Isogai has no difficulty communicating his thoughts via the written text of his letter, bypassing the need for speech in the first place. If he is isolated by his disability, it is not because he is unable to "speak" in the broader sense, but rather because the disability marks him as other. His case highlights the gap between written and spoken media as they relate specifically to the body, in addition to foregrounding the ableism inherent in the reduction of political articulation to speech.

Isogai's confessional letter also offers an implicit critique of autobiographical narrative as transparent window to the self.[32] Isogai's letter disrupts the flow of Kin Kakuei's I-novelesque narrative and reconfigures the structure of the novel as a confession within a confession, creating a series of doubles that accompany this telescoping structure. Whereas the structure itself doubles the layers of written media obstructing what is supposed to be a transparent communication from the narrator-as-author's self to the audience, the doubling of the "self" in question further undermines this communication. By virtue of their shared struggle with stuttering, Sai views Isogai as a part of himself, which is perhaps one reason that Isogai's personal narrative is embedded in his own. The two "selves" being revealed here, due to the doubled structure of the novel, begin to overlap and eventually to blur into each other. As a result, Kin's "I-novel" has no consistent "I," even in terms of the first-person pronouns used by its narrators. There is the "boku" (I) of the main narrative, and the "ore" (I) of Isogai's letter, and even this choice of pronoun is transferred to Sai at least once following the suicide note.

In a segment of Sai's inner monologue, when his Korean friend has just asked him to attend a political event, he thinks to himself, "But it's only my body I will be carrying there. My mind will be trapped somewhere else altogether. Somewhere else, not outside of me but within, inside my stutter" (85). In each case here the personal pronoun is "ore" rather than "boku," despite the fact that prior to this, Sai's inner monologue has always used the "boku" of the narrator's discourse. Not only does this pronoun slippage introduce a slippage into the "I" or "self" being related in the novel, this passage reiterates the mind-body fissure that is at issue throughout the narrative. In addition, the destabilization of the "I" reintroduces the question of whether interiority can ever be transmitted to the outside—in other words, whether the whole exercise in self-revelation of the I-novel is inherently futile.[33]

This questioning of the possibility of self-revelation is a refrain throughout Kin's text. Isogai opens his confession with doubts about whether even Sai, his closest friend, could ever really understand him. Near the end of the same letter, Isogai introduces yet another corporeal metaphor for human isolation, quoting the Book of Exodus wherein Moses refers to himself as "[I] who am of uncircumcised lips" (74).[34] As Isogai explains, Moses argues that he should not serve as God's messenger because of his "uncircumcised lips," which Isogai interprets as a stutter or other speech impediment. Immediately after quoting this passage, Isogai rewords it as "[I] who am of uncircumcised heart," invoking another scriptural circumcision metaphor as a description of his own condition: "My heart will die without ever being circumcised, and thus, I will never have truly touched my heart to that of another" (74).

This analogy serves as yet another mechanism for binding Sai and Isogai not only to each other, but also to an abstracted universal human condition. As Sai muses on Isogai's letter at the end of the novel, he universalizes the notion of the uncircumcised heart. He asks, "Couldn't these words apply to every human being, not just Isogai? . . . Can mutual understanding ever really go beyond an understanding of mutual isolation?" (96). He then extends this discussion to incorporate the metaphor of the "uncircumcised lips" as well, arguing it is not only stutterers who can never fully express their thoughts to those around them, but all human beings:

> When Moses uttered these words, 'I who am of uncircumcised lips,' they were not just the words of Moses the stutterer. Wasn't he speaking as a representative [*daihyōsha*] of all humankind, including non-stutterers? The only one with truly circumcised lips, or as Isogai put it, the only one with a circumcised heart is God, and before him human beings, all of them, have uncircumcised lips which can never be circumcised, and their hearts remain uncircumcised as well (97).

This, the conclusion of the novel, is its central conceit: that the stutterer is the "representative" of the world, trapped in her own mind, unable to make a real connection with another. In the end, the stutterer is normalized, assimilated into "all humankind." In this way, at least, *Kogoeru kuchi* still falls into the trap of narrative prosthesis, and the stutterer is explicitly "representative" of everything but the particularity of disabled experience.[35]

Even this representation, however, is not direct, but rather filtered through the sets of doubles created by the novel's narrative structure.[36] Sai and Isogai are the most obvious set of doubles, both acting as the stuttering "representatives" of all humankind, as if to de-emphasize their ethnic difference. But there are also the two Sais, presenting the ethnic version of this isolation. Furthermore, I-novel discourse suggests yet another double to add to this set—the author himself. By layering these figures together, just as Isogai's narrative is layered into Sai's, Kin is able to destabilize the equation of author with protagonist. In the same way, the various stuttering representatives of the human condition, each with his own particular set of ethnic circumstances, sabotage the universalizing function of the novel's logic of representation.

Curiously, even as Kin deploys these doppelgangers, he eschews what is arguably the most visible instrument of doubling in the genealogy of colonial and Zainichi Korean literature in Japanese: textual heteroglossia. *Kogoeru kuchi* displays none of the visible linguistic hybridity we have observed up to this point. As I argued in the case of Kim Sŏkpŏm's work, the insertion of Korean-language glosses between the lines of Japanese text creates a sonic doubling effect that draws attention to the text as medium and frustrates its claims to transparent representation. The layers of text created by such interlinear glosses are not dissimilar in function to the layers Kin creates with his nested autobiographical narratives. It is surprising, then, that he would not make at least some use of the bilingual *furigana* technique employed by other Zainichi writers.

Where this effect is most striking is in Kin's refusal to attach a *furigana* gloss to Sai's name. Even in texts of Zainichi literature that forgo extensive glossing, the readings of proper nouns are usually provided. Kin could easily have included a single gloss of the name in the first instance to determine whether it should be pronounced "Sai," as in the Japanese reading of the character, or "Ch'oi," as in the Korean. With the practice of *furigana* glossing so common in Korean and other (post)colonial Japanese-language texts, the lack of even a single gloss in *Kogoeru kuchi* is, counterintuitively, the more conspicuous choice. Especially with such a common Korean name, even Japanese-language readers with little to no background in Korean topics may be aware that this character is often glossed as "Choi" (チョイ) in katakana for the Korean "Ch'oi." Thus, even readers with the strongest preference for reading the character as "Sai" may hesitate to wonder whether that reading is correct. Conversely, it is also possible to imagine a reader, perhaps one with a Korean-language background, with a strong preference for reading the name as "Ch'oi." In the absence of *furigana*, this reader too may hesitate, reproducing a sort of stuttering within the process of reading itself. Transliterating the name into English, needless to say, requires a blunt decision, or perhaps a textual representation of the undecidability: Sai/Ch'oi. The ambiguous reading of the name, then, is another marker of the gap between text and speech as linguistic media, but is also a specific *political* choice. Rather than legitimizing one side of the fraught battle over how Zainichi Koreans should pronounce their names—which is itself a product of the history of imperial assimilation efforts to alter or erase those names—Kin leaves the reading ambiguous, such that this battle is refought each time the reader encounters the name and cannot decide how it should sound.

This insistence on ambiguity, or the invisible doubling of sound, is perhaps an even more radical practice than the insertion of the double directly into the text. Even in this case, when the possibility of reading the name as "Ch'oi" is not explicitly suggested by a gloss, the suggestion still emerges from the history in which the text is embedded.[37] In other words, the double layers of sound attached to the character 崔 are still there, even when they are not visibly or materially present.[38] This invisible doubling, occurring on the central character's name, creates one final set of doppelgängers: "Sai" and "Ch'oi." This coexistence of two "selves" doubles the narrative itself, creating two separate paths for reading the novel once the split is made. There is the version of the story revolving around "Ch'oi," and a different version revolving around "Sai." In a text so concerned with the politics of sound and self-definition, and to a lesser extent with ethnicity and colonial history, the reader's choice of name for the novel's central character cannot help but color the entire story.

Moreover, a third option exists for naming the character, one that is enabled by the *absence* of speech: the strictly visual element of the name, the always not yet pronounced textual component itself, 崔. The tension between the visual representation of the name and its multifarious pronunciations draws our attention yet again to the particularity of linguistic media. Just as the visual medium of text enables the speech-disabled characters to "speak," the rupture of text from sound draws attention to the somatic implications of the gap between writing and speaking. The disabled body insists on this kind of specificity. At the same time, it points us in the direction of silence, and all the possibility it entails as an alternative to the foreclosures of coherent representation.

6

Words that Hurt

Yi Yangji's Yuhi *and the Embodied Subject in Transit*

Not long after the death of Kin Kakuei in 1985, literary critic Kuroko Kazuo offered a bleak assessment of the state of Zainichi literature as it transitioned from Kin and Kim Sŏkpŏm's second-generation era to that of the third. These younger writers—whose chief representative in Kuroko's reckoning was Yi Yangji, the subject of this chapter—are conscious of themselves as "strangers" in a strange land (*ihōjin*), subject to discrimination in Japan, yet equally alienated from a Korea to which they cannot return. This sense of in-betweenness, of being violently removed from both Korea and Japan, is found in the work of first- and second-generation writers as well, Kuroku notes, as it is arguably the very meaning of being "Zainichi." The problem, according to Kuroko, is that whereas previous generations responded to this issue with political engagement, either battling Japanese discrimination or fighting for reunification, these younger writers turn inward, more interested in the psychological than social aspects of their identities. His critique recalls those aimed at Kin Kakuei—that he subordinated the political to the personal.

Moreover, he echoes much broader contemporary criticism of Japanese literature as a whole, even making this comparison explicit:

> It can be said that the tendencies shared by the third generation are utterly in accord with the younger generation of writers debuting in contemporary Japanese literature, such as Shimada Masahiko and Kobayashi Kyōji, or even going back to Murakami Haruki and the like, who are content to revel in their own inner emptiness, without turning their attention to the world, society, or revolution. In other words, at least for now younger Zainichi writers avoid falling into "literarism" by relying on the sense of being a "stranger" that defines their existence—or to put it another way, by centering the ethnonation [*minzoku*], which acts as a kind of raison d'etre for Zainichi Korean

> Literature. Still, they are in jeopardy of assimilating into the troubling mainstream of contemporary Japanese literature. In fact, Yi Yangji's [recent work] strengthens this trend toward existentialism, and there is not a trace of ethnic consciousness to be found.[1]

Kuroko's worry here is not that Zainichi writers are abandoning the political in favor of the personal. His position is that unlike the Japanese authors he cites, Yi Yangji cannot simply detach from the political—her existence *as Zainichi* precludes such a move. This comes through especially in Kuroko's reading of the recently deceased Kin Kakuei in the same essay. Kin's tragic life story cannot be told without reference to the peninsular divisions fracturing Zainichi politics and alienating him from the community.[2] Rather, Kuroko's fear is that Zainichi Koreans might *become Japanese*, and via this assimilation also conform to the melancholy apolitical current of Japanese literature.[3] What began with Kin Kakuei comes to a head with Yi Yangji: the rejection of Zainichi nationalism in favor of a personal (read intersectional) politics is dismissed as assimilation.

Notably, the politics of gender are elided here, similarly to the elision of disability politics in criticism of Kin Kakuei. In fact, serious considerations of gender have only belatedly arrived on the scene of Zainichi literary criticism.[4] Rather, the difference between Kin and Yi for Kuroko and other critics sympathetic to Zainichi nationalism is really about their stances vis-à-vis Japan, or the prospects of being or becoming Japanese. Whereas Kin, despite his allegedly reactionary or solipsistic politics, narrates his own awakening to his Korean identity and thereafter remains tied to it, Yi's story is one of her failure to properly become Korean.

Yi grew up in a thoroughly assimilated home, her parents having naturalized (thereby conferring Japanese citizenship on her) when she was nine years old. She attended Japanese schools and went by the name Tanaka Yoshie. Her passing was so effective that she did not recall facing any discrimination as a child. However, as a young adult she became more involved in ethnic politics, and eventually traveled to Seoul to study Korean folk music and dance, in the hope of better understanding her ethnic heritage. By this point her parents had divorced, and while she was pursuing a degree in Korean literature at Seoul National University, both of her brothers died suddenly. Her life was touched repeatedly by tragedy, up to and including her untimely death in 1992. The fracturing or in-betweenness of her identity is one element of this tragic life story.

Ironically, as we can see from the description of third-generation writers as *ihōjin*, by the time Yi Yangji debuted, Zainichi identity had come to be defined by the very sense of "in-betweenness" that for writers like Kim Sŏkpŏm was destructive of Zainichi coherence. But in between what? As previously discussed, *zainichi* is a spatial descriptor, its literal meaning denoting nothing more than presence in Japan. Of course, as we have also seen, to be "in Japan" can connote much broader kinds of being than embodied presence—a being in the language, the history, the post-imperial politics that go into making Japan as much as the boundaries of its archipelago. In the same way, to be "in between" Japan and Korea has little to do with the positioning of the physical body between the two landmasses corresponding to the Japanese and Korean nation states. This territorialized language is not dissimilar from narrative prosthesis, in that it relies on the body as metaphor but ignores its physical realities.

In this chapter, I unpack and interrogate configurations of speech, text, and body in Yi Yangji's *Yuhi* (1988) in order to arrive at a clearer picture of what exactly falls "between" what in notions of Zainichi identity. "In-betweenness," like "transgression" and "hybridity," can imply coherence in the two entities whose boundaries it ostensibly blurs. *Yuhi* belies the blithe assumption of the internal coherence of languages through the figure of the translator, and explodes the condition of possibility for empathy and mutual understanding itself through the figure of the never-quite-present body. Through these figures, Yi is able to explore the affective potential of non-meaning sound and meaningful silence, as well as the violence of legibility and speech.

THE TRANSLATOR-NARRATOR AS SUBJECT IN TRANSIT

Among the most intriguing aspects of *Yuhi* is the gap it creates between the Japanese text and the voice of the narrating character, who has no knowledge of Japanese. The novella tells the story of Yuhi,[5] a Zainichi woman who comes to Korea seeking to reconnect with an ethnic homeland from which she feels alienated. The narrative begins at the moment of this mission's failure, with Yuhi abruptly returning to Japan. Her time in Korea is related in flashback, as her elderly landlady (referred to as "Oba" [Aunt]) and the narrator, "Onni"[6] (Oba's live-in niece), recall the time they spent with Yuhi while she lived in their home for the final six months of her sojourn. Thus, the narrative present of the story is set entirely in Korea, from which Yuhi (the only Japanese-speaking character) is already absent. Yet, it is rendered in Japanese, a language that is foreign to both the narrating character and the geographical space she occupies throughout. This leads to moments of uncanniness, as when the narrator states (in Japanese), "I couldn't read Japanese at all."[7]

In fact, this choice of narrator has caught the attention of critics and readers of the work since its publication. The standard interpretation of the narrative gap tends to conclude that the choice of the nameless Korean "Onni" as narrator allows for a more "objective" look at Yuhi that could not be achieved without some distance from the character.[8] Indeed, the author herself endorsed this view in the afterword to the Korean translation of *Yuhi*, stating that "the original motivation for my attempt to portray the figure of a Zainichi Korean through the eyes of a Korean living in Korea was the need to understand myself more objectively, more thoroughly."[9] Yi's stated intentions notwithstanding, the consequences of her choice lead to a narrative that is much more suggestive than a mere examination of the self from an "outside" or "objective" perspective—a project whose possibility is dubious in the first place. Instead, because the narrating perspective lies outside the narrative language of the text, to read *Yuhi* is to experience a text always already in translation.[10]

What I want to propose at the outset of my reading of *Yuhi* is that the novel's narrative voice—not "Onni" per se but rather the translating presence rendering the text in Japanese—constitutes what Naoki Sakai calls a "subject in transit." In other words, this narrator, as translator, "must be internally split and multiple, and devoid of a stable positionality."[11] If, in the narrative present, Onni is positioned stably within Korea and Yuhi is positioned stably outside it, then the narrator-translator exists not in the gap between, but rather in a plane where such a gap (whether between languages or geopolitical spaces) is unrepresentable. This allows the text to expose the limitations of spatial metaphors for language, subjectivity, and sociality, just as *Kogoeru kuchi* dismantles standard bodily metaphors of isolation and oppression.

Whereas translation is typically understood as an act of transmission between two bounded entities (such as Korean and Japanese) that are external to each other, as Sakai points out, it is the act of translation itself that "borders" languages in the first place. Translation is a practice of rendering radically incommensurable nonsense into sense, such that the difference of that nonsense can be represented as *distance*. In Sakai's words:

> Translation pertains to two dimensions of difference that must not be confused: radical difference of discontinuity that does not render itself to spatialized representation, and measured difference in continuity that is imagined in terms of a border, gap or crevice between two spatially enclosed territories or entities, figuratively projected as a distance between two figures accompanying one another. And the transition from the first to the second we often call 'translation.'[12]

With the thoroughly territorialized (or bordered) entities of Japan and Korea looming large in *Yuhi*, the deterritorialized figure of the translator-narrator becomes a discomfiting presence, betraying the spatial logic of Korean difference from Japan.

This uncanny narration provides the backdrop for a novel more generally concerned with displacement in time as well as space. Because the majority of the plot is related through Onni's flashbacks, the narrative is constantly shifting between the present time—the day that Yuhi has departed for Japan—and the past, when Yuhi is still in Korea. At times, this broken narrative can leave the reader confused about what is happening when and where. Early in the novel, Onni is on her way home from work the day of Yuhi's departure. The narrator tells of her hurried trip home, and of the deserted, empty feeling of the neighborhood when she finally reaches her street:

> The memory of Yuhi's voice prodded me in the back. I could sense her shifting gaze, seeping as it had into the sound of that voice. Beckoned by that voice, by that gaze, I turned around. Yuhi was standing beside me. I could clearly remember her face in profile looking up toward the top of the hill. Just like that day six months ago, I stood next to Yuhi, looking up at the bare rocks on the peaks that stretched back in the distance (276).

Here, the narrative suddenly and seamlessly shifts to the past, and it is unclear for just a moment whether Yuhi is actually there or Onni is merely envisioning her there. It is not until later, when we are told that Yuhi has left the country, that it becomes clear that this is Onni's memory. For the time being, the line between past and present is blurred, and it is possible that Yuhi is, in fact, presently standing beside Onni, looking up at the mountain, just as she had in the past.

Even later in the novel, when it has been established that Yuhi has left the country and is no longer present, traces of her remain—in Onni's memory, as well as in the flow of the novel. Yuhi's character is a constant presence in the narrative, despite being completely absent from its present time. For example, once inside the house, after being scolded by her aunt for failing to properly say goodbye to Yuhi, Onni goes up to Yuhi's now vacated room, where she continues to feel her presence:

> Somehow the empty room felt smaller than it had when it was full of her things.
>
> Yuhi was still in this room.
>
> I was arrested by the traces of her that remained. They drew me back whenever I thought about getting up to leave, and kept me grounded to that spot (284).

Here, despite the fact that the reader knows that Yuhi is not actually in the room, the narrator continues to relate her nagging sense that Yuhi is still in the house, making her presence felt. Though this passage lacks the ambiguity of the one above, it is no less effective at trapping the reader between times through the narrator's own ambiguous temporal location. Even as Onni remembers Yuhi from months ago, she cannot physically conjure Yuhi's presence in the room. It is only the floating presence of the narrator, the disembodied translator, who can occupy these two positions simultaneously. Moreover, though it is clear that the character of Onni is placed firmly in Korea throughout the novel (in both its past and present), the location of the narrator is undetermined both spatially and temporally. The moment of narration is necessarily later than the moment the story takes place, opening up the possibility of its narration from a space outside Korea, outside Japan, or even from an imaginary space open to ambiguity or contradiction.

Atsuko Ueda takes up this issue in her incisive reading of the novel, wherein she demonstrates how the ironic linguistic construction of the narrative lends ambiguity to the novel's sense of place. In the course of her analysis, Ueda notes that the text rarely refers explicitly to "Japan" or "Korea," but more often uses terms like *uri nara* (our country) or *i nara* (this country). Moreover, these Korean terms usually appear with their Japanese equivalents or "translations" (*bokoku* [motherland] for *uri nara*, and *kono kuni* [this country] for *i nara*). These glosses are meant perhaps as a convenience for Japanese readers, but Ueda sees a more complicated picture. In nearly all instances of the appearance of these terms in the novel, the most obvious reading would assume that they refer to Korea rather than Japan, but Ueda argues that the presence of these "translations" introduces doubt. She writes, "The juxtaposition of the hangŭl with its translation (in Japanese characters) renders the antecedent ambiguous. Does *uri nara* (*bokoku*) refer to Korea, or to Japan? Do *uri nara* and *bokoku* even have the same antecedent? Because of the ambiguous relationship between these symbols and their referents, it is impossible to decide with any certainty."[13]

Though Ueda's focus here is on ambiguity in language, I would argue that these uncertain referents also serve to muddle the reader's sense of the spatial location of the narrator. After all, if it is possible that *uri nara*, or especially *bokoku*, refers to Japan, then the possibility exists that the narrator is located in Japan. The narrator is not only translator, but in transit. In another passage earlier in the novel, the Korean words "i nara" (this country) appear juxtaposed with the Japanese "kono kuni" more or less without context, allowing for perhaps greater referential ambiguity than even *uri nara* and *bokoku*:

> Why had she left? Why couldn't Yuhi have stayed in this country [*kono kuni*]? These questions were pointless now, but still I felt flushed with anger as they came to mind.
>
> '*I nara* (*Kono kuni*).'
>
> As I stood there, Yuhi's voice flitted through my mind. I thought back on all the times Yuhi had spoken these words, all the different looks on her face, all the different ways the words sounded coming out of her mouth. There was the day she muttered them under her breath, seemingly out of contempt for herself. The day she spat them out carelessly mid-sentence, sarcastically, scornfully. The day she mumbled them tentatively, as if struggling to find some other words to use and coming up empty. The day she uttered them as a desperate plea (282).

Here, it is not quite clear who is uttering this "i nara" or "kono kuni," or even perhaps which of the two is being spoken. It could just be a reference to a time when Yuhi spoke these words, since it is apparent from the paragraph that follows that she did in fact utter them on a number of occasions. It is also possible that Onni herself is speaking them as she recalls these instances of Yuhi's use of the words, "i nara."

However, what seems to prompt the narrator to recall these words is her own use of the Japanese equivalent, "kono kuni," in the preceding sentence. This raises the question of what is being quoted here. Is it the narrator's own use of "kono kuni" beforehand? Or is it perhaps the use of "i nara," prior to hypothetical translation? Or does it refer to her memories of Yuhi's use of "i nara," albeit prior to their representation in text? Is it possible that this might even refer to memories of Yuhi uttering the Japanese words "kono kuni"? None of these questions have clear answers, and without knowing exactly what is being spoken and by whom, it is impossible to be certain whether this "i nara" or "kono kuni" refers to Korea or Japan. Though in the reality of the story, the narrator's first question—"why couldn't Yuhi have stayed in this country?"—seems to ask why she was unable to remain in Korea, there may be some room to interpret this question (especially since it appears in Japanese, using the Japanese phrase "kono kuni" rather than the Korean "i nara") as a question of why Yuhi was unable to remain in Japan, or why she felt the need to search for herself in Korea.

In any case, this moment of heightened confusion of spaces and languages allows the disembodied translator-narrator to come to the fore. Without a subject transversing the spaces and translating the words of "kono kuni" and "i nara," the two are unable to come into contact, creating the uncanny sensibility present in this and other passages of the novel. The translating narrator enjoys greater freedom not only to float through and across these colliding spaces, but also to call into question their very distinction. Due to the narrator's ability to seamlessly traverse the two, "i nara" and "kono kuni" collapse into one and the same entity, offering a moment's respite from the conflict between politically bounded Korea and Japan that drives Yuhi's (or Yi Yangji's) entire struggle. By positing an extraspatial, extralinguistic narrating voice, Yi is able to effect a fleeting escape from the impasse in which she is embedded, by imagining a realm in which the impasse is null and void.

ABSENCE AND THE AFFECT OF ILLEGIBILITY

If the narrator of *Yuhi* is unlocatable due to her being in transit, then the title character is similarly unlocatable, but due to absence. Although Yuhi too is technically in transit, en route to Japan, this is less important to the story than the fact of her being missing from it. The narrative repeats the refrain that Yuhi is not there: not in the country, not in the house, not in her room, and in multiple instances, "not anywhere" (*doko ni mo inai*) (326, 335). For Onni, this is a bitter reality, each successive realization of which shocks her anew. This shock is often described as physically impacting her body, perceived as a wriggling lump inside her, or as a piercing or percussive sensation. Yuhi's lack of corporeal presence does little to limit her corporeal effects on Onni.

In fact, the novel is structured as a series of scenes in which Onni visits sites where Yuhi's absence is palpable and narrates the memories triggered by physical presence in these spaces. Unsure how to cope with the loss of Yuhi, Onni moves vicariously through the spaces she occupied in an attempt to bring her back, even if only in spirit. As mentioned above, when Onni first returns from work at the beginning of the story, she stands outside the house looking up at the rocks on the mountainside, with Yuhi "standing beside [her]" (276). This turns out to be a reenactment of a moment when Yuhi gazed up at the same rocks before she left. As Onni moves into the house, she pauses in the entryway to recall a moment Yuhi did the same. After entering the house, she stands behind the living room sofa, recalling that this is where Yuhi sat the day she first came to their house. Then she is arrested by the illusion that Yuhi is sitting there even now. In all of these cases, the memory of a past Yuhi collapses into the present moment, such that her body is brought back to the place it once was, further disorienting the sense of time and space in the novel.

Eventually, Onni moves to Yuhi's now vacated bedroom, where even more memories return to life. At first Onni sits in the place she always occupied when she visited Yuhi in her room. As she continues to reminisce, however, she unfolds Yuhi's portable desk and sits at it as if she were Yuhi herself. This shift from attempts to recreate co-presence with Yuhi to what seems like an attempt to physically embody her occurs at a moment of frustration, when Onni is confronting the sheer weight of what she did not know about Yuhi and her experience. Upon entering the bedroom, Onni recalls a phone conversation she had with Yuhi earlier that day. Calling from the airport, Yuhi asks Onni to retrieve a packet of writing she left in the top drawer of her dresser because she could not bring herself to take it with her back to Japan. She tells her she can do as she pleases with it, either keeping it as a memento or disposing of it, but the question of her reading the text is moot. When Onni opens the dresser drawer, she finds an envelope stuffed with 448 pages of writing in Japanese. The bulk of this unknown and unknowable text in her hands testifies to all that Onni does not and could not understand about Yuhi. This woman she thought she knew intimately had the time and inclination to surreptitiously write 448 pages, and all in a language Onni herself cannot read. It is perhaps the chagrin she feels at this realization that causes her to try not only to bring Yuhi back but to become her, to attempt to see the world through her eyes.

Onni also attempts, quite literally, to speak in Yuhi's voice. Many of the instances in which she vicariously positions her body in spaces Yuhi occupied conjure not only a visual image of Yuhi's ghostly presence, but also resurrect the sound of her voice. Some of these moments are marked conspicuously in the text, as the recreation of Yuhi's voice is represented in hangŭl, which contrasts sharply with the surrounding Japanese characters. The first case of this occurs, again, in the blur of time and space in which Onni gazes up at the rocks on the mountains with the Yuhi of the past standing next to her. When sound is introduced to this confusing visual scene, it is in a similarly disorienting manner, the origins of the voice initially unclear: "바위 (岩) [*pawi* (rocks)]" (277). The first instance of dialogue in the novel is thus rendered in a bilingual textual mode familiar from the work of Kim Sŏkpŏm and his colonial predecessors. A word whose pronunciation is unclear is glossed with katakana that transcribes its Korean pronunciation, while a parenthetical gloss follows to fill in the meaning. Yi takes this practice a step further, however, by replacing the shared language of sinographs with the opacity of hangŭl, as if to emphasize the unbridgeable difference of the languages rather than their historical unity.

Furthermore, the text introduces this utterance without clarifying whose voice is producing it. The reader experiences a brief moment of uncertainty as to whether it is Onni spontaneously naming the rocks in her view, or whether the "Yuhi" standing beside her made this declaration in the past (or its phantasmic reproduction in the present). The answer turns out to be both, in a way. The quoted "*pawi*" is attributed as follows: "I recalled Yuhi's voice and murmured the word, trying to mimic her pronunciation. I could still hear her voice as she stressed the *wi* sound, trying her best to pronounce it correctly, but sounding all the more awkward for her effort" (277). In the end, it remains possible to attribute the sound represented by these hangŭl to both the voice of Yuhi resurrected from the past and the voice of Onni performing that resurrection by embodying Yuhi, down to the sounds that came out of her mouth.

Nevertheless, the source of Onni's frustration throughout the novel is that these efforts fail. She can no more speak in Yuhi's voice than she can literally embody her, just as she is unable to decipher the Japanese text Yuhi leaves behind. Although the novel is presented in the form of pseudo-translation, it is thematically focused on the *impossibility* of transmission and communication rather than its potential. What Yi described as an effort to understand herself through the character of Yuhi, and what critics have described as a journey toward greater empathy for the *ihōjin* or the in-between subject,[14] is, I would argue, anything but. The novel is rather a depiction of the limits of empathy as an ethical value founded on the assumption that the other can be understood. Whatever relationship Onni is able to have with Yuhi is necessarily built from at best a partial and fractured understanding of her emotions and experiences.

Onni herself even acknowledges the hubris of her presumption of understanding Yuhi. As she reflects on how she viewed Yuhi before the shock of her departure, she begins to see that her image of Yuhi was colored by her own self-consciousness. "Maybe I saw a bit of myself in her. Or maybe I unilaterally decided that she somehow resembled me, projecting my own brooding, introverted character onto her" (289). Onni provides anything but an "objective" perspective on Yuhi. Everything we know about Yuhi is filtered through Onni's projections, or serves only to emphasize how little she knows—and how little we can know in the first place.

This failure of communication and mutual understanding is underscored in *Yuhi* through its emphasis on the incommensurability of speech, body, and text. As with other examples of Zainichi literature, *Yuhi* shows an outsized concern not only with language in general, but with the particularities of their spoken and written forms. This is yet another effect of the uncanny translator-narrator, whose presence brings into relief the pseudo-translation between speech and text that goes unremarked in most texts. Instead of an assumption of one-to-one correspondence between the sounds of the characters' spoken dialogue, the narrative of *Yuhi* openly displays the multi-step process of "translation" undergone between the Korean "speech" of the characters and the Japanese text of the final product. After the phonetically and semantically glossed hangŭl text of the first line of dialogue, the next lines occur in katakana transcription of Korean accompanied by parenthetical translations of meaning in Japanese, leaving out the hangŭl "original" (which is already a pseudo-translation of the original speech posited by the text):

ヌグセヨ？	（誰ですか）	Nuguseyo? (Who is it?)
. . .	. . .	
チョエヨ	（私です）	Chŏ yeyo. (It's me.) (277)

This serves to establish that in the world of the story, Onni and her aunt are speaking to each other in Korean throughout. This device in place, the dialogue then immediately transitions to being presented more or less exclusively in Japanese "translation," completing a progression from the purportedly strictly phonetic (though in this case unpronounceable for target readers) hangŭl, to the somewhat awkward phonetic transcription represented by the katakana, to a supposedly more transparent transcription of meaning rather than sound.

Exceptions to this rule, those points in the text when hangŭl or katakana-transcribed Korean language reemerge, have the effect of disrupting the narrative and causing the reader to pause and wonder why the particular language in question was untranslatable. Some Korean words, like *chŏnse* (a large deposit made in lieu of rent), appear in katakana in dialogue exchanged between Onni and her aunt, presumably for lack of clear Japanese equivalents, and as a reminder of the linguistic setting of their speech. In other cases, particularly Onni's further recollections (or reenactments) of Yuhi's voice speaking Korean phrases such as "이 나라 (この国)" (*i nara* [this country]) and "이 나라 사람 (この国の人) (*i nara saram* [this country's people]), the baggage involved in reproducing the Korean characters along with both interlinear and parenthetical glosses is clearly deployed for more weighty political purposes (282). The same goes for "uri nara," which is similarly glossed as Onni repeats the words, again in Yuhi's voice, while tracing their corresponding hangŭl characters with her finger on the surface of Yuhi's written (but illegible) testament (300). Here, the hangŭl characters presented to the Japanese reader reproduce not only Onni's experience of confronting an illegible text, a text not meant for her, but also her embodied performance of tracing their shapes. The affective potential of these characters and the performance they generate stands in contrast to their inefficacy as conveyors of meaning in their function as text on a page.

An even better example of the affect of illegibility comes a few pages later, when Onni removes Yuhi's Japanese text from its envelope and encounters the written characters themselves. She states—paradoxically, as the statement appears in Japanese—that she cannot read a word of it, then nevertheless relates her feeling that the Japanese words on the page are speaking to her in Yuhi's voice:

> I couldn't read a word of Japanese. There were some kanji that I knew. I tried to follow along with those characters and puzzle out what she was writing about. But I soon gave up. It was no use. Still, I couldn't take my eyes off it.
>
> The characters [*moji*] were breathing.
>
> They were looking up at me, speaking to me. Just looking at them, I could hear Yuhi's voice, the sound of it filling my head and rushing through my veins (308).

Somehow, despite her inability to translate those written characters into decipherable *meaning*, she is able to translate them into *sounds*. Moreover, the words on the page, described as "breathing," are personified, animated, perhaps even embodied. They affect Onni's body in turn.

This dynamic intensifies as Onni continues looking at the text she cannot read, still conjuring the image of Yuhi's body through her vicarious placement at her desk and proximity to this product of her hand. Eventually the sounds she "hears" take on more specific form:

> 'A, I, U, E, O.'
>
> I knew these sounds. A, I, U, E, O, I whispered. I tried to make Yuhi say them too. Yuhi came to me in the form of the characters on the page, with their particular shapes and contours, whispering back at me. . . .
>
> I looked around the room once more, feeling as if I had become Yuhi herself. Her words stared back at me as well (309).

This merging of text, voice, and body finally allows Onni to feel at one with Yuhi. Yet it is not through reading the text she left behind and understanding what she wrote that this comes about. Rather, it happens via her confrontation with what she cannot understand. She is able to reach out to Yuhi with her imagination, even if she cannot bridge the gap between them by communicating linguistically.

What I want to emphasize here is that this suggests a generalizable mode of "reading" texts. The acknowledgment of remnants outside what text is capable of representing—the voice, the body, the "other"—allows for a relaxation of the impulse to interpret or critique. Instead, the text can prompt its readers to imagine what is not represented. As we see with Onni, this can be a more ethical, less solipsistic exercise than an ultimately futile quest to mine the meaning from a text. That meaning, like Yuhi, may always be absent.

However, Onni's moment of oneness with Yuhi soon gives way to the anger and frustration that characterizes the narrative as a whole, upon the realization that she will never know what Yuhi has written in this text. She notes, with somewhat ironic phrasing, "I couldn't help thinking that Yuhi had revealed herself in these pages. That she had poured her heart and soul into these words, the innermost parts of herself that she never let anyone see. But all in Japanese" (309). What Onni speculates here is that Yuhi has written a confession of sorts, but one that will never reach an audience, and therefore cannot function as a confession. It is a confession that is arrested in its pre-revealed state.

As the implications of Yuhi's refusal to share her inner life with her in legible form dawn on Onni, she continues:

> I had felt so close to Yuhi, so connected to her. I had thought of her as a sister. And like a sister I had worried about her, commiserated with her, and sometimes I was even truly angry at her. I thought she cared for me like a sister too. I thought we both felt this way, that we were kindred spirits, drawn together by our mutual isolation.
>
> But the whole time, Yuhi had been so far away.
>
> Perhaps it was because I was so used to reading her writing in hangŭl, but somehow her writing in Japanese didn't seem unfamiliar to me. And yet the fact that she had sat here writing it, alone, was a testament to just how far away she had been. To the unbridgeable distance that remained between us (309).

Onni's anger throughout the novel arises essentially from the inaccessibility of this text and the distance it represents, a distance she had failed to recognize before Yuhi's sudden departure. The illegible text becomes an object of suspicion—like any text in the eyes of a critic—possibly precisely because it is produced at a distance. In contrast to the proximity of speech, text engenders a nagging skepticism in that the reader can never be sure that it is not a product of translation. Yuhi's written Korean, which Onni remarks is less awkward than her Korean speech, nonetheless reads as if it is translated directly from Japanese. Even if the text, in this case, is more apt to communicate meaning clearly, speech is still privileged as a means of accessing the authentic self. Its source absent, text betrays its own mediated quality.

Thus, the absence of Yuhi functions similarly to the floating positionality of the narrator-translator, in that they both preclude proximal access to the embodied speaking voice. The fundamental unknowability of these subjects, coupled with the unilateral desire to know them, gives rise to the anxiety of translation, or the anxiety of language itself. To return to Naoki Sakai's formulation of the subject in transit, the political work of transforming nonsense into sense is not confined to the realm of "translation proper," which is to say translation between two supposedly unified and mutually exclusive national languages. Rather, "translation introduces a disjunctive instability into the putatively *personal* relations among agents of speech, writing, listening and reading."[15] In other words, the gap between speech and text, as with the gap between languages, comes into being at the moment of translation between the two. Translation disrupts not only the internal coherence of language communities but also the coherence of the speaking subject, even within a single language. To understand speech as a communicative medium offering transparent access to the self requires the assumption that embodied experience is translatable into speech. This, as we have seen, is impossible. There is a more fundamental inaccessibility that the corporeal mediation of language, as social act, overcomes.

Indeed, as Yuhi and Onni's stories demonstrate, speech as embodied practice has poietic qualities even if it is never translated out of incoherence. As the portion of the novel taking place in Yuhi's room comes to a close, Onni recalls the tone and rhythm of Yuhi reading Japanese aloud, which she would sometimes overhear from outside the room. At the same time, Onni clutches Yuhi's text to her chest, forging a connection between Yuhi's written and spoken words, even as she understands neither:

> I was holding this bundle of Yuhi's writing in my arms. I felt like she had become the characters, and I was hugging her tightly to my chest. . . . The voice I was hearing was the characters. It was as if the words on the page had become audible sound. The pages I held to my chest seemed to reach through my body and touch [something within], making it cry out in Yuhi's voice from deep inside me (316).

Again, Onni's access to Yuhi's voice is not a product of her ability to translate between the written artifact she holds—the two may not even be commensurable in the first place. Instead, it is the bodily act of holding onto the text as tactile object that enables Onni to reanimate her own embodied memories of hearing Yuhi's voice. The text has this affective power even in the absence of meaning, but only insofar as it comes into contact with Onni's body, causing her to recall Yuhi's bodily state when she wrote it, or when she spoke in the voice that haunts it.

More often than not, her body was in pain. It is clear that Yuhi experiences the Korean language as an assault, often retreating to the safe haven of Japanese. In one instance, caught in a cacophony of Korean voices on a crowded city bus, Yuhi breaks down and starts muttering under her breath in Japanese. Onni, desperately trying to help her, eventually protests, "If you won't talk to me, I can't understand what's wrong" (306). Rather than responding, Yuhi drops her head to her knees and clasps both hands over her ears, trying to quiet the noise. Yuhi's visceral aversion to the sounds of the Korean language causes her to censure herself for her perceived betrayal of her national language and community, and plays no small part in giving rise to Onni's bitterness toward her.

In another case, a severely intoxicated Yuhi has another breakdown in speech, but this time compensates by writing in hangŭl rather than speaking in Japanese. She writes a line or two at a time, with Onni's reactions interspersed between, though it is not a conversation as such. One line of Yuhi's writing links continuously to the next without responding to Onni's dumbfounded interjections. Compiled together, they appear in the text as follows, the longest occurrence of glossed hangŭl in the novel:

언니 (オンニ)	Ŏnni
저는 위선자입니다 (チョヌン ウィソンジャイムニダ)	Chŏ nŭn wisŏnja imnida
저는 거짓말장이입니다 (チョヌン コジンマルジャンイイムニダ)	Chŏ nŭn kŏjinmaljang'i imnida

(オンニ	(Onni
私は　偽善者です	I am a hypocrite
私は　嘘つきです)	I am a liar)
. . .	. . .
ウ リ ナ ラ 우리나라	Uri nara
(母国)	(Motherland)
. . .	. . .
サ ランハル ス オプスムニ ダ 사랑할 수 없읍니다	Sarang hal su ŏpsŭmnida
(愛することができません)	(I cannot love it)
. . .	. . .
テ グム チョワ ヨ 대금 좋아요	Taegŭm choayo
テ グム ソ リ ヌン ウ リ マルイムニ ダ 대금소리는 우리말입니다	Taegŭm sori nŭn uri mal imnida
(テグム　好きです	(I love the taegŭm
ウリマル テグムの音は　母語です)	The sound of the taegŭm is my mother tongue [uri mal]) (313–14).

Here Yuhi's self-flagellation echoes the aphorism of the translator as traitor. And in fact, she is performing an act of translation by presenting these fragments of text to Onni. Perhaps they are a transcription of the Korean words she would have spoken, or perhaps they are direct translations from the Japanese words that might come more naturally to her—which the text of the novel then reproduces, but as a translation of the Korean text rather than the other way around.

In any case, the sense of suspicion, falseness, or hypocrisy ingrained in her use of the written Korean language comes from the sense that this language does not belong to her. Because she cannot love "uri nara"—glossed in Japanese as *bokoku* (motherland) but literally "our country"—she cannot apply the collective possessive pronoun "uri" to herself. To utter or even to write the words "uri nara" or "uri mal" (our language) would be to lie, to betray. Here the ambivalent antecedents of the translated words "this country" or "our country" have heavy emotional consequences.

This becomes especially poignant when Yuhi is explaining to Onni why she cannot stay in Korea and finish her degree. It is her hatred of spoken Korean that prevents her from remaining any longer:

> At school, in the city, everywhere I go, the Korean everyone speaks—it's like tear gas. It burns, it stings. Just hearing it makes it hard to breathe. . . . I hated their voices. The voices of their actions, the voices of their gazes, the voices of their facial expressions, the voices of their bodies—I couldn't stand them. It was like breathing tear gas (321).

One can hardly begrudge Onni her anger at the offensive terms in which Yuhi describes Korea and its language. More suggestive, however, are the corporeal terms she employs here. It is not only literal speech that bothers her, but a much broader set of gestures and actions that she lumps in with spoken Korean. At the same time, these voices have physical as well as mental impacts, ostensibly disrupting the fundamental bodily act of breathing. Yuhi goes on to say that this hatred of the language—and her disgust with herself for harboring it—physically prevented her hand from moving to write the characters "uri nara" on an exam. This stutter in written form is the moment she decides she must return to Japan. A complex confluence of speech, writing, and embodied affect excise her from the "uri" of "uri mal" and ultimately the very space of "uri nara."

HOMOSOCIALITY AND HOMOLINGUAL ADDRESS

This returns us to the question of spatial metaphor and the politics of belonging, as Yuhi feels that she was always somehow outside "uri nara" even as she was literally within it. In fact, as she is explaining her decision to leave and its connection to the Korean language soundscape, she redraws the boundaries of *where* she was during the novel: "I like the sound of the Korean you and Oba speak. Just knowing there were people who spoke that kind of Korean made it worth staying in this country (*kono kuni*). Or at least staying in this house. Maybe I was never really in this country, just in this house" (315).

Of course, the exception she carves out for Onni and Oba as she expresses her disdain for the Korean language does little to temper this statement. Onni's offense is understandable, especially when considered against the backdrop of Yuhi's larger pattern of painting Korea with a broad brush. Onni's recollections of Yuhi voicing the words "i nara" (this country) and "i nara saram" (this country's people) are particularly painful, as Yuhi always follows these words with stereotypes, stated definitively as if she is an authority. This leaves Onni galled not only at Yuhi's presumption of qualification to speak for or about Korea and its people, but also certain that Yuhi would revise her negative view of the country if only she would get to know it better. One wonders just how much knowledge would be required for a statement beginning with "This country's people . . ." not to end in a similarly totalized and presumptuous fashion. Instead, the real root of this tension is the troubled logic of representation. The limited cross section of Korea that Yuhi has experienced cannot possibly stand for the richer and more complex whole, but this whole cannot be grasped without flattening out its nuances. This may be what Yuhi is getting at when she says that if she was in a particular space, it was the house, not the country.

However, tracing Yuhi's path to arriving in the house—as well as the country—complicates this picture somewhat. As Onni and Oba learn when they first meet her, Yuhi has moved out of many boarding houses and rooms for rent already, though she is not eager to say why. Months after she moves in, and unbeknownst to Onni, Yuhi gives her aunt a glimpse into the problems she faced in previous housing situations. She describes an altercation between a former landlord's two sons that starts over a minor disagreement and turns violent, eventually resulting in one of the brothers punching through the window of the house's front door. Yuhi is shocked that this would happen right before her eyes—and that her fellow tenants are not taken aback—but Oba has trouble holding back laughter as she tells the story. The normalcy of this kind of toxic masculinity drives her toward a female-only house.

Similarly, it is a fraught reaction to patriarchy that drives Yuhi to Korea in the first place. In another reveal made via Oba rather than Onni, Yuhi explains that her father was once swindled by a fellow Korean in Japan, such that any mention of Korea he made to his family thereafter was to malign it. This also meant that her family tried aggressively to assimilate into Japanese society, with Yuhi attending Japanese schools and only belatedly awakening to her Korean identity. At some level, it is her father's recent death that prompts her journey "back" to Korea, an attempt to rehabilitate the country in her mind after so much negative indoctrination. Yuhi's love-hate relationships with Korea, then, cannot be disentangled from the same conflicted emotions she holds toward her father.

An underexplored aspect of the novel, then, is the homosociality of the space where it all takes place. The house is distinguished by the palpable absence of men. Oba's husband, whom she describes as a Korean nationalist, harboring anti-Japanese sentiments originating in the colonial period, is dead. Her married daughter has emigrated to the United States with her husband. Onni is unmarried in her thirties, a state that is treated as almost pathological by those around her. Yuhi's father has passed away, as noted above, and she leaves behind brothers in Japan. If the house lends her a sense of belonging unavailable to her in the larger Korea outside (or for that matter in Japan), then it has as much to do with gender as national identity. At the same time, the way Yuhi and Oba discuss their departed father and husband, respectively, both unable to fully accept the nationalist or assimilationist outlooks they represented, illustrates the intersecting and contradictory allegiances that Korean women must navigate on either side of the straits.

However, the homosociality between these women exists on a continuum that slides into homoerotic territory as well.[16] Beyond Onni's unmarried status and the way she describes her inability to connect with others, the narrative drops hints that her fascination with Yuhi goes beyond sisterly affection, including her constant remarks on Yuhi's mesmerizing androgynous appearance. This possibly sexual tension comes to a head when Onni attempts to hold Yuhi's hand on an outing, a culturally normative practice between young women in Korea but not in Japan. Despite understanding the cultural difference in question, Yuhi is uncomfortable with the touch. The novel leaves plenty of space to interpret this as just one more instance of Yuhi's general discomfort with Korea and experience of culture shock, often portrayed as a will to guard her body against the sensations of being in Korea. Yet it is also possible to read this awkward moment as an unspoken and subconscious realization by both women that Onni's affinity for Yuhi is not strictly sisterly. Whether it verges on the erotic or not, Onni's desire for Yuhi—including desire for bodily closeness—goes a long way toward explaining the obsessive bitterness or even rage that characterizes her reaction to Yuhi's departure.

This anger at Yuhi's disappearance and the shattering of the family these three women created is connected to deeper anxieties Onni and Oba share about their actual family. Yuhi's leaving is perhaps a painful reminder of the absence of Oba's daughter. As if to confirm this emotional overlap, the day Yuhi leaves Oba calls her daughter at an unreasonable hour for her time zone and talks for so long that Onni retires for the evening before the conversation ends. The daughter's migration to the United States is one of many subtle background reminders of Cold War vectors of power in the story. Yuhi's very ability to come to Korea is a product of Japan's economic dominance in the region, itself enabled by American Cold War policy. Oba vacillates between relief that Yuhi does not conform to the stereotyped image of Zainichi Koreans as lavish consumers of Seoul's nightlife and vague apprehension that she may sympathize with the communist North. In this way she serves as a reminder of not only this family's geographical separation, but also South Korea's place in the geopolitical order, particularly the division of the peninsula along ideological and geographical lines.

This politics of the fractured nation—so often, as here, read allegorically onto the fractured family—collides with the politics of sexuality at the site of Onni's body. Her refusal or inability to perform her reproductive duty to the patriarchal nation-state exacerbates her and Oba's anxiety over their disappearing family.[17] The intersecting imperial histories and intersecting normative demands on her body turn Yuhi's absence into a personal and political disaster. If Onni is angry at Yuhi's failure to assimilate as a proper Korean national subject, then this necessarily overlaps with her failure (in the eyes of her father) to assimilate into proper Japanese national subjectivity, and with Onni's own perceived shortcomings as a Korean woman, including but not limited to her failure to reproduce the family and the nation. As with Yuhi's conclusion that she cannot use the collective possessive "uri" because she does not belong to the Korean "we," neither does Onni in any neat or unproblematic way. The difference is one of mobility: whereas Yuhi escaped, Onni cannot.

This opposition between stasis and movement brings us to the enigmatic conclusion of the novel, where Yuhi discusses her "language crutch" (*kotoba no tsue*). She uses this metaphor—once again latching onto the figurative language of disability—to describe her own feelings of stasis within language. She tells Onni that when she first wakes up every morning, a sound like "ah" escapes her lips, falling somewhere between the sound of breathing and the sound of spoken language. As it happens, this sound also falls between the Japanese and Korean languages.

Both syllabaries begin with this same vowel sound. Thus, when Yuhi awakens from dreams, she stands fixed at the crossroads of the two languages:

> Is it an 아(ア), or is it an あ? If it's an 아, then I grab the crutch that goes 아(ア), 야(ヤ), 어(オ), 여(ヨ). But if it's an あ, then it's the crutch that goes あ、い、う、え、お. But I never know for sure if it's an 아 or an あ. It's always been that way. And it just keeps getting harder to tell which it is. I can't grab the crutch (335).

Although this passage is represented as dialogue in the text, notably it would be difficult for Yuhi to convey the sense of this to Onni through speech alone, since it is impossible to distinguish between 아 and あ in spoken language without some additional reference or gesture. This 아/あ, then, is the site of intersection of Japanese and Korean, of speech and text, and as Yuhi suggests here, of sense and nonsense. It is the primordial speech act prior to the coherence imposed by the systematized ordering of sounds in a syllabary. She cannot linger in this pre-linguistic space, even as proceeding along one path and abandoning the other entails a sense of pain and loss.

The metaphor of the crutch frames this ordering of nonsense into sense as the device that enables her mobility in the language, but it is unclear that such mobility is an improvement over the momentary stasis of the 아/あ. Even if this nonsensical sound cannot be translated into meaning that could make Yuhi understood, it does provide the potential for an embodied empathy that does not require being understood. The novel closes with Onni uttering her own 아, whereupon she feels unable to walk, "as if my crutch were taken from me" (335). She also finds that the sounds that should continue from the 아 do not come to her, as if she too is uncertain whether this sound exists in Korean or Japanese—the latter completely unknown to her, a wall that cuts her off from Yuhi.

There can be no doubt that this is an empathetic moment. Onni shares with Yuhi the emotional experience of searching for a language crutch, and either not finding it, or not finding it particularly enabling. The "ah" sound they both make will never act as a medium for mutual understanding, but it can offer an embodied connection based on mutual experience. Perhaps they are both feeling the frustration of in-betweenness and non-belonging in this moment, and Onni is finally able to understand Yuhi's plight. But what the collapse of 아 into あ suggests is that there is no gap for Yuhi to occupy, no two bounded entities to fall between. Instead, I would propose that what Yuhi and Onni experience here, in the moment before sound becomes language, is the radical social act of encountering the incommensurable.

. . .

To conclude, I want to point to one other potential basis for solidarity between Onni and Yuhi that runs parallel to communication and mutual experience: shared history. As with their views of Korea as a whole, the two women's understandings of Korean history overlap and conflict, one of many sources of tension in the novel. One of the more uncomfortable moments when this contestation of history comes to the surface happens in the realm of literary history in particular. Upon learning that Onni majored in Korean literature in college, Yuhi asks about the topic of her thesis. Onni responds that she wrote on Yi Sang, and in the course of their conversation asks Yuhi which Korean authors she likes. She replies, abashedly, that she does not read much fiction in Korean because it is difficult for her, but that the author who intrigues her the most is Yi Kwangsu.

The awkwardness of this exchange is due to the very different connections these two women have to the Korean literary past. Yi Sang is perhaps the most revered writer of the colonial period, but died before Japanese mobilization for total war and thus never confronted the dilemmas presented by the loss of the Korean language and the collapse of artistic freedom. Yi Kwangsu, on the other hand, embodies all of the messiness that Yi Sang avoids. By mentioning him here, Yuhi explicitly positions herself as the heir to these contradictions and failures. It is the first hint she gives of her betrayal of the Korean nation, linking her own assimilation and affinity for Japan to collaboration with imperialism. Perhaps it would not be unfair to say that *Yuhi* goes further than any other work we have seen to make this link explicit, to position Zainichi literature as an alternate future for colonial Korean literary history: for some a dystopia in which the Japanese assimilation project and disappearance of literature in the Korean language are carried out; for others, the condition of possibility for a kind of writing outside the burden of representation for a monolithic nation or linguistic community.

7

What Was Zainichi Literature?

Temporalities of Silence and the Incoherent Future in Yū Miri's Hachigatsu no hate

"When I die, Zainichi literature will be over." So declared Kim Sŏkpŏm at a recent symposium in his honor. A bold statement, to be sure, but as discussed at the outset of this book, Kim is by no means the first or only member of the Zainichi literary establishment to predict that the genre may soon be a thing of the past. Indeed, the twenty-first century has been marked by anxiety over the future of Zainichi literature, as well as the unavoidable questions about the past and present that accompany such anxieties. It is not as if the prophets of Zainichi literature's doom expect the population of Koreans in Japan to disappear or stop writing altogether. Rather, it is the erosion of certain boundaries—temporal and otherwise—that has raised doubts as to the future *coherence* of Zainichi literature as a literature. As I will argue here, the question invariably becomes, was there ever such a coherence in the first place?

Of course, the context for this anxiety is assimilation. As noted in previous chapters, even by the 1960s and 1970s, only a minority of Koreans in Japan attended ethnic schools or spoke Korean at home. The use of Japanese names and marriage to Japanese spouses were also on the rise, as was naturalization, despite vocal disapproval of the latter from Zainichi intellectual leaders. These trends have only intensified in the decades since. Passing is so commonplace that Yi Yangji's story of discovering her Korean heritage in adulthood is not an uncommon one.[1] Without questioning the validity of the choices younger Koreans in Japan are making, it is easy enough to imagine that these trends toward assimilation, which mirror the explicit goals of the Japanese colonial government, are painful to witness for the older Koreans who lived through that very regime.

Meanwhile, the stated political project of the Zainichi (nationalist) literature nurtured by this older generation—the reunification of the Korean peninsula as the condition of possibility for eventual return—has become all but irrelevant in the present day. Reunification may still be a worthy enterprise, but return as such is for all intents and purposes already impossible, as Yi so eloquently and tragically demonstrated. The Korea of the past can never be made whole, if it ever actually existed as imagined. In the aftermath of this temporal shift, with "Korea" now an object of nostalgia rather than aspiration, it is no wonder that an affect of impending loss should permeate the discourse on Zainichi literature.

This is not to imply universal agreement that the loss is to be mourned. Other (typically younger) voices argue that "Zainichi," with its latent implication that Koreans in Japan are somehow out of place, is no longer or never was a viable framework for Koreans who wish to remain in Japan. As previously noted, Kaneshiro Kazuki is among the most vocal literary figures to push for alternative modes of Zainichi identification, such as "Korean-Japanese," an embrace of ethnic minority status. Recognizing the limitations of this position, however, Kaneshiro has also expressed a desire to be read not as a writer belonging to any particularized category, longing for the day when such frameworks are superseded by his recognition as a universalized "human" writer.[2] This sentiment is by no means unique among Zainichi writers, or indeed among writers of minority, postcolonial, diasporic, or otherwise particularized literatures the world over. There is no shortage of critics arguing that such frameworks, with all the representational burdens and restrictions they impose on subjects within their spheres (as this book has discussed in detail), are best moved beyond once their political purposes have been served. The real question concerning the future of Koreans in Japan and their literary production is: whose political ends are actually served by Zainichi literature or even identity? Or, to put it another way, insofar as Zainichi ever existed, what was it founded upon, and should that foundation be preserved or dismantled as we turn toward the future?

These tensions came to a head with the 2006 publication of the eighteen-volume anthology *"Zainichi" bungaku zenshū* (*Collected Works of "Zainichi" Literature*).[3] Notably missing were the works of the aforementioned Kaneshiro Kazuki and another of the last scions of Zainichi literature: Yū Miri. Since winning the Akutagawa Prize in 1996—third in a line of Zainichi writers to do so, after Ri Kaisei in 1971 and Yi Yangji in 1989[4]—Yū has achieved enormous success as a writer and public intellectual in the Japanese mainstream. As such, the Zainichi establishment seems keen to claim her as one of their own, while also being critical of her failure to toe the party line in terms of the subject matter and political disposition of her work. Though she is hardly the first to be put in this position by Zainichi critics—as we have seen in the last two chapters with Kin Kakuei and Yi Yangji—Yū's omission from the *zenshū*, her unmatched popularity, and her frequent refusal to center ethnic issues in her work make her a particularly troublesome figure for those contemplating the "end" of Zainichi literature as well as the problems and possibilities engendered by a "post-Zainichi" framework.

In this chapter, I read Yū Miri's career in conversation with the discourse of the "post-racial" in the United States, particularly its implications for literary historiography. In both cases, I argue that an intersectional lens is crucial for understanding the gendered and class exclusions that go into constructing a coherent literary history, and that the (re-)emergence of these excised voices challenges the notion of a coherent future for a literature. Then, by thinking through "colorblindness" as a specifically corporeal metaphor for an imagined post-racial temporality, I ask what happens if, as in the case of the Zainichi, difference is less visual than sonic. What would it mean to hear, in an embodied sense, the voices of the post-difference future? I explore these questions through a reading of Yū's *Hachigatsu no hate* (*The End of August*, 2004), wherein the author's attempt to reconstruct the silenced voices of the past, including so-called "comfort women" and other victims of wartime and postcolonial atrocities, suggests alternative modes for listening—not only to the past, but also to the future, with all the endings and beginnings it contains.

TOWARD AN INTERSECTIONAL LITERARY HISTORY

As noted above, Zainichi literature is hardly unique in its contemplation of its own demise. I begin by discussing the implications of "the end" for the project of Zainichi literary history in comparative frame with African American literature, which is undergoing an eerily similar critical debate. This comparison is fruitful not only due to the parallels of "post-racial" discrimination surviving a coherent notion of difference, but also because of the specific manifestation of this crisis in terms of a perceived ending of the corresponding literary genre. On the American side, Kenneth Warren's *What Was African American Literature?*—whose polemical title this chapter echoes—is a case in point.[5]

Warren's position is that African American literature as such emerged in the context of the Jim Crow social order of segregation and state-sanctioned discrimination arising post-Reconstruction, and ended with the collapse of this social order in the Civil Rights era. The crux of his argument is that during this period, African American literature was characterized by a set of shared assumptions between writers and critics regarding the political orientation of the literature they were creating: they proceeded with the understanding that their work would be judged both "instrumentally," in terms of its usefulness for combating the injustices of Jim Crow, as well as "indexically," as a barometer of racial progress or solidarity.[6] In other words, what makes (or made) African American literature a genre was not a set of abstract characteristics that could be projected onto black writing across history. Rather, it was defined by the knowledge that texts within would be read according to frameworks imposed by the genre itself. By now, what Warren calls the instrumental and indexical modes of reading should be recognizable as a hermeneutics of representation. A text is African American literature so long as it is *read as* African American literature, which is to say read as representing (in both instrumental and indexical senses) African Americans. The same can be said of Zainichi literature.

No wonder that when these hermeneutical frames begin to crumble, suddenly the end is nigh—but the end of what? The most obvious counter to Warren's claim (and one that he of course anticipates) is that the oppressive social order to which African American literature was conceived as resistance still exists, and so therefore must the literature. Even if we accept that African American literature is historically bounded by the specific political project of dismantling Jim Crow racial hierarchy, we need not concede that this project is finished. Though Warren readily acknowledges the continuing legacy of Jim Crow and the ongoing salience of racism, he argues that "with the legal demise of Jim Crow, the coherence of African American literature has been correspondingly, if sometimes imperceptibly, eroded as well."[7] As ever, the culprit for eroding this "coherence" is the admission of a broader range of voices into the cacophony of those representing the larger group. Conversely, it was the exclusion of all but the most elite black writers from recognition by the American literary scene that created a semblance of coherence in the first place. These writers ended up inadvertently reinforcing the disenfranchisement of black people

> by giving credence to the idea that certain African American individuals and cadres by virtue of their achievements, expertise, and goodwill could direct and speak on behalf of the nation's black population. Such was the context that gave rise to African American literature—one in which the black literary voice could count for so much because, in political terms, the voice of black people generally counted for so little. . . . The ending of legalized segregation, however imperfect it has been in desegregating American society, could not but change this situation.[8]

The end of Zainichi literature obviously cannot be tied to such a specific point as the Civil Rights era and the end of Jim Crow, even as the community has seen undeniable political progress on issues of fingerprinting, citizenship, and political participation in recent decades. But that is precisely the point: it is not the end of oppression that brings about the end of the literature, but rather the end of its internal coherence. This coherence, as Warren shows in the case of African American literature and as this book has detailed in the case of Zainichi literature, is a product of ignoring *intersecting* oppressions that are mutually constitutive of the oppression faced by the group in question. In both cases, anxieties toward the fraying of collective ties and the erosion of political solidarity—without an accompanying disappearance of racial or ethnic discrimination—coincide with increased attention to intersectional concerns within the collective. Moreover, if the coherence of an ethnic literature comes into question when its standard bearers are no longer elite (mostly male) writers of high-brow or "pure" literature, then intersectionality implies not so much an end to that literature as a never having been.

The distinction between pure literature (*jun bungaku*) and mass literature (*taishū bungaku*) in Japanese-language literary circles is certainly a factor in producing the fear that Zainichi literature is ending. Indeed, no small part of what makes Kaneshiro Kazuki and Yū Miri problematic in the eyes of the Zainichi literary establishment has been their mass appeal, as well as their willingness to cross over into popular media.[9] Nonetheless, perhaps an even more visible fracture in Zainichi literary history falls along gender lines. In fact, it would not be unfair to say that standard accounts of Zainichi literary history fail to mention a single woman before Yi Yangji.[10]

Recent years have seen attempts to rectify this imbalance, the most thorough of which is Song Hyewon's provocatively titled *"Zainichi Chōsenjin bungaku shi" no tame ni: Koe naki koe no porifonī* (*Toward a "Zainichi Korean Literary History": The Polyphony of Voiceless Voices*, 2014).[11] Song's main contention is that the received history of Zainichi literature focuses so myopically on its origins in the male colonial elite writing for high-brow Japanese readers as to render "voiceless" a rich array of other "voices," especially women and Korean-language writers.[12] She critiques the generational narrative of Zainichi literature's origins and trajectory, with Kim Talsu as its patriarch and the male bundan figures of Zainichi nationalism as its heirs. She demonstrates that this narrative was essential for constructing the coherence of Zainichi literature and its history. Reintroducing women's writing, Korean-language literature, and the work of postwar Korean migrants to Japan makes for a much messier history, generating anxiety for those invested in its coherence.

How, then, does Yū Miri fit into this picture? Yū certainly has moments at which her attitude seems to skirt toward the erasure of Zainichi specificity in a way we might deem "post-racial" or "post-Zainichi." Nevertheless, it would be a stretch to claim that she shows a desire to move past Zainichi identity as it pertains to the ethnic discrimination that has its roots in the colonial oppression of the past and continues into the present. Rather, if she takes part in deconstructing the category of Zainichi and hastening its end, she does so by exposing the failures of Zainichi as a framework to accommodate the internal heterogeneity of its community members and the intersectionality of race with gender and sexuality especially.[13] To get a glimpse at the politics of this, I examine here two interviews taking place in 1997, on the occasion of her being awarded the Akutagawa Prize.

The first is a conversation between Yū and Ri Kaisei, published in the literary magazine *Gunzō*.[14] In one of the first exchanges in the interview, Ri objects to Yū Miri's characterization of her own place within the Zainichi community.

> Ri: By the way, Ms. Yū, you often refer to yourself as second-generation, so I'd like you to correct yourself on this point. I am second-generation, you are third-generation, and the generation after you will be fourth-generation. Did you think of yourself as second-generation?

Yū: I say I am second-generation because my mother and father were born in South Korea and came to Japan where they had me. Wouldn't that make me second-generation?

Ri: I suppose you could say that, but in any case, since I'm second-generation, I wondered how you could be when our ages are so different—you're the same age as my second son. (Laughs.)[15]

This is a prototypical example of what is known as "mansplaining."[16] Ri feels the need to ask Yū to "correct herself" on a matter about which she is better positioned to be an authority—in this case, her own generational identity. But more than simply an example of paternalism from the Zainichi old guard, this exchange is noteworthy for Ri's assumption of the role of arbiter of who gets to identify how. He allows that Yū might have a sense of herself as second-generation, but at the same time dismisses that kind of autonomous identification in favor of an arbitrary age-based scheme of his own. He has the final word on the generation to which Yū Miri belongs—never mind that Yū's understanding of what "second-generation" means is more standard across migrant communities. More than that, however, what this minor disagreement on Yū's status illustrates is a larger problem with Zainichi identity, or perhaps even identity in the abstract. Namely, if the terms of identity discourse impose a schema like Ri's, that a given subject simply *is* in one category or another, then there is no room for self-determination, for the active sense of identification. Conversely, no matter how one might choose to identify in this autonomous sense, one is nevertheless beholden to the recognition of such an identity by others in order for it to function socially.

Finally, by adding that he is old enough to be her father, he stops one step short of making explicit what seems to be implied by all of this: that he is her daddy. As the conversation goes on, Ri continues to invoke this generational logic to frame the ways that Yū and other young writers will inherit the projects and concerns of elder Zainichi writers. Most prominently, Ri sees promise in Yū's probing of the relationship between the broken homes portrayed so often in her stories and the politics of the Korean peninsula, broken in half by postwar division. However, what pleases him most is her statement that she plans to continue to "bear the burden" of Korean identity:

Yū: I am grateful that my father never naturalized. To exist in the space between Japan and Korea, to be placed in a situation I have to think about has been good for me as a writer, I think. I myself never think of naturalizing. There is plenty of baggage that comes with that, but it's a burden I want to bear. I never wish to run from it.

Ri: That's such a wonderful thing. Once when I was out drinking with someone or other somewhere, you came up in conversation, so I said something like 'That Yū Miri is a dutiful daughter'—as if I knew anything about it. (Laughs.) But to hear you talk just now, that's what I feel.[17]

Here, Ri's troubling paternalism returns in perhaps more explicit terms. Nevertheless, even in his position as father-figure, he appears to be the more vulnerable in this instance. Where he could have said that Yū cannot help but bear those burdens because she *is* Zainichi, he instead recognizes the volition she ascribes to herself. Perhaps this is simply a reflection of Ri's agreement that an identity that navigates "between Japan and Korea" is the proper one for Zainichi Koreans to espouse. At the same time, it also seems to reflect an anxiety on Ri's part that so many in Yū's generation choose not to bear that burden, whether by passing, naturalizing, or simply not going to the considerable lengths required to "awaken" to a Zainichi identity—a process described by earlier Zainichi writers like Yi Yangji and Kin Kakuei. The impression Ri gives here is one of relief, that the "end" of Zainichi literature will be forestalled, at least as long as Yū Miri continues to shoulder the burden of carrying it forward.

This exchange highlights the temporality of the post-Zainichi, in addition to the centrality of assimilation to the anxieties and reorientations that create it. The "post-racial," in the Zainichi context, is rarely presented as a utopian fantasy. Even aside from the emptiness of its promise of an end to discrimination within the present climate, the "post-racial" for Koreans necessarily reanimates a history of imperial Japanese efforts to eradicate Korean difference through assimilation and imperialization. Particularly fraught is Zainichi literature's position vis-à-vis the colonial Korean practice of writing in Japanese, which produced the very founders of what is now considered Zainichi literature, but has also been viewed as a sort of complicity in the assimilation project. The "end" of Zainichi is terrifying precisely because it presents itself as a return to the beginning.

On the other hand, Ri also betrays a concern about the loss of patriarchal control within a post-Zainichi world. After all, what makes Yū Miri a "dutiful daughter" (*oyakōkō*) is her choice to remain within a Zainichi framework. That is, her claim to ownership of such an identity—which emerges alongside the specter of naturalization that she raises here—belies the possibility that she may also choose to be disobedient, to abandon her father along with her ethnic heritage. This is the flip side of the contradiction in their earlier exchange on the generation to which Yū Miri belongs. In this case, when Yū Miri explicitly identifies as Zainichi (insofar as Zainichi can be conflated with the sense of inbetweenness that Yū affirms), she undermines the logic of Zainichi as an ontological category to which she simply belongs or does not belong. If she can opt in, she may be able to opt out. In this way, the boundaries of the Zainichi community become impossible to police—yet another process by which the "end" of Zainichi might come about.

Compounding this problem, from the perspective of a Zainichi patriarch demanding filial piety from his daughter, is that his faith may be misplaced. Too much is riding on his assumption that Yū's statement here is a commitment to carry on the legacy of Zainichi literature as Ri understands it. In another interview from the same year, this one with novelist Hayashi Mariko, Yū takes a strikingly different tone: "I do not possess an awareness of being a Zainichi South Korean writer." She goes on: "If I write about South Koreans, my works are framed as 'Zainichi literature.' And that is what I don't like."[18] The remarkable difference in stance here is not necessarily indicative of disingenuousness on Yū's part. It may simply arise as a result of different understandings of what it means to be a Zainichi writer or to perform Zainichi identity. Still, it is intriguing that Yū's framing of her own commitment to the project of reproducing Zainichi literature changes so starkly depending on her audience. Even if this project was not specifically what she had in mind when she refers to the "burden" she wishes to bear, she raises no objection to Ri Kaisei's repeated implication that she is situated firmly within the genealogy of Zainichi literature. If that is indeed something to which she objects, as she seems to say to Hayashi, then she does not voice such an objection to Ri. Perhaps we could see Yū's slipping in and out of the Zainichi literature framework as a part of the post-Zainichi temporality. Either way, the dutiful daughter would eventually betray her daddy: Yū Miri's declining to have her work included in the "*Zainichi*" *bungaku zenshū* undermined its claims to comprehensiveness and authority, and triggered anew a sense of the looming "end" of Zainichi literature.

In the end, the controversy around the anthology may actually give us the clearest sense of what Zainichi literature actually means for the authors working within. It is a "textual identity."[19] It is not useful as a map of an ontologically definable collective, though it may often be presented or received as such. Rather, it is nothing more than an understanding of how a text will be read within its rubric. Signing onto this understanding allows access to a network of publishing venues and contacts that, depending on one's standing, may be a useful conduit for gaining access to readership. For Yū Miri at this point in her career, inclusion in the anthology was not necessary for this kind of access, especially when her work's presence in a Zainichi literature anthology would inevitably frame her readers' reception of it in ways she might find undesirable. It is thus not necessary to make any determination of Yū Miri's personal identification with or outside the framework of Zainichi-ness in order to uncover the practical consequences of naming her work "Zainichi literature" or not.

In this way, a "post-racial" or "post-Zainichi" framework, while making us aware of the historicity of ethnic categorization, has further potential to alert us to the intersectional nature of such categories. This is meant not only in the common sense of intersectionality, which insists that race, gender, and other identity categories are mutually dependent. It also suggests a shift away from a concern with the internal coherence of collective categories produced by single-axis frameworks and toward a praxis that asks first *how* such frameworks are working, and more importantly, *for whom*. If Yū Miri can be said to have rejected Zainichi, it may just be that Zainichi rejected her first.

At the same time, if the previous generation is anxious about the end of Zainichi, what that really indicates is that they perceive a benefit to be derived from Zainichi as a mode of identity or a publishing network. Neither can this anxiety be separated from the history of violent assimilation and collaboration in which it is embedded. In the end, we may find ourselves looking for a way to define Zainichi such that Yū Miri is at once the dutiful daughter and the liminal presence. What the notion of the post-racial or post-Zainichi offers us—as long as we fully appreciate the irony of its failure to overcome actual racial oppression—is the opportunity to bring the contradictions of the present into the light and demand alternative futures. It is toward the future that we now turn.

THE "COLORBLIND" FUTURE AND THE POETICS OF PASSING

If there remains an uneasiness with the notion that Zainichi (or African American) literature is over, how then are we to imagine its future? As with the question of literary history, it is easier to expose the limitations of existing understandings of what Zainichi literature is or was, or its place within larger categories of Japanese-language or even World Literature, than it is to articulate a positive vision for what it can or should be. Moreover, it is far from clear to all involved that the framework of Zainichi is worth maintaining in the first place. Is it better to set our sights on a speculative post-Zainichi future? In this section, I examine the discourse of the "post-racial," specifically the ambivalent corporeal metaphor of "colorblindness," to tease out the pitfalls and potency of imagining such a future.

By "post-racial" I am referring to the white American fantasy that the country's long history of racial oppression and injustice is now over, and the problem of systemic racism is no longer relevant to American politics. Yet more insidiously, this myth further entails the notion that it is now *white* Americans who are the main target of discrimination.[20] The fallacy of a "post-racial" America has of course been obvious to people of color all along, and the disastrous consequences of its circulation are underscored by the current climate. Japan is not without its parallels to this kind of post-racial thinking, from the increasing potency of ethnonationalism on the national political scale to the slow creep of far-right fringe ideas from the dark corners of the internet to the mainstream. One of the main hate groups emerging from the latter calls itself the "Zainichi tokken o yurusanai shimin no kai," or "Citizens Against Zainichi Privilege," an accident of translation echoing the language of white privilege and "reverse racism."

Aside from such explicit outpourings of racial animus, post-racial rhetoric shifts the burden of responsibility onto the minority to move past or overcome the history of racism. Indeed, its successes are visible in the occasional reactionary embrace of this kind of logic by members of the minority group. Among the more prominent American examples of this was recording artist Pharrell Williams's statement in an interview with Oprah Winfrey that "The New Black doesn't blame other races for our issues. The New Black dreams and realizes that it's not pigmentation: it's a mentality, and it's either going to work for you or it's going to work against you."[21]

On the Zainichi side, Tei Taikin articulates similar sentiments in his book *Zainichi Kankokujin no shūen* (The Demise of Zainichi Koreans, 2001), arguing that Koreans in Japan need to let go of their victimhood mentality and stop clinging to the history of colonial violence.[22] The fault in this reasoning arises in part from a paradoxical temporality. If the post-racial *precedes* the imperative to relegate racism to the past, then it engenders dual impossibilities: first, it becomes impossible to insist that racism precedes race, and second, it becomes impossible to conceive of race as anything other than victimhood. In fact, as in the case of "post-racial" America, the emergence of what could be called a "post-Zainichi" era predates the demise of the discrimination to which an organized Zainichi politics is a necessary response. Perhaps the most prominent and troubling emblem of ongoing discrimination is the rise of anti-Korean hate speech in the public sphere.

Worse still, as in the case of "colorblind" racism in the United States, the goal of equal treatment is easily co-opted in the service of maintaining an unequal status quo.[23] In *Seeing a Colorblind Future*, Patricia Williams connects the ideology of colorblindness—the notion that the path to racial equity lies in ignoring racial difference—to the incoherent temporality of the post-racial. If a colorblind future is to exist, she argues, it cannot emerge from a colorblind present that erases a past that is anything but colorblind:

> While I do want to underscore that I embrace color-blindness as a legitimate hope for the future, I worry that we tend to enshrine the notion with a kind of utopianism whose naïveté will ensure its elusiveness. . . . 'I don't think about color, therefore your problems don't exist.' If only it were so easy. But if indeed it's not that easy then the application of such quick fixes becomes not just a shortcut but a short-circuiting of the process of resolution.[24]

The willful blindness as "quick fix" that Williams describes recalls the politics of Japanese reckoning with wartime atrocities on the Asian continent. In a 2016 agreement between the Park Geun-hye and Abe Shinzo administrations, the Japanese government agreed to create a restitution fund to compensate the victims of its program of military sex slavery, in exchange for which the South Korean government committed to silence on the so-called "comfort women" issue. The sense was that if we would all just agree not to talk about it anymore, we could move on. Here, redress becomes a way to silence the voices pointing out injustice rather than to enable their speech—both of which have their problems, as I further discuss below in the context of Yū Miri's fiction writing.

However, what I want to focus on here is the strangeness of referring to this ideology in the language of physical impairment as "colorblindness," or even "blindness" full stop. This corporeal metaphor has gone largely uninterrogated since it appeared in Justice John Marshall Harlan's famous dissent in *Plessy v. Ferguson*.[25]

That the making of racial knowledge should be located literally in the eye of the beholder, whose *inability* to see constitutes the utopian ideal, is a much more suggestive notion than it is given credit for.

Williams comes close to acknowledging this uncanniness when she opens her essay with an anecdote about her son. When his nursery school teachers report that he is colorblind, Williams takes him to an ophthalmologist who "pronounce[s] his vision perfect."[26] An actually colorblind or otherwise visually impaired person might reasonably ask whether their eyes are not also perfect, but the point of the story turns out to be that his diagnosis never had anything to do with his eyes. Rather, his teachers had been assuring the whole class that color "doesn't matter" as a direct response to racist incidents among the children (so obviously color did matter). Williams's son had extrapolated from there to insisting that the colors of everyday objects did not matter, leading to the initial misunderstanding. Only a child could mistake one kind of colorblindness for the other.

Despite, or perhaps because of, this distinction, Williams and other critics of colorblind racism generally do not question its specific sensory framing in terms of visual impairment. They even reappropriate the metaphor to refer to colorblind racism's constituent "blindness" to inequity rather than blindness to visually presented difference. In either case, it goes without saying that the blindness in question is not a problem of bodily impairment, but rather an unwillingness to admit the consequences of the racial hierarchies that have been inscribed as visual signs apparent on the body. That this is spoken of in terms of the body actually provides a useful reminder of how this racial meaning is made: it does not exist *a priori* in or on the body of a person of color, but must be *read* on such bodies in order to come into being.

Lurking beneath the surface of this discussion is the problem of passing, which opens up a fissure between knowledge of difference and difference itself, between perception and ontology. If one were reducible to the other, then passing would eliminate difference itself, but clearly it does not. Instead, those who experience passing describe crushing anxieties that accompany it, whether from fear of being found out, fear of the failure to represent oneself authentically, or uncertainty of or ambivalence toward one's own identity.[27] The problem of passing makes it clear that a utopian post-racial or post-difference future cannot be founded merely on the lack of *knowledge* of difference, since passing cannot produce equity when its burdensome psychology is taken into account.

Passing further menaces the idealized post-racial future in the case of Koreans in Japan, where it is frequently the voice that betrays. Most prominently, in the aftermath of the Great Kantō Earthquake, thousands of Koreans were massacred by vigilante groups, which gave pronunciation tests to determine the ethnicity of their victims. Many Zainichi writers, including Yū Miri, have written fiction portraying the "becoming Korean" that occurs in the moment of speaking one's own name. These figures are presented with a choice between passing and speech itself—assimilation versus giving voice to their difference—where neither option presents a tenable path to an ethical post-difference future.

It seems worth asking, then, what might be gained from considering the issue of racial knowledge in a sonic rather than visual register. What happens when difference (or the injustice that co-figures it) is heard rather than seen, or better yet, silent rather than invisible? Perhaps more fundamentally, why frame the speculative future disappearance of racial knowledge in terms of bodily impairment in the first place? Thus, whether the imagined future is difference-deaf or colorblind, it remains a struggle to conceive of such a future as anything other than assimilation on the terms of past or present-day hegemonies. Just as the post-racial body shades toward whiteness, and just as the utopian medical rhetoric of "cure" posits a future absent of disabled bodies, the body of the future may only be able to speak in the language of the powerful.[28]

Thus, the question I want to keep in mind for the remainder of the chapter is: what happens to language in the post-difference future? Can the post-racial, post-able body speak? How might it engage with its history? Does it need to forget the past in order to live in the future it inhabits? To imagine this future body is to rethink basic assumptions about language, commensurability, and the notions of subjectivity and otherness they entail. Speculative futures of the post-racial, the post-disability, and the post-Zainichi all produce versions of the same anxiety toward the threat of assimilation on the terms of the powerful—the eradication of alternative modes of speech or representation. It is this silence and its accompanying anxieties that Yū Miri deals with in her magnum opus, *Hachigatsu no hate*, to which I now turn.

THE SILENT PAST AND FUTURE IN *HACHIGATSU NO HATE*

Yū's project in *Hachigatsu no hate* echoes Song's book title and so many other projects of a similar nature: recovering lost voices from the past. The novel, clocking in at over eight hundred pages, is a meditation on the violence of Korean history from roughly the 1920s to the 1970s, viewed through the life of Olympic hopeful long-distance runner Yi Uch'ŏl and his sprawling family.[29] It is a story of movement and rupture, following Uch'ŏl as he moves between Korea and Japan, narrating the turmoil in his own childhood home and its repetition in subsequent generations. The family is devastated by the untimely deaths of all his siblings except for his youngest brother Ugŭn—a promising runner in his own right—and the illegitimate half sister born to his father's mistress. Despite Uch'ŏl's anger at his father for betraying his mother, he goes on to engage in a series of dalliances, eventually abandoning four different mothers of his children. At every turn this family chaos is exacerbated by the turbulence of the historical context: colonization and an escalating total war effort, the short-lived liberation and long-term occupation and division of the peninsula, the Korean War, and the violent suppression of leftist activity in South Korea under Rhee Syngman and Park Chung Hee.

This cross section of national history is oriented around a family history, as Yi Uch'ŏl is a fictional stand-in for the author's grandfather, whose personal life and running career Yū meticulously researched for the book. Moreover, the novel employs a framing device in which Uch'ŏl's story—and the larger family history and national story in which it is embedded—is initiated by the character "Yū Miri," who actively seeks to reconstruct it. As with many of texts covered in this book, then, *Hachigatsu no hate* operates in a strained and self-conscious relationship to the I-novel mode, as well as the larger question of personal versus political narrative raised by literary taxonomies—I-novel, Zainichi, or otherwise.

Ultimately, I would argue, what *Hachigatsu no hate* portrays is a sense of Korean colonial and postcolonial history as a burden, its telling and retelling a painful exercise that its subjects endure rather than relish—in other words, the burden of representation. If the novel represents an attempt to "recover" silenced voices from the past, that effort results in the reimposition of this burden and runs the risk of serving the "listener" (or, perhaps, the reader) more than the voices themselves. In this way, Yū's texts suggests the limitations of empathy, perhaps even representation more broadly, as the aim of literature. In reading *Hachigatsu no hate*, I hope to tease out these limitations and begin to suggest alternative readerly affects, which might allow for a less violent or assimilative mode of engaging with the radical others of the past and future.

Hachigatsu no hate opens on an instance of silence: "Even though I am running along the river, the water doesn't make a sound. Neither does the wind. . . . The only sound that can be heard is the sound of my breath: ssu ssu hah hah (すっすっはっはっ)."[30] This sound of a runner's breathing (much more awkward to render in English than in the original Japanese) will be a refrain throughout the novel. The first few pages of the text continue to repeat the sound of breath, interspersed between the fragmented narrating voice, here the spirit of Yi Uch'ŏl, who recalls moments, images, names, and even songs (rendered in boldface text) from his life. The narrative then shifts abruptly to the scene of a *ssikkim-kut*, a shamanistic ritual for cleansing the spirits of the dead of bitterness and attachment, allowing their souls to leave the world.[31] In the process of this ritual, performed by several female shamans (*mudang*), their male accompanist (*paksu*), and "Yū Miri" as hostess, Yi Uch'ŏl and other figures from his family are resurrected, possessing the bodies of the shamans and borrowing their voices to narrate their stories of resentment. From the start, the novel asks the reader to be conscious of voice as a matter not only of history and narrative, but of sound and embodiment.

This first chapter, by way of the *ssikkim-kut*, tells in condensed form the story the rest of the novel will go on to detail. Yi Uch'ŏl is a talented distance runner whose hopes of appearing in the Olympics are dashed when the 1940 Tokyo games are canceled. Shortly thereafter Uch'ŏl escapes to Japan to avoid being drafted into the war, abandoning his family in the process. After a brief return to Korea following the Japanese defeat and Korean independence in 1945, Uchŏl runs away to Japan again, this time to escape the violence of the Korean War. He starts a new life, running a pachinko parlor and marrying a Japanese woman who bears his youngest son. He also begins a second running career in his middle-aged years, but eventually gives it all up again to return to Korea, where he dies alone. Also appearing in the *ssikkim-kut* are the angry spirits of his abandoned wives and lovers, his youngest brother and running partner Ugŭn, and a young girl from their hometown of Miryang who was infatuated with Ugŭn. Both of the latter, we learn, met with tragic ends. Ugŭn was shot by the South Korean police for leftist activities and buried alive. The girl was trafficked into sex slavery at a "comfort station" for the Japanese military, and threw herself overboard after serendipitously meeting and confessing her story to Uchŏl on a ship returning to Korea after the war. Yū Miri leaves the ceremony with instructions to have Ugŭn and the girl posthumously married in another shamanistic ritual, bringing both of their spirits back to Miryang and within the fold of the family's enshrined ancestors. In many ways, the opening chapter frames the novel as literally a project of resurrecting the lost voices of the past.

The next chapter complicates this framing by once again offering embodiment of the deceased as a means of accessing the personal and national histories they witnessed, but in a completely different context. In this case, Yū Miri is running a marathon in Seoul. The narrative is once again punctuated by the onomatopoetic refrain of the breath: ssu ssu hah hah (すっすっはっはっ). This time it is not Uchŏl's breath but Yū Miri's, as she struggles to complete the longest distance she has ever run while nursing the pain of an injured knee. Whereas the other runners, like her grandfather, "run for the sake of running," Yū "runs for the sake of writing" (48), ostensibly in order to reconstruct her grandfather's experience and provide inspiration for the very novel in which this appears.

What she finds, however, is that even within the secularized shamanistic ritual she has set up for herself by running the marathon, it proves impossible to live the experience of another. As the pain in her knee spreads throughout the rest of her body with the finish line still miles away, she ponders the fate of her grandfather's brother, Ugŭn, who was "stronger than pain," (56) refusing to give up the names of his leftist associates in the face of torture by the police (and his eventual live burial). However, as soon as she has these thoughts, she rejects her own implicit comparison of her suffering to that of her great-uncle:

> ssu ssu hah hah Trying to imagine his pain through my pain ssu ssu hah hah Is a waste of time ssu ssu hah hah 'Put yourself in someone else's shoes' or 'I feel your pain' ssu ssu hah hah That's just shit people say ssu ssu hah hah ssu ssu hah hah You can't really feel someone else's pain ssu ssu hah hah No matter how much you care about the person suffering, no matter how much you might want to take their place ssu ssu hah hah The only pain you can feel is the pain of not being able to feel their

> pain ssu ssu hah hah ssu ssu hah hah ssu ssu hah hah ssu ssu hah hah ssu ssu hah hah (56–57).

If her project in running this race or even writing this book was to empathize with her long-deceased family members and the larger Korean nation they might be read as representing, then this early framing of that project already suggests its limitations. Neither "Yū Miri" nor Yū Miri (nor indeed the reader of this text) can access their experiences. Instead, Yū begins to feel her grandfather running alongside her, hearing his breath in the same すっすっはっはっ rhythm as her own. His spirit encourages her to keep going, to embrace the pain as her running companion. She cannot run *as* Uch'ŏl, but she can run *with* him.

At the end of the chapter, Yū Miri finishes the marathon, but Yi Uch'ŏl's spirit keeps running, arriving at his childhood self on the day his brother Ugŭn was born. This flashback marks the beginning of the main story, taking up the vast majority of the novel, nested within the dual framing devices of the *ssikkim-kut* and the marathon. The novel's ponderous pacing within this main narrative defies its sweeping historical scope. The sense of time here feels quotidian rather than historical; it lingers rather than flows. This stilted temporality is especially palpable in the stories of the women in Uch'ŏl's life, who are usually depicted as waiting bitterly for the return of their perpetually absent husband or lover. These narratives are almost always confined to a single day or even part of a day, focusing on the sights, sounds, and scents of the scene at hand. Most of the female characters introduced are found cooking, doing laundry, or performing other ritualized household duties. The text offers vivid descriptions of the sequence of tasks they perform, listing every ingredient added in preparation of the dinner menu, the sounds of knives chopping and water boiling always rendered in Korean transcribed into katakana and glossed with Japanese equivalents. These sensory details facilitate the imagination of a shared corporeal presence with these women, stopping time in a moment of everyday life which the reader's senses are drafted into co-creating.

This is part of what makes it so devastating when the day-in-the-life presented is that of a so-called "comfort woman." Her story, arriving in the second half of the novel, is where the smooth flow of the everyday meets the traumatic rupture of violent historical events. For her, this violence becomes matter-of-fact, each day bringing a new repetition of rape after rape after rape, presented in all the vivid, now horrifying detail of the previous chapters. What has been a hotly contested footnote in the history of the Asia-Pacific War—taboo for decades in Korea, to say nothing of the reluctance to speak of it in Japan—takes on all the weight of embodied experience in *Hachigatsu no hate*.

At the same time, the comfort woman's story of corporeal violence dovetails with the novel's more general exploration of the violence of language and speech. Woven into the story of her sexual exploitation and forced labor are descriptions of the women's struggles to pronounce Japanese accurately in order to avoid beatings, reminiscent of the violence in the aftermath of the Kantō Earthquake. Their training in the Japanese language, adoption of Japanese names, and recitation of the Imperial Subject Oath recall Yi Uch'ŏl's experience of the same as part of his primary and secondary education. In both contexts, speech is compelled for the purpose of disciplining colonial subjects.

By contrast, the comfort woman's story ends with a steadfast refusal to speak. When the news of Japan's military defeat reaches the comfort station, the girl escapes and ends up on a ferry to Korea, where she crosses paths with Uch'ŏl. She remembers him due to his status as a minor celebrity in Miryang, where he is known as the Olympic runner who might have been. Despite this tenuous connection, she confesses that she admired his brother Ugŭn from afar, and once wished to marry him before her hopes of marriage were dashed by her experiences in the comfort station—or, more accurately, her correct assumption that she will bear the shame for those experiences. Uch'ŏl consoles her, assuring her that, to the contrary, she can hold her head high in the newly liberated Korea.

As they near the shores of the peninsula, Uch'ŏl asks her name. The girl refuses to answer, other than to give him her comfort-woman name, Namiko, and her "*sōshi kaimei* name," Kanemoto Eiko. Within the novel to this point, including the introductory *ssikkim-kut*, the reader is also not given her name. She is introduced when her main storyline begins as Eiko, then is referred to more and more often as "the girl" (*shōjo*), her name slowly vanishing as she approaches the site of her trauma. In the comfort station, she is assigned the name "Namiko," and the narrative refers to her as such thereafter. It is perhaps a safe assumption that she has an "original" Korean name, but it never comes up until Uch'ŏl asks and she refuses to tell.

Uch'ŏl then retires for the night, leaving Eiko/Namiko alone on deck. By this point she knows that she cannot bring herself to set foot back on the Korean peninsula:

> **Kim Yŏnghŭi!** Namiko screamed her own name. Father! If nothing else, the name you gave me has never been raped. Mother! No one has laid a finger on the name you called me. **Kim Yŏnghŭi!** The name of a thirteen-year-old virgin. Namiko held the name **Kim Yŏnghŭi** close. **Kim Yŏnghŭi!** Namiko cried, throwing herself into the sea. No one saw it. No one heard it. (642–43; emphasis original).

Yŏnghŭi's careful guarding of her real name offers a twist on the trope of passing that appears in so much Zainichi literature. Rather than posing as Japanese in order to avoid the violence enacted on Koreans, Yŏnghŭi (Namiko) is always recognized as Korean and thus subject to this violence. What she hides is the name itself, rather than the identity it is supposed to represent. When she finally shouts her name into the void, it is clear that *not* being heard is more liberating for her than the recognition and patriarchal absolution Uch'ŏl provides. Nonetheless, her eternal silence is underscored by the scene immediately following her death, in which the ferry passengers wake and spot the Korean coastline in the distance, shouting "Long live Korea!" (万歳！万歳！　大韓独立万歳！) as they rejoice in its liberation (643).[32] Yŏnghŭi's absence—or silence—is conveniently forgotten.

As the discourse on colorblind racism makes clear, a future that depends on willful forgetting of past and present injustice offers no path to the post-racial utopia it promises. The celebration of a liberated Korea depicted in *Hachigatsu no hate* rings hollow precisely because it is enabled by the erasure of comfort women's experiences. As such, the project of recovering and recognizing the "silenced" voices of the past is certainly a noble one. However, as the thorny case of comfort women demonstrates, recognition does not necessarily lead to redress, and a reckoning with the past may be necessary but not sufficient for imagining a better future.[33] I would also suggest that the straightforward interpretation of silence as victimhood implied by the impetus to recover lost voices from the past is flawed. Yŏnghŭi's refusal to speak is her one tether to agency, and seems to provide her with a semblance of comfort in her tragic final moments. Her voice, like so many others, is ultimately unrecoverable. Rather than forcing such voices to speak, in some cases the more compassionate move may be to learn to cope with their silence, on their terms rather than our own.

Yŏnghŭi's climactic silence encapsulates much of how *Hachigatsu no hate* deals with the trauma of *sōshi kaimei* and its reverberations in the present day.[34] In fact, Yŏnghŭi is not the only character to keep her name a secret. Ugŭn does so as well, albeit in reverse: he adopts a new name to keep hidden since, unlike Yŏnghŭi, he considers "the name his father gave him"[35] sullied by its pronunciation in Japanese to conform to *sōshi kaimei* policy. On the fateful August evening Uch'ŏl leaves for Japan, perhaps never to see his brother again—the same night Yŏnghŭi leaves for what she believes is a job sewing military uniforms—Ugŭn asks his brother to give him a new name. He knows that Uch'ŏl had been thinking of names for his baby brother, and asks him to give him one of them as a pseudonym.

「. . . 号？　なぜ号が必要なんだ」

「戸籍上は倭奴(ウエノム)に隷従して国本雨根(くにもとうこん)になってしまったけれど、こころまで服属したわけじゃない証(あかし)に倭(ウエ)の戸籍から離脱したいんだ。恥辱にまみれた国本雨根という名を使うわけにいかない。抵抗をつづけるための、立ち向かうための、闘うための砦(とりで)として新しい名前が必要なんだ。おれは今日から李(イ)春植と名乗るよ。ヒョンがいったじゃないか. . .春に植える. . .芽を出してすくすく伸びて大きな樹になるという希望を込めた名前だって」

「あぁ　いい名だ」

'A pseudonym? What do you need that for?'

'On my *koseki*, it says I am Kunimoto Ukon, a slave of the Japs (*waenom*). So as a sign that they haven't yet conquered my heart and soul, I want to break away from my

> Jap *koseki*. There's no way I can use the name Kunimoto Ukon, which is covered in shame. I need a new name as a fortress from which to resist, to stand up to them, to fight them. From today forward, I will be known as Yi Ch'unsik. You said so yourself, didn't you *hyŏng*? It means "planted in spring." It's a name filled with the hope that what starts as a tiny bud will soon grow into a towering tree.'
>
> '**Yes, it's a fine name.**' (467; emphasis original).

Despite Ugŭn's declaration that he will now call himself Ch'unsik, he of course still uses his *sōshi kaimei* name in public-facing situations, and continues to use "Yi Ugŭn" in the same contexts after the war. Only his closest friends know him as Yi Ch'unsik. Not unlike the case of Kim Yŏnghŭi, Ugŭn's situational usage of his names is ostensibly about preserving a sense of purity in private where such purity is publicly lost. In both cases, however, the guarding of the name essentially boils down to a preservation of agency. By using, or more suggestively, by refusing to use their names, Ugŭn and Yŏnghŭi have some measure of control over what is known about them. They both show a desire not to speak, not to reveal, *not to be known*.

Ultimately, this desire is betrayed by their representation in the novel itself. Almost in spite of itself, *Hachigatsu no hate* reveals Ugŭn and Yŏnghŭi's inner secrets. In the moment of Yŏnghŭi's death, the reader learns her name even if no one in the universe of the story ever does. But in the end, even that silence is broken. The novel concludes with a return to the framing devices of its opening chapters. The penultimate chapter narrates another shamanistic rite, this time a *sahu kyŏlhonsik*, a posthumous wedding ceremony that serves a similar function to the *ssikkim-kut*, allowing the couple to leave the world behind and enter the afterlife together. In this case, the couple is Yŏnghŭi and Ugŭn. Before the two can be "wed," however, "Yū Miri" and the shamans have to coax Yŏnghŭi into revealing her name, which she eventually does. With this, the couple is supposed to be cleansed of their bitterness, their spirits finally able to rest. However, when the two dolls representing the bride and groom are placed on a raft and floated down the stream, the female doll falls off into the water, eerily reenacting Yŏnghŭi's suicide.

This lack of resolution is in keeping with the righteous anger and resentment these two characters hold onto up to this point. Yū spends the entire novel building up a dissonant, unresolved sense of history, which the "Yū Miri" character within the story attempts to undermine by producing a happy ending for the couple. One cannot escape the sense that what the *sahu kyŏlhonsik* achieves is not a comforting of the dead, but rather a comforting of Yū Miri. The rage of Yŏnghŭi and Ugŭn—again, the one sure sign of their agency—must be quenched for our benefit, not for theirs.

The last chapter, however, the shortest of the entire novel, returns to the figure of a breathing runner. This runner may be Uch'ŏl, or possibly Ugŭn or Yū Miri, or possibly anyone, identifiable only by the sound and rhythm of the breath: すっすっはっはっ. The text here returns to the absence of sound with which it started, noting once again that the water flowing along the river cannot be heard, nor can the buzz of cicadas that would ordinarily monopolize the August soundscape. The narrating runner also begins to feel disembodied, noticing the absence of sweat, and the sense that they could run as fast as they wanted without ever tiring. Finally, the runner begins to detach from language itself:

> なにかいいたいのか？ すっすっはっはっ アニヤ（いや） なにもいいたくない すっすっはっはっ もう言葉を追いかけたくはない すっすっはっはっ 言葉に追いつき すっすっはっはっ 言葉から抜け出し 言葉がついてこられない速度で すっすっはっはっ 言葉という言葉を振り切って すっすっはっはっ すっすっはっはっ 言葉から遠く離れたところですっすっはっはっ 走る
>
> Is there something I want to say? ssu ssu hah hah *Aniya* (no), nothing at all ssu ssu hah hah I'm tired of chasing after the words ssu ssu hah hah Catching up to the words ssu ssu hah hah Slipping past the words, moving so fast they can never catch up ssu ssu hah hah Shaking loose the word "words" itself ssu ssu hah hah ssu ssu hah hah In a place far removed from language ssu ssu hah hah I am running (824).

Having broken loose from language, the runner then moves past time itself, the narrative breaking down into nothing more than the sound of the breath, until its final boldface word: "**Freedom!** (自由 !)" (825).

The runner's escape from language suggests a way of imagining a future liberation, one that is enabled by silence itself. Crucially, this muteness is enabled and enabling not as the suppression of speech, but only insofar as it represents an end to the burden of speech, where that burden is understood as the demand that others make themselves known. It requires a different kind of listening, or perhaps even a departure from listening, a willingness simply to be and to breathe together. What Uch'ŏl's story comes down to, like that of Ugŭn and Yŏnghŭi, is the gap between what goes down on paper—a *koseki*, an official history, a newspaper article reporting on the achievements of a promising marathon runner—and the unknown remnant shared only with the most intimate loved ones, or perhaps no one at all. This gap represents a sort of agency, to not speak, to not be known, to arrive at a place beyond words. Moreover, to accept this kind of relationship with the other, in which the other is allowed to remain unknown, is to open up more ethical possibilities for engaging with the radical others of the past and future. By learning to cope with silence, we may begin to imagine ways of being that do not depend on normative modes of speaking, providing hope for an unassimilated future.

Epilogue

Global Zainichi Literature

If Zainichi literature is indeed reaching its end, it is doing so at a moment when the Zainichi community is more globally visible than at any point in its history. Min Jin Lee's *Pachinko* (2017), a widely decorated bestseller in the United States, has been translated into nearly thirty languages. The novel, along with Soo Hugh's television adaptation for Apple TV+, has brought the stories of Koreans in Japan to broader and more international audiences than ever before, albeit through the conduit of English-language media. At the same time, efforts to translate Zainichi literature have ramped up considerably, particularly for South Korean and Anglophone markets.

Translations into Korean have existed at least since Yi Yangji's *Yuhi* was published nearly simultaneously with the original in 1989. Yū Miri and Gen Getsu were translated into Korean upon receiving the Akutagawa Prize, marketed as winners of the same. But the last decade has seen a sharp increase in Korean-language translations of, and research on, Zainichi literature. Kim Sŏkpŏm's massive *Kazantō* was released in a twelve-volume Korean translation in 2015, followed by the final installment of a five-volume collection of Kim Saryang's work and related secondary scholarship in 2016.[1] Since the *Kazantō* translation, the same press has continued to publish translations of fiction and non-fiction by Zainichi writers, especially those concerned with the Cheju 4.3 Incident, such as Kim Sŏkpŏm and Kim Shijong. Kim Sŏkpŏm's *Kotoba no jubaku* and *Mandogi yūrei kitan*, both addressed in chapter 4, were released in Korean translation in 2022.[2]

Meanwhile, in English, the same trend has occurred, both within and outside the academic press. On the academic side, a second anthology of short fiction and other writings by Koreans in Japan was released in 2018, following the first of its kind in 2011.[3] Meanwhile, in the popular press, Takami Nieda's translation of Kaneshiro Kazuki's *GO* appeared in 2018.[4] Most notably, Yū Miri's *JR Ueno-eki Kōenguchi* (2014) won the 2020 National Book Award for translated literature as *Tokyo Ueno Station*, translated by Morgan Giles.[5] Giles's translation of *Hachigatsu no hate* was published as *The End of August* in 2023.[6] Possibly due to this increased attention in English, Korean translations of *JR Ueno-eki Kōenguchi* and *GO* were released in 2021 and 2023 respectively, the former titled after the English version, *Tok'yo Ueno Sŭt'eishŏn*.[7]

At this moment of increased visibility for the Zainichi community, one can sense the gravitational pull of South Korean soft power initiatives and the global hegemony of English, as in the relatively belated Korean translations of *GO* and *Tokyo Ueno Station*. Most emblematic of these forces, perhaps, is the Korean Diaspora Literature series, sponsored by the Literature Translation Institute of Korea (LTI Korea), a state organization whose mission is to increase South Korea's cultural influence by disseminating Korean literature to the world. The 2022 publication of several volumes of Zainichi literature in English translation, through LTI sponsorship, instantly doubled the quantity of texts available in English.[8] These volumes, appearing alongside works by Koreans in China and Russia, are marketed as simultaneously Korean and global, with very little to indicate that these texts were written in Japanese rather than Korean.

Much like the use of *Chainich'i*, after the Anglophone pronunciation of Zainichi, rather than *Chaeil*, the Korean sinographic equivalent (discussed in chapter 1), this pattern is indicative of the ways that the English language is implicated in the discursive formation of Zainichi literature. If ever it was tenable to discuss these works under the umbrella of Japanese or Korean national literatures—or indeed, a binary opposition of the two—that time is now past. Perhaps *Pachinko* and *Tokyo Ueno Station*, the two prime examples of Zainichi literature's globalization and increased reach, can both be dismissed as failing to fall within the taxonomical boundaries of the genre itself. *Pachinko*, of course, is not written by a member of the Zainichi community, whereas the content of *Tokyo Ueno Station* has nothing obvious to do with the diasporic Korean experience in Japan. Yet even contemporary works that fall more squarely within the purview of Zainichi literature, such as Sagisawa Megumu's "Hontō no natsu" ("The True Summer," 1992), Kim Masumi's "Moeru Sōka" ("The Burning Grass House," 1997), and Che Sil's *Jini no pazuru* (Jini's Puzzle, 2016), introduce what David Roh has called the "tertiary national space" of the United States as a means of teasing out the contours of Zainichi identity in a globalizing world.[9] These texts are interested in the mobile, deterritorialized Zainichi subject, particularly as it travels to and from the United States.

As the history narrated in this book demonstrates, there is nothing particularly new about this. These forms of movement and contact across intersecting imperial hegemonies have been with Zainichi literature since its beginnings, and even before, in the Korean- and Japanese-language writings of colonial Korea.

Nevertheless, the frameworks through which we have viewed these works have not allowed these transnational, intersectional elements to come into focus. In Anglo-American academia in particular, it is not only the siloed nation-state sectors of area studies that have been a barrier. To reiterate, Zainichi studies has been at the center of successful efforts to explode those siloes, and border-crossing inter-Asian exchange now has a firm place within Asian studies disciplines. The problem, however, is that these transnational phenomena are still ostensibly bounded within the area of Asia "over there," alienated from the hegemonic English-language production of knowledge "over here."

What this book has attempted is a move beyond what Donna Haraway has called a "conquering gaze from nowhere," probing instead the possibilities of a kind of knowledge production answerable and accountable for its own "semiotic technologies for making meanings."[10] In fact, perhaps its primary concern has been the implication of normative "semiotic technologies" themselves in creating the silence or incoherence of certain voices. Among these voices are those of Koreans in Japan, situated at the intersection of Japanese imperialism, Western (or more specifically American) global hegemony, and now even an ethnocentric South Korean soft power machine. A recognition of this global entanglement, as well as the reader's own location within it, is necessary for engaging with the sometimes silent, sometimes incoherent voices it produces. After Haraway's "situated knowledge," we might call this kind of approach *situated reading*.

In that spirit, I would like to conclude by further suggesting that Zainichi literature in its deterritorialized form can reveal the ways that the American academic "gaze from nowhere" obscures an important truth: that Zainichi stories *are* American stories. Here, of course, I do not mean to imply that Zainichi stories are commensurate to the American experience, wholly knowable as objects of empathy or interpretation. Rather, they are our stories because we are involved, and have been from the start. The struggle of Koreans in Japan for rights, recognition, and representation, often implicitly presented as *paralleling* the struggles of ethnic and racial minorities in the United States (or worse, divorced entirely from Western contexts), is in fact deeply *entangled* with American imperialism, Cold War politics, and global hegemony. That struggle is also imbricated with the history of Japanese imperialism and perhaps, in the twenty-first century, the rise of an appropriative global Korean cultural imperialism.

If this book asks, at some level, what it means for American readers—or *an* American reader—to take up Zainichi literature, then it must first be said that there is no Zainichi literature to take up. Zainichi literature does not cohere, precisely because of these intersectional entanglements, as well as those more typically conjured by intersectionality discourse: race, ethnicity, gender, sexuality, (dis)ability. And second, even a single text that has traveled to readers along the pathways enabled by the taxonomical framework of Zainichi cannot be grasped as something that exists in the world *outside*, alien to the American experience.

But even if such a reader recognizes her involvement and entanglement with the text, it does not follow that it appears in a form that is fully legible, assimilated into the modes of expression and representation she expects. Instead, these texts—exemplified by but by no means limited to the works discussed in this book—are often presented as challenges to blithe assumptions of legibility and commensurability within a global literary market, where global equals "in English."

This radical illegibility or incoherence is more visible through the lens of intersectionality. Such a lens allows for the recognition that barriers to legibility and coherence are erected in part by the intersection of empires and other forms of hierarchy. At the same time, an intersectional framework reveals the entire question of legibility to be a practical one: there is no legibility in the abstract. The question is always: legible *to whom?* Just as there is no coherent Zainichi literature, much less a uniform Zainichi community, there is no representative American reader, no cohesive American experience or history outside those constructed through the suppression of internal difference and transnational entanglement. Recognizing the positioned nature of the reader, with a gaze from *somewhere*, in turn gives rise to an ethical demand for self-consciousness of the ways that a given audience, its modes of listening and reading, are complicit in limiting or producing the possibilities for what can and cannot be said.

I want to end, then, by exploring the Zainichi-adjacent text that has resonated most powerfully with American readers and literary circles. Through a situated reading of *Pachinko*, conscious of both reader and writer's respective positions, the ethical demands of reading from somewhere can come into focus. These demands are made all the more poignant by the uncanny familiarity of the novel, presented both as a story that history has excised from the very possibility of coming into global view, yet at the same time as an object for international empathy and understanding. Like so many texts treated in this book, it asks readers who encounter it to recognize the violence they do by ignoring them as well as the violence they do by understanding them, if understanding is only possible on the reader's terms.

PACHINKO AND THE FAILURES OF HISTORY

Pachinko narrates four generations of a family history, starting from a poor couple in Yeongdo whose first several children die at a young age before their one surviving daughter, Sunja, is born. The novel's story largely coincides with Sunja's lifetime, though the central focus eventually shifts to her sons, Noa and Mozasu, and finally to her grandson, Solomon. Whether at the intimate level of the family or in terms of the grand narratives of nations, *Pachinko* is concerned with history. Better yet, it is concerned with the absence of history, paradoxically telling the stories that have not been told. As *Pachinko* famously begins, "History has failed us, but no matter."[11] Christina Yi has interrogated this opening line in terms of its use of "us," probing the conditions for being included in the "us" whose absent history the novel sets out to narrate.[12] Yi compares the global reach of *Pachinko*, via English, to works of Zainichi literature that have been rendered "untranslatable" by the very Japanese terms for referring to the community inscribed in this "us."

Following Yi, I would like to consider another kind of "us" that is implicated in this failure of history. After all, for the presence or absence of Zainichi history to come into question in the first place, there must be an audience for that history. Lee's opening line is enigmatic, perhaps merely meant to convey that the events of history have been cruel to Koreans in Japan. But it could also suggest that history has failed to record or narrate the experiences of Koreans in Japan, though Lee's own thorough research for the book contradicts this notion. I read this line instead as a declaration that nobody *knows* this history, that it is under- or unrepresented—a problem for which the novel acts as a corrective. Of course, it is not that nobody knows this history, but rather that "we" as global (read English-language) readers are presumed never to have encountered it. Thus, history has failed—or has been failed by—yet another "us."

Speaking for myself, to read *Pachinko* as an American immersed in the Zainichi literary tradition is to feel an uncanny sense of my own position. In a way, I am not the target audience. The novel seeks to introduce and explain things I already know. Yet at the same time, the story feels out of sync with the texts by Zainichi writers that taught me those things in the first place. Its project is different. This difference arises precisely from the novel's assumption of an American audience with a particular understanding of the relationships between race, ethnicity, and nation—and here I am very much included in the target audience. What feels so strange about *Pachinko* has everything to do with the problem of representation that this book sets out to critique: like so much English-language knowledge making, it sets out to bring into "our" sphere of vision a history that has been invisible, but it can only do so on "our" terms, even as the ostensible purpose of representing the un(der)represented is to disrupt those very terms.

This problem, as well as the centrality of American modes of thinking through questions of national belonging and racial justice, comes to the fore in Lee's framing of her own response to Zainichi stories. In an interview with *The Atlantic*, Lee says:

> I realized that I was more upset about what had happened to them, in many ways, more than they were. I think I was more upset because, as an American, I feel a sense of indignation at injustice, and I also feel like I can have redress. As a lawyer, I know that I can seek justice in a very specific formal way. Not that these efforts have always had a good outcome in our legal history, and they can require people to take continuous action for a very long time. But in America there have been some wonderful overturning of inequitable things, even if it's taken 20 years or 50 years or 100 years. As Americans, we know it's possible. But this was a reminder that, in other parts of the world, there is often no redress for suffering or inequity.[13]

Lee's perspective on injustices faced by the Zainichi community, both here and in the novel, seems unaware of the rich history of Zainichi activism, and the extent to which it has in fact sought and won many forms of redress.[14] Of course, much of this activism has been geared toward reunification and other forms of justice for Koreans on the peninsula, rather than aimed at carving out a space for Koreans in a liberal pluralist Japan. Organized Zainichi politics was supported by and aligned with North Korea for much of its postwar history, and even outside the purview of Ch'ongryŏn, Koreans in Japan have opposed and sought redress for American militarism and imperialism, often in fraught solidarity with the Japanese left. If Lee or her readers set out looking for a history of Zainichi activism that mimics or parallels that of Asian Americans or other racial minorities in the United States, then of course they may find little worth mentioning. But if there is indeed "no redress for suffering or inequity," then surely that is a product of American power itself, not the result of a lack of some uniquely American "sense of indignation at injustice."

Indeed, in many ways, *Pachinko* orients the story toward the United States as a sort of teleological end goal of the Zainichi history it tells in microcosm. The characters idolize the United States, often simply as a status symbol—Solomon's education at Columbia University a case in point—but at times ideologically, as a bastion of justice and freedom. In the end, when Solomon abandons his (or his family's) dream of employment at an American bank to follow in his father's footsteps in the pachinko business, this is perhaps meant to signal what Lee calls, in the interview quoted above, Zainichi "graciousness in response to their suffering."[15] What could easily be read as political quietism is cast as the strength to endure, rather than fight, injustice. In either case, the entire story is couched in the assumption that redress for Koreans in Japan would take the forms it has taken in the United States, and that these forms are perhaps impossible in the Japanese context.

The impossibility of reconciling American multiculturalist views of justice and redress with the Japanese setting in which the novel takes place comes through particularly clearly in the character arc of Phoebe, a Korean American woman introduced as the story is drawing to a close. Phoebe is Solomon's girlfriend, whom he meets in college. She stands in stark contrast to the main female characters, all of whom echo the novel's refrain, "a woman's lot is to suffer."[16] In line with the way Lee describes the Zainichi Koreans she spoke to as part of her research for the book, these women do not respond with indignation to their suffering, but rather find ways to survive and even thrive despite their lot in life. By comparison, Phoebe has no patience for the injustices they face, and has no qualms about saying so aloud. A review of the Japanese translation of *Pachinko* calls her "fortissimo."[17]

The casual misogyny here, from a reader of the novel, echoes that confronted by the characters, including Phoebe, within the story itself. In fact, Kang Yujin connects Sunja's departure for Japan with a long and ongoing history of Koreans emigrating in an attempt to escape patriarchy and heterosexism.[18] Indeed, as the novel moves forward in time from colonial Korea to imperial and post-imperial Japan, and eventually expands in geographic scope to include the United States, the freedoms women enjoy continually expand. This is one of many ways that the novel sets up an implicit teleology that moves inexorably toward a liberated, idealized America. Within this schema, Japan can be viewed either as a stepping stone toward the real prize of American immigration and assimilation, or as a deviation that hinders the family's smooth journey toward this ultimate goal.[19]

This hierarchical configuration leads to a disconnect for Phoebe, who cannot reconcile the modes of Korean identification she encounters in Japan with her own Korean American positionality. Nor does Solomon's family seem to be able to comprehend Phoebe's experience. This disconnect comes into relief when Solomon brings Phoebe to a family gathering at which Sunja and her sister-in-law Kyunghee are preparing a feast. Kyunghee and Sunja are shocked when Phoebe reveals that her own mother does not cook, and she "grew up eating pizza and hamburgers" because her mother worked as an office manager in her father's practice (449).

> 'Mom was always working. She did all the medical paperwork at the dining table next to us kids while we did our homework. I don't think she ever went to bed until midnight—'
>
> 'But you didn't eat any Korean food?'
>
> Kyunghee couldn't comprehend this.
>
> 'On the weekends we ate it. At a restaurant' (449).

As the conversation continues, Phoebe is almost dismissive of Kyunghee and Sunja's seeming obsession with Korean food, which for them has been a source of pride, income, and community throughout the novel. At the same time, the gap in their respective Korean immigrant experiences is couched precisely in terms of the roles for women, with Phoebe's mother "out of the kitchen," so to speak, suggesting the beginning of a more complete liberation that Phoebe appears to enjoy. As the scene concludes, this is all made more explicit through Sunja's inner monologue: "Her mother used to say a woman's life was suffering, but that was the last thing she wanted for this sweet girl who had a quick, warm smile for everyone. If she didn't cook, then so what?" (451).

Phoebe clearly stands in contrast to the longsuffering Zainichi women in Solomon's family, but is nevertheless connected to them via Korean ethnicity, which is what seems to count. In the same scene, it is noted that Solomon feels pressure from his grandmother and aunt to marry a Korean woman, and Sunja's narrated train of thought goes on to mention that "she hoped that Phoebe wanted children." Even if Phoebe does not share the family's particular immigrant experience, she belongs to the same "imagined community" of the global

Korean diaspora. Min Jin Lee goes out of her way to frame the diaspora as such, using an extended quotation from Benedict Anderson as the epigraph to Book III (which contains this scene and the entirety of Phoebe's arc), following the Book II epigraph, "I thought that no matter how many hills and brooks you crossed, the whole world was Korea and everyone in it was Korean."[20] Much like the South Korean soft power machine, Lee is interested in the Korean diaspora as a global entity, bound together by connections imagined rather than real.[21] But at the same time, I would maintain that forging even spurious connections across these disparate communities might nevertheless be productive, along the lines of what Andrea Mendoza theorizes as "nonencounter," a means of contesting the bounded and ostensibly coherent siloes of knowledge production that render illegible non-Western modes of thinking race, gender, sexuality, and so forth.[22] Ironically, the entire conversation takes place in Korean, a language Phoebe shares with Sunja and Kyunghee, but not Solomon. Her Korean, like English, connects her to the global Korean diaspora in a way that is inaccessible to Zainichi Koreans who speak only Japanese.

This is not to say that the bridge between Korean Americans (or the broader Korean diaspora) and a globalized South Korea is erected via suppression of the history of Japanese colonization. If anything, the reverse is true, as exemplified by Phoebe. Living in Japan to be close to Solomon, Phoebe becomes more and more disillusioned with Japan, and eventually their relationship deteriorates as a result. When Solomon accuses her of bigotry against the Japanese, she responds, "You're going to say that I've been reading too much about the Pacific War," suggesting that Solomon resents her constant reminders of the atrocities committed by the Japanese empire (470). In fact, Solomon offers as a rebuttal a reminder of Japanese victimhood during the same period: "The Japanese have suffered, too. Nagasaki? Hiroshima? And in America, the Japanese Americans were sent to internment camps, but the German Americans weren't. How do you explain that?" (470). He thus repeats the rhetoric of victimhood and defeat that is so often leveraged in Japan to avoid reckoning with the victims of Japan's wartime aggression, including colonial Koreans. If only one of these histories can be relevant at once—in other words, without attending to the intersection of Japanese and American imperialisms—then the history of Koreans in Japan becomes impossible to articulate.

Positioned at this intersection, Solomon's frustration with Phoebe becomes a bit clearer. As noted above, part of what is difficult about Solomon's situation arises directly out of the history of Japanese imperialism, particularly his alienation from the Korean language. But it is largely the history of American imperialism—leading to the division of the peninsula, the suppression of Korean ethnic schools and activist organizations in occupied Japan, and the precarious and limited citizenship status of Koreans in Japan—that causes the issues that Phoebe finds so inscrutable. In one moment, it is the internal division of the Zainichi community itself that sets her off:

> 'In America, there is no such thing as a *Kankokujin* or *Chosenjin*. Why the hell would I be a South Korean or a North Korean? That makes no sense! I was born in Seattle, and my parents came to the States when there was only one Korea,' she'd shout, relating one of the bigotry anecdotes of her day. 'Why does Japan still distinguish the two countries for its Korean residents who've been here for four fucking generations? You were born here. You're not a foreigner! That's insane. Your father was born here. Why are you two carrying South Korean passports? It's bizarre' (435).

It is notable that the situation that Phoebe decries as "insane" and "bizarre" is also the one that she cannot articulate strictly in English. She must resort to the terms *Kankokujin* and *Chosenjin*, left somewhat opaque, though vaguely understood as referring to South and North Korea respectively. She neglects to mention that there is no neutral term outside the Anglophone "Korean." Suggestively, in the Korean translation of the novel, these terms are rendered as *Kangkkokkujing* and *Chosenjing*, transliterating into Korean the Japanese pronunciation of the terms rather than translating them into their Korean equivalents, *Hangugin* and *Chosŏnin*.[23] The translator understands the illegibility here as vital to Phoebe's position. If the two terms are fully legible, then the difference between them is fully legible, and the insistence on distinguishing can hardly be described as "insane."

Indeed, so much of what remains illegible in *Pachinko*, despite its overall success in representing Zainichi Koreans and correcting the history that has "failed" them, are all the ways that the United States is implicated in that very history. Instead, it is portrayed a sort of paradise on the horizon, "this magical place so many Koreans in Japan idealized" (336). The few characters who might be inclined to criticize the United States, such as those aligned with Ch'ongryŏn, are portrayed as misguided, and bound for a North Korea that functions as a black hole in the novel, where people go to disappear. And yet, the broader Cold War politics in East Asia, responsible for so much of the injustice that Lee sets out to narrate, warrant barely a mention. This is the part of the story that Phoebe—and likely most readers of *Pachinko*—cannot see.

Perhaps it is this unspoken difference in perspective that ultimately alienates Phoebe from Solomon. As he decides to end their relationship, at essentially the same moment he chooses to abandon his career in global finance for his father's line of work, Solomon muses that he "was Japanese, too, even if the Japanese didn't think so. Phoebe couldn't see this. There was more to being something than just blood. The space between Phoebe and him could not close, and if he was decent, he had to let her go home" (471). In this way, Solomon's story eventually undermines the teleological march of the family toward success and liberation in the United States, and the importance of their location in Japan is reasserted over the globalized Korean (ethnocentric) identity that Phoebe stands in for. It falls to Solomon, the character most deeply entangled with the United States itself, to insist on the unbridgeable chasm between the Zainichi experience and the American perspective.

. . .

Perhaps it is strange to end a book on the representational impossibilities faced by Zainichi writers with a reading of a bestseller overtly aiming for Zainichi representation. And of course, some readers may object that Min Jin Lee's work, like that of Yi Kwangsu and perhaps even Kim Saryang, is not "Zainichi." By now I hope it is clear that this distinction can only matter if we begin from the assumption that Zainichi literature is a coherent and knowable entity "over there," removed from the production of anglophonic knowledge. Instead, I have argued that the more salient function of literary taxonomies, such as Zainichi literature, is to create encounters. The textual encounters narrated in this book can enable an ethics that goes beyond empathy and understanding.

In this sense, when nations, cultures, languages, and other modes of taxonomizing literature come into question, perhaps it is more important to describe the location of the audience than the author. It is through situated reading that the ethical potential of literature is unlocked. What is exciting about reading Zainichi literature from somewhere rather than nowhere is that it reveals the ways that the same intersecting power relations that define Zainichi positionality also define our own. It allows us to be affected by the texts, rather than constantly seeking to know them as something over there, not here. Properly situated as such, the reading of *Pachinko*, in places and languages all over the world, has this potential as well.

Indeed, it is only by suppressing the myriad ways that the United States is implicated in Zainichi history that it becomes possible for American readers to experience *Pachinko* at a distance, to empathize with characters facing an injustice "over there." Its release coincided with the start of the Trump presidency, and its popularity continued into the COVID-19 pandemic, which brought further attention to racial inequities, particularly anti-Asian hate crimes and police killings of black Americans, including George Floyd in May 2020, sparking massive protests in the summer of that year. In the midst of this heightened awareness of American racism, the novel perhaps provided an outlet for readers to engage with issues of race and national identity in the abstract. American readers could sympathize with Zainichi Koreans, secure in the knowledge that they have nothing to do with "us." But as the very narrative of *Pachinko* tacitly reveals, and as this book has argued, Zainichi history has everything to do with us.

NOTES

INTRODUCTION: EAVESDROPPING ON ZAINICHI LITERATURE

1. The word "Zainichi" almost always appears in quotation marks in contemporary Japanese discourse on Zainichi literature and culture, with authors and critics explaining that this allows them to acknowledge the fluidity and diversity of the community of people to whom the term has been applied. I have dropped the scare quotes for the sake of convenience, but the reader can assume that I use the term advisedly. I discuss the usage and meaning of these quotation marks at length in chapter 1.

2. For a range of contemporary perspectives on the meaning of and reasons for maintaining *Chōsen-seki* (stateless Korean nationality, as opposed to *Kankoku-seki*, South Korean citizenship), see Ri Rika, ed., *Chōsenseki to wa nani ka: Toransunashonaru no shiten kara* (Tokyo: Akashi Shoten, 2021).

3. "Kankoku-kei Nihonjin" and "Chōsen-kei Nihonjin" (ethnically Korean Japanese) are also in use, but are generally applied to naturalized citizens of Japan with Korean heritage, who are marginalized within the Zainichi community itself.

4. I do not think this woman intended to other North Korea or those who identify as "Zainichi Chōsenjin" in this way, but this is precisely the point. The language itself forces speakers to choose a side.

5. See, for instance, Pak Chungho, "'Zainichi' bungaku wa shōmetsusuru no ka," *Shakai bungaku* 26 (2007): 187–90. Pak states in the essay that "a certain Zainichi writer" has publicly wondered whether Zainichi literature may cease to exist in the future (187). He is likely referring to Kim Sŏkpŏm (b. 1925), who has declared at numerous symposia and other events that when he dies, Zainichi literature will be over. I unpack the discourse surrounding the "end" of Zainichi literature in chapter 7, and take up Kim's work in chapter 4.

6. Vera Mackie, Brian Dowdle, Joshua Fogel, Stefano Romagnoli, and Davinder Bhowmik, "The Death of Japanese Studies" (Roundtable Discussion, Association for Asian

Studies Annual Conference, Denver, Colorado, March 22, 2019). A follow-up discussion was moved online in the midst of the COVID-19 pandemic, which brought death in the straightforward sense of the word, but also ushered in hiring freezes, deep funding cuts to academic programs, and an increased urgency to justify the "relevance" of the humanities. Despite attempts to maintain the optimistic future-oriented framing of the roundtable as organized, the deep sense of anxiety and precarity brought about by the pandemic in the spring of 2020 is palpable throughout the panelists' initial remarks and the responses from the community. "The 'Rebirth' of Japanese Studies" is available at http://prcurtis.com/events/AAS2020/.

7. John Whittier Treat, "Japan Is Interesting: Modern Japanese Literary Studies Today," *Japan Forum* 30, no. 3 (March 2018): 421–40. See also John Whittier Treat, *The Rise and Fall of Modern Japanese Literature* (Chicago: University of Chicago Press, 2018), which takes up the sense of crisis in Japanese literature in the existential terms of the "end of literature."

8. The most incisive response to the "death" of Japanese studies along these lines was Grace En-Yi Ting, "Negativity and Hope, or Addressing Gender and Race in Japanese Studies," *Gender and Sexuality* 15 (2020): 67–81.

9. Shu-mei Shih, "Against Diaspora: The Sinophone as Places of Cultural Production," in *Global Chinese Literature: Critical Essays*, ed. Jing Tsu and David Der-wei Wang (Leiden: Brill, 2010), 39.

10. See David Murphy, "Literature after Empire: A Comparative Reading of Two Literary Manifestos," *Contemporary French and Francophone Studies* 14, no. 1 (January 2010): 67–75.

11. Daniel Simon, trans., "Toward a 'World-Literature' in French," *World Literature Today* 83, no. 2 (April 2009): 54.

12. Simon, "Toward a 'World-Literature' in French," 55.

13. Salman Rushdie, "'Commonwealth Literature' Does Not Exist," in *Imaginary Homelands: Essays and Criticism 1981–1991* (London: Granta Books, 1991), 61–70 (quotes from 62).

14. Rushdie, "'Commonwealth Literature' Does Not Exist," 62.

15. See Thérèse Migraine-George, *From Francophonie to World Literature in French: Ethics, Poetics, and Politics* (Lincoln: University of Nebraska Press, 2013), xxi–xxvi, for a detailed discussion of this backlash in the wake of the *Le Monde* manifesto. Another telling example is the lengthy debate within Comparative Literature on how the field can cohere when confronted with demands for greater inclusivity. See Charles Bernheimer, ed., *Comparative Literature in the Age of Multiculturalism* (Baltimore, MD: Johns Hopkins University Press, 1995). Gayatri Chakravorty Spivak's *Death of a Discipline* (New York: Columbia University Press, 2003) is written partially as a response to these debates and to globalization writ large, and, notably, couches the problem in the same language of ending and "death."

16. Harumi Befu, *Ideorogī to shite no Nihon bunkaron* (Tokyo: Shisō no Kagakusha, 1987); Oguma Eiji, *Tan'itsu minzoku shinwa no kigen: "Nihonjin" no jigazō no keifu* (Tokyo: Shin'yōsha, 1995).

17. See, for instance, John Maher and Gaynor Macdonald, eds., *Diversity in Japanese Culture and Language* (New York: Kegan Paul International, 1995); Donald Denoon et al., eds., *Multicultural Japan: Palaeolithic to Postmodern* (Cambridge, UK: Cambridge University Press, 1996); Michael Weiner, ed., *Japan's Minorities: The Illusion of Homogeneity* (New York:

Routledge, 1997); John Lie, *Multiethnic Japan* (Cambridge, MA: Harvard University Press, 2001).

18. For an early synopsis of critiques of multiculturalism, see Henry Louis Gates Jr., "Beyond the Culture Wars: Identities in Dialogue," *Profession* 1993 (1993): 6–11.

19. An early example of a critique of nationalist narratives of Korean cultural essentialism from within Korean studies can be found in James Palais, "A Search for Korean Uniqueness," *Harvard Journal of Asiatic Studies* 55, no. 2 (December 1995): 409–25. The specific framing of this critique around "uniqueness" echoes some of the early anti-*Nihonjinron* discourse, e.g. Peter Dale, *The Myth of Japanese Uniqueness* (New York: St. Martin's Press, 1986).

20. In the twenty-first century alone, Anglophone academics have produced many studies of the Zainichi community and its literature, including but not limited to: Sonia Ryang, ed., *Koreans in Japan: Critical Voices from the Margin* (New York: Routledge, 2000); Melissa Wender, *Lamentation as History: Narratives by Koreans in Japan, 1965–2000* (Stanford, CA: Stanford University Press, 2005); John Lie, *Zainichi (Koreans in Japan): Diasporic Nationalism and Postcolonial Identity* (Berkeley: University of California Press, 2008); David Chapman, *Zainichi Korean Identity and Ethnicity* (New York: Routledge, 2008); Sonia Ryang, *Writing Selves in Diaspora: Ethnography of Autobiographics of Korean Women in Japan and the United States* (Lanham, MD: Lexington Books, 2008); and Sonia Ryang and John Lie, eds., *Diaspora Without Homeland: Being Korean in Japan* (Berkeley, CA: University of California Press, 2009). It has also been the subject of numerous PhD dissertations, including Christopher Scott, "Invisible Men: The Zainichi Korean Presence in Postwar Japanese Culture" (Stanford University, 2006); Nikki Dejan Floyd, "Bridging the Colonial Divide: Japanese-Korean Solidarity in the International Proletarian Literature Movement" (Yale University, 2011); Jonathan Glade, "Occupied Liberation: Transforming Literary Boundaries in Japan and Southern Korea, 1945–1952" (University of Chicago, 2013); Nathaniel Heneghan, "Floating Signifiers: Tracing Zainichi Korean Identity in Postcolonial Literature and Visual Media" (University of Southern California, 2015); and Soo Mi Lee, "Performing Postcolonial Feminine Identity as Shaman: Building Narrative Bridges Between Two Worlds" (University of California, Berkeley, 2015).

21. Chris Burgess, "Multicultural Japan? Discourse and the 'Myth' of Homogeneity," *The Asia-Pacific Journal: Japan Focus* 5, no. 3 (March 1, 2007): Article ID 2389.

22. This led to a flurry of monographs whose focus is the Japanese empire rather than simply Japan, encompassing the Korean peninsula and other former colonies and examining in detail their mutual influences, conflicts, and ambivalences. See, for example, Karen Thornber, *Empire of Texts in Motion: Chinese, Korean, and Taiwanese Transculturations of Japanese Literature* (Cambridge, MA: Harvard University Asia Center, 2009); Robert Tierney, *Tropics of Savagery: The Culture of Japanese Empire in Comparative Frame* (Berkeley: University of California Press, 2010); Kimberly Kono, *Romance, Family, and Nation in Japanese Colonial Literature* (New York: Palgrave Macmillan, 2010); Mark Driscoll, *Absolute Erotic, Absolute Grotesque: The Living, Dead, and Undead in Japan's Imperialism, 1895–1945* (Durham, NC: Duke University Press, 2010); Samuel Perry, *Recasting Red Culture in Proletarian Japan: Childhood, Korea, and the Historical Avant-Garde* (Honolulu: University of Hawai'i Press, 2014). Two earlier yet still vibrant forerunners of this wave of scholarship are Leo Ching, *Becoming "Japanese": Colonial Taiwan and the Politics of Identity Formation*

(Berkeley: University of California Press, 2001); and Faye Yuan Kleeman, *Under an Imperial Sun: Japanese Colonial Literature of Taiwan and the South* (Honolulu: University of Hawai'i Press, 2003).

23. Serk-Bae Suh, *Treacherous Translation: Culture, Nationalism, and Colonialism in Korea and Japan from the 1910s to the 1960s* (Berkeley: University of California Press, 2013); Nayoung Aimee Kwon, *Intimate Empire: Collaboration and Colonial Modernity in Korea and Japan* (Durham, NC: Duke University Press, 2015); Christina Yi, *Colonizing Language: Cultural Production and Language Politics in Modern Japan and Korea* (New York: Columbia University Press, 2018).

24. Travis Workman offers a detailed discussion of this potential in "Locating Translation: On the Question of Japanophone Literature," *PMLA* 126, no. 3 (May 2011): 701–8.

25. Kim Sŏkpŏm, "'Nihongo bungaku' to rekishisei," *Kokyō: Nihongo bungaku kenkyū (Border Crossings: The Journal of Japanese-Language Literature Studies)* 2, no. 1 (June 2015): 4–6. Nayoung Aimee Kwon offers a similar critique in "Japanophone Literature? A Transpacific Query on Absence," *MFS Modern Fiction Studies* 64, no. 3 (Fall 2018): 541–46.

26. Naoki Sakai and Hyon Joo Yoo, eds., *The Trans-Pacific Imagination: Rethinking Boundary, Culture and Society* (Singapore: World Scientific Publishing Company, 2012), 27, 34–37.

27. For a review of the early literature in the field, see Lisa Yoneyama, "Toward a Decolonial Genealogy of the Transpacific," *American Quarterly* 69, no. 3 (September 2017): 471–82.

28. Sakai and Yoo, *The Trans-Pacific Imagination*, 37.

29. Sakai and Yoo, *The Trans-Pacific Imagination*, 5, emphasis added.

30. Yoneyama, "Toward a Decolonial Genealogy of the Transpacific," 478.

31. Simon Critchley, *The Ethics of Deconstruction: Derrida and Levinas*, 3rd ed. (Edinburgh: Edinburgh University Press, 2014), 9.

32. Emmanuel Levinas, *Totality and Infinity: An Essay on Exteriority*, trans. Alphonso Lingis, 4th ed. (Dordrecht: Kluwer Academic Publishers, 1991), 44.

33. Jacques Derrida engages directly with Levinas's writing in "Violence and Metaphysics: An Essay on the Thought of Emmanuel Levinas," in *Writing and Difference*, trans. Alan Bass (London: Routledge Classics, 2001), 97–192. On the interplay between Levinasian ethics and the critical tradition of deconstruction, see Critchley, *The Ethics of Deconstruction*. My own understanding of this theory has benefited enormously from its applications in Suh, *Treacherous Translation*, and Erin Graff Zivin, *Anarchaeologies: Reading as Misreading* (New York: Fordham University Press, 2020), both of which focus on the failures, errors, and aporias that necessarily arise in the processes of reading, writing, and translation.

34. Idelber Avelar, "The Ethics of Interpretation and the International Division of Intellectual Labor," *SubStance* 29, no. 1 (2000): 98; emphasis original.

35. Avelar, "The Ethics of Interpretation," 96.

36. As Naoki Sakai and others have illustrated, this hierarchy in which Western theory is purported to explain non-Western practice or experience is not a result of universality versus particularity, but rather the West's power to claim a universal subject position. See *Translation and Subjectivity: On Japan and Cultural Nationalism* (Minneapolis: University of Minnesota Press, 1997), especially chapter 5.

37. Jennifer Nash, *Black Feminism Reimagined: After Intersectionality* (Durham, NC: Duke University Press, 2019), 3.

38. Nash, *Black Feminism Reimagined*, 2.

39. Kimberlé Crenshaw, "Demarginalizing the Intersection of Race and Sex: A Black Feminist Critique of Antidiscrimination Doctrine, Feminist Theory, and Antiracist Politics," *University of Chicago Legal Forum* 1 (1989): 139–67.

40. For a concise intellectual history of intersectionality, see Nash, *Black Feminism Reimagined*, 6–11. For a more in-depth perspective looking further into the past, see Vivian May, "Intellectual Genealogies, Intersectionality, and Anna Julia Cooper," in *Feminist Solidarity at the Crossroads: Intersectional Women's Studies for Transracial Alliance*, ed. Kim Marie Vaz and Gary L. Lemons (New York: Routledge, 2012), 59–71.

41. Kathy Davis argues that intersectionality's success as social theory is precisely because it is so vague and open-ended that it fails to cohere; see "Intersectionality as Buzzword: A Sociology of Science Perspective on What Makes a Feminist Theory Successful," *Feminist Theory* 9, no. 1 (April 1, 2008): 67–85.

42. Patricia Hill Collins, *Black Feminist Thought: Knowledge, Consciousness, and the Politics of Empowerment*, 2nd ed. (New York: Routledge, 2000), 18.

43. Combahee River Collective, "A Black Feminist Statement," in *This Bridge Called My Back: Writings by Radical Women of Color*, ed. Cherríe Moraga and Gloria Anzaldúa, 4th ed. (Albany: State University of New York Press, 2015), 210–18.

44. Audre Lorde, "Age, Race, Class, and Sex: Women Redefining Difference," in *Sister Outsider: Essays and Speeches*, rev. ed. (Berkeley, CA: Crossing Press, 2007), 122–23.

45. Kimberlé Crenshaw, "Mapping the Margins: Intersectionality, Identity Politics, and Violence against Women of Color," *Stanford Law Review* 43, no. 6 (1991): 1242, emphasis added.

46. Mecca Jamilah Sullivan, *The Poetics of Difference: Queer Feminist Forms in the African Diaspora* (Champaign: University of Illinois Press, 2021), 20.

47. Sullivan, *The Poetics of Difference*, 11.

48. Here I am envisioning something close to what Sullivan calls "interstitial hermeneutics," a type of reading that queer poetics demands of its audience, and which causes an encounter with one's own lack of knowledge or centeredness (*The Poetics of Difference*, 21–22). Again, I read this as a fundamentally ethical approach.

49. Paul Ricoeur, *Freud and Philosophy* (New Haven, CT: Yale University Press, 1970), 32–34. See also Rita Felski on the limitations of this mode of interpretation in *The Limits of Critique* (Chicago: University of Chicago Press, 2015), 1–13. I am also indebted to Will Bridges, whose post-critical approach to Japanese-language literary production has informed my own; see *Playing in the Shadows: Fictions of Race and Blackness in Postwar Japanese Literature* (Ann Arbor: University of Michigan Press, 2020).

1. THE UNTIMELINESS OF "ZAINICHI": LITERARY HISTORY AND THE CONSTRUCTION OF COHERENCE

1. For a more detailed discussion of the contested origins of Zainichi literature, see Cindi Textor, "Zainichi Writers and the Postcoloniality of Modern Korean Literature," in *Routledge Handbook of Modern Korean Literature*, ed. Yoon Sun Yang (New York: Routledge, 2020), 225–38.

2. One of the best is Ko Youngran, *"Sengo" to iu ideorogī: rekishi, kioku, bunka* (Tokyo: Fujiwara Shoten, 2010).

3. I distinguish between *Zainichi*, a proper noun denoting a mode of (ethnic) identification or the community of people identifying as such, and *zainichi*, which I use in its literal sense, "in Japan."

4. Kawamura Minato, *Umaretara soko ga furusato: Zainichi Chōsenjin bungakuron* (Tokyo: Heibonsha, 1999), 112.

5. Kawamura, *Umaretara soko ga furusato*, 113.

6. John Lie, *Zainichi (Koreans in Japan): Diasporic Nationalism and Postcolonial Identity* (Berkeley: University of California Press, 2008), 118.

7. Kawamura, *Umaretara soko ga furusato*, 14–15.

8. See, for instance, Isogai Jirō, *"Zainichi" bungakuron* (Tokyo: Shinkansha, 2004), 9–19, for another version of the generational narrative, which inevitably centers the second-generation writers who were themselves instrumental in defining Zainichi Korean literature and its foils.

9. Song Hyewŏn, *"Zainichi Chōsenjin bungaku shi" no tame ni: Koe naki koe no porifonī* (Tokyo: Iwanami Shoten, 2014).

10. Andre Schmid, *Korea Between Empires, 1895–1919* (New York: Columbia University Press, 2002), 8.

11. Schmid, *Korea Between Empires*, 12–13.

12. Lydia Liu refers to these asymmetrical negotiations of meaning as "translingual practice," uncovering their impact on modern Chinese literature in *Translingual Practice: Literature, National Culture, and Translated Modernity—China, 1900–1937* (Stanford, CA: Stanford University Press, 1995). On the formulation of terms for literature in Japan and Korea respectively, see Atsuko Ueda, *Concealment of Politics, Politics of Concealment: The Production of "Literature" in Meiji Japan* (Stanford, CA: Stanford University Press, 2007) and Yoon Sun Yang, *From Domestic Women to Sensitive Young Men: Translating the Individual in Early Colonial Korea* (Cambridge, MA: Harvard University Asia Center, 2017).

13. Yi Kwangsu, "What Is Literature? (Munhak iran hao)," trans. Jooyeon Rhee, *Azalea: Journal of Korean Literature and Culture* 4 (2011): 310.

14. Yi, "What Is Literature?," 312.

15. Yi, "What Is Literature?," 305.

16. Travis Workman shows that Yi was less concerned with national sovereignty than with cosmopolitan moral subjectivity, to which his notion of national culture (including literature) was a means rather than an end in itself. If Korean literature (*Chosŏn munhak*) provided this means in the early colonial period, then Japanese national literature (*kokumin bungaku*) was just as suited to the task in the late colonial period. This offers an answer to the enduring question of how Yi could transform from a nationalist advocating Korean independence to a pro-Japanese collaborator in the span of a few short decades, and would also explain the relative lack of emphasis on Japan here (in addition to censorship and other constraints on what Yi could write in this context). See Travis Workman, *Imperial Genus: The Formation and Limits of the Human in Modern Korea and Japan* (Berkeley: University of California Press, 2016), 91–92.

17. Mark E. Caprio, *Japanese Assimilation Policies in Colonial Korea, 1910–1945* (Seattle: University of Washington Press, 2011), 129–30; 153.

18. Leo Ching, *Becoming "Japanese": Colonial Taiwan and the Politics of Identity Formation* (Berkeley: University of California Press, 2001), ch. 3.

19. On the Korea boom of the late 1930s and early 1940s, see E. Taylor Atkins, *Primitive Selves: Koreana in the Japanese Colonial Gaze, 1910–1945* (Berkeley: University of California Press, 2010), 129–61.

20. On the broader contexts and consequences of this conundrum, see Nayoung Aimee Kwon, *Intimate Empire: Collaboration and Colonial Modernity in Korea and Japan* (Durham, NC: Duke University Press, 2015); Workman, *Imperial Genus*; Christina Yi, *Colonizing Language: Cultural Production and Language Politics in Modern Japan and Korea* (New York: Columbia University Press, 2018).

21. Workman, *Imperial Genus*, 56–57.

22. Kwon, *Intimate Empire*, 6–16; Yi, *Colonizing Language*, 72–94.

23. On the fraught politics of memory surrounding Japanese militarism and imperialism see, for instance, Yoshikuni Igarashi, *Bodies of Memory: Narratives of War in Postwar Japanese Culture, 1945–1970* (Princeton, NJ: Princeton University Press, 2000); and Lisa Yoneyama, *Cold War Ruins: Transpacific Critique of American Justice and Japanese War Crimes* (Durham, NC: Duke University Press, 2016).

24. Notably, the occupation had been present for months in Okinawa, which marks the end of the war at the conclusion of the Battle of Okinawa on June 22, 1945. The discrepancy in memory of the end of the war and beginning of the occupation further highlights the slippery nature of the divide between *naichi* (Japan proper, which ostensibly included Okinawa) and *gaichi* (the colonies).

25. The Ryukyu Kingdom, currently Okinawa Prefecture and under United States authority until 1972, is a notable example.

26. Chikako Kashiwazaki, "The Politics of Legal Status: The Equation of Nationality with Ethnonational Identity," in *Koreans in Japan: Critical Voices from the Margin*, ed. Sonia Ryang (New York: Routledge, 2000), 20–21.

27. On the "complicity" of US imperialism and East Asian nationalisms see Naoki Sakai and Hyon Joo Yoo, "Introduction: The Trans-Pacific Imagination—Rethinking Boundary, Culture and Society," in *The Trans-Pacific Imagination: Rethinking Boundary, Culture and Society* (Singapore: World Scientific Publishing Company, 2012), 1–44. On the role of militarization in halting the progress of decolonization in Asia, see Setsu Shigematsu and Keith L. Camacho, eds., *Militarized Currents: Toward a Decolonized Future in Asia and the Pacific* (Minneapolis: University of Minnesota Press, 2010).

28. Ko Youngran, *"Sengo" to iu ideorogī*, 281–329.

29. Minsook Lee, "The Japan-Korea Solidarity Movement in the 1970s and 1980s: From Solidarity to Reflexive Democracy," *The Asia-Pacific Journal: Japan Focus* 12, no. 38 (September 21, 2014): Article ID 4187.

30. Also at issue is the more familiar intersectional problem of how to mount a feminist critique of Japanese and Korean societies from within this double bind. I discuss this in further depth in chapters 6 and 7.

31. Kin Kakuei (discussed in chapter 5) is also known as Kim Hagyŏng. Ri Kaisei is the pen name of Yi Hoesŏng. Though Ri/Yi has no stated preference, I refer to him as Ri Kaisei throughout the book.

32. Isogai, *"Zainichi" bungakuron*, 12.

33. I use *Zainichi Chōsenjin bungaku* (translated as Zainichi Korean Literature) to distinguish a more narrow, unbracketed notion of the category from the looser, bracketed "Zainichi" Literature that elides the word for "Korean" and is applied less strictly (perhaps more incoherently).

34. 在日朝鮮人連盟 (J: Zainichi Chōsenjin Renmei; K: Chaeil Chosŏn'in Yŏnmaeng).

35. Before disbanding the organization entirely, the American occupation ordered a mass closing of Korean schools in Japan in 1948. See Hiromitsu Inokuchi, "Korean Ethnic Schools in Occupied Japan, 1945–1952," in *Koreans in Japan: Critical Voices from the Margin*, ed. Sonia Ryang (New York: Routledge, 2000), 146–54.

36. 在日朝鮮統一民主戦線 (J: Zainichi Chōsen Tōitsu Minshu Sensen; K: Chaeil Chosŏn T'ong'il Minju Chŏnsŏn).

37. Sonia Ryang, "The North Korean Homeland of Koreans in Japan," in *Koreans in Japan: Critical Voices from the Margin*, ed. Sonia Ryang (New York: Routledge, 2000), 35.

38. 在日本朝鮮人総聯合会 (J: Zai Nihon Chōsenjin Sōren Gōkai; K: Chae Ilbon Chosŏn'in Ch'ongryŏn Haphoe).

39. As Sonia Ryang puts it, "The repatriation zeal has to be seen in conjunction with Ch'ongryŏn's goal of unifying all Korean forces in Japan and its self-definition as a North Korean organization based in Japan, working for the prosperity of the homeland and its people, not an organization of Koreans in Japan with an eye to their future well-being in Japan" ("The North Korean Homeland of Koreans in Japan," 36). Also of note is that many of those "repatriated" were in fact born in Japan.

40. Lie, *Zainichi (Koreans in Japan)*, 42.

41. The abbreviation by which the organization is commonly known is coincidentally rendered *Mindan* in both Korean and Japanese. The organization's official name was originally 在日本大韓民国居留民団 (J: Zai Nihon Daikan Minkoku Kyoryū Mindan; K: Chae Ilbon Taehan Minguk Kŏryu Mindan), but was changed in 1994 to 在日本大韓民国民団 (J: Zai Nihon Daikan Minkoku Mindan; K: Chae Ilbon Taehan Minguk Mindan), deleting the compound 居留, which implies temporary status.

42. John Lie puts it at 90 percent support for Ch'ongryŏn over Mindan in the late 1950s, despite the vast majority of Koreans in Japan at this time tracing their family roots (or actual birthplaces) to the southern half of the peninsula (*Zainichi (Koreans in Japan)*, 42).

43. J. Mark Mobius, "The Japan-Korea Normalization Process and Korean Anti-Americanism," *Asian Survey* 6, no. 4 (April 1966): 241.

44. David Chapman, *Zainichi Korean Identity and Ethnicity* (New York: Routledge, 2008), 32.

45. Ri Yuhwan, *Nihon no naka no sanjūhachidosen: Mindan, Chōsōren no rekishi to genjitsu* (Tokyo: Yōyōsha, 1980).

46. Ch'ongryŏn membership and Chōsen-seki nationality became even more precarious positions after the Cold War, when North Korea lost Soviet backing and came under international scrutiny for its nuclear program and human rights violations. Sonia Ryang details the situation for Ch'ongryŏn Koreans in the 1990s in *North Koreans in Japan: Language, Ideology, and Identity* (Boulder, CO: Westview Press, 1997).

47. Yasunori Fukuoka, *Lives of Young Koreans in Japan* (Melbourne: Trans Pacific Press, 2000), 22.

48. For more on the politics of passing for Zainichi Koreans, see Christina Yi and Jonathan Glade, "The Politics of Passing in Zainichi Cultural Production," *Azalea: Journal of*

Korean Literature and Culture 12 (2019): 235–56, and other contributions to the special issue of *Azalea* on this topic.

49. Lie, *Zainichi (Koreans in Japan)*, 44–48.

50. Lie, *Zainichi (Koreans in Japan)*, 98–99.

51. Kim Sŏkpŏm, "Ima, 'Zainichi' ni totte 'kokuseki' to wa nani ka: Ri Kaisei-kun e no tegami," *Sekai* 653 (October 1998): 131–42. As I discuss in chapter 4, now that Kim has himself traveled to the Korean peninsula and witnessed the changes wrought by decades of division and, in the case of South Korea, American hegemony, even he recognizes that there is no going back to the unified Korea of his youth. He acknowledges that his connection to Korea is now purely fictive, even if he might argue that this imagined Korean homeland is no less politically forceful than the actual Koreas.

52. Ri Kaisei, "'Mukokusekisha' no yuku michi: Kim Sŏkpŏm-shi e no hentō," *Sekai* 657 (January 1999): 257–69.

53. Fukuoka, *Lives of Young Koreans in Japan*, 38–39.

54. Fukuoka, *Lives of Young Koreans in Japan*, 24–33.

55. Yi Yangji, discussed further in chapter 6, relates such a story in "Watashi wa Chōsenjin," in *Yi Yangji zenshū* (Tokyo: Seikōsha, 1993), 579–91.

56. Yoon Keun Cha, *"Zainichi" no seishinshi* 3 (Tokyo: Iwanami Shoten, 2015), 160. See also So Hye Kim, "Questioning Authenticity: On the Documentary Film *Reclaiming Our Names*," *Azalea: Journal of Korean Literature and Culture* 12 (2019): 335–63 on the documentary film representations of the *honmyō sengen* movement in Osaka schools.

57. Kang Yun'i, "Yū Miri *Hachigatsu no hate* ni okeru hi-'honmyō': Sōshi kaimei no kage to shite no gō to genjina," *Shōwa bungaku kenkyū* 74 (March 2017): 157–71.

58. See Mizuno Naoki, *Sōshi kaimei: Nihon no Chōsen shihai no naka de* (Tokyo: Iwanami Shinsho, 2008) for a reevaluation of the policy.

59. Kang Yun'i, "Yū Miri *Hachigatsu no hate* ni okeru hi-'honmyō,'" 168.

60. Fukuoka, *Lives of Young Koreans in Japan*, 30–33.

61. Takeda Seiji, *"Zainichi" to iu konkyo: Ri Kaisei, Kim Sŏkpŏm, Kin Kakuei* (Tokyo: Kokubunsha, 1983). Takeda discusses his own name in an essay included in the 1995 *bunkobon* version of the book, which I cite in subsequent chapters: Takeda Seiji, "Mittsu no namae ni tsuite," in *"Zainichi" to iu konkyo* (Tokyo: Chikuma Shobō, 1995), 273–79.

62. I discuss Kin's ambivalent belonging to the canon of Zainichi literature in chapter 5.

63. For examples of attempts to recuperate the lost voices of non-canonical (female) writers from the Zainichi community, see Melissa Wender, *Lamentation as History: Narratives by Koreans in Japan, 1965–2000* (Stanford, CA: Stanford University Press, 2005), 91–125, and Catherine Ryu, "Introduction to Chong Ch'u-wŏl's 'Ningo,'" *Azalea: Journal of Korean Literature and Culture* 12 (2019): 415–23.

64. See, for instance, Isogai's explanation of the distinction between *"Zainichi" bungaku* and *Zainichi Chōsenjin bungaku* in *"Zainichi" bungakuron*, 16–17.

65. Kaneshiro discusses this in Kaneshiro Kazuki and Oguma Eiji, "Sore de boku wa 'shiteiseki' o kowasu tame ni *GO* o kaita (kōhen)," *Chūō kōron* 116, no. 12 (December 2001): 334–36.

66. Lie, *Zainichi (Koreans in Japan)*, x.

67. Kazuki and Oguma, "Sore de boku wa 'shiteiseki' o kowasu tame ni *GO* o kaita (kōhen)," 336.

68. Hara Hitoshi, ed., *Yū Miri: 1991–2010* (Tokyo: Kanrin Shobō, 2011), 7.

69. Workman discusses both writers in these terms in *Imperial Genus* (see chapters 2 and 5).

70. Japan ratified the International Covenant on Civil and Political Rights and the International Covenant on Economic, Social and Cultural Rights in June 1979.

71. David Roh analyzes this failed return in *Minor Transpacific: Triangulating American, Japanese, and Korean Fictions* (Stanford, CA: Stanford University Press, 2021), ch. 4.

72. Before *Gold Rush* (trans. Stephen Snyder [New York: Welcome Rain, 2002]), the Akutagawa Prize-winning stories by Yi Yangji and Ri Kaisei had appeared in English translation (heavily abridged, in the case of *Yuhi*). See Yi Hoe-song, "The Woman Who Fulled Clothes," trans. Beverly Nelson, in *Flowers of Fire: Twentieth-Century Korean Stories*, ed. Peter Lee, rev. ed. (Honolulu: University of Hawai'i Press, 1986), 344–72, and Yang Ji Lee, "Yu-Hee," trans. Constance Prener, in *New Japanese Voices: The Best Contemporary Fiction From Japan*, ed. Helen Mitsios, (New York: Atlantic Monthly Press, 1991), 55–68.

73. For instance, compare the titles of Richard H. Mitchell, *The Korean Minority in Japan* (Berkeley: University of California Press, 1967) and Changsoo Lee and George De Vos, eds., *Koreans in Japan: Ethnic Conflict and Accommodation* (Berkeley: University of California Press, 1981) to those of Lie, *Zainichi (Koreans in Japan)* and Chapman, *Zainichi Korean Identity and Ethnicity*, both from 2008.

2. QUEER(ING) LANGUAGE IN YI KWANGSU'S *MUJŎNG*: GENDER, SEXUALITY, AND COLONIAL MODERNITY

1. Kim Tong'in, "Ch'unwŏn yŏngu," *Samch'ŏlli* 6, no. 7 (July 1934) and no. 8 (August 1935). Internal quotations from Yi Kwangsu, "Ŏrin pŏt ege," *Ch'ŏngch'un* 9–11 (1917).

2. Kim Tong'in, "Ch'unwŏn yŏngu," *Samch'ŏlli* 6, no. 8: 147.

3. Yi Kwangsu [Ch'unwŏn], "Munhak iran hao," *Maeil sinbo*, 10–23 November 1916, no. 2 (November 11, 1916). Translation from Yi Kwangsu, "What Is Literature?," trans. Jooyeon Rhee, *Azalea: Journal of Korean Literature and Culture* 4, no. 1 (2011): 295. I discuss this essay in more detail in chapter 1.

4. Yi Kwangsu [Ch'unwŏn], "Munhak iran hao," *Maeil sinbo*, 10–23 November 1916, no. 4 (November 15, 1916); Yi, "What Is Literature?," 301. These and other ideas found in Yi's essay are similar to the philosophy of literature in Tsubouchi Shōyō's "Shōsetsu shinzui" (The Essence of the Novel, 1885), of which Yi was a reader. See Michael Shin, "Interior Landscapes: Yi Kwangsu's 'The Heartless' and the Origins of Modern Literature," in *Colonial Modernity in Korea*, ed. Gi-Wook Shin and Michael Robinson (Cambridge, MA: Harvard University Press, 1999), 255.

5. Michel Foucault, *The History of Sexuality, Volume I: An Introduction*, trans. Robert Hurley (New York: Pantheon Books, 1978), 43.

6. Eve Kosofsky Sedgwick, *Between Men: English Literature and Male Homosocial Desire* (New York: Columbia University Press, 1985), 201–2.

7. J. Keith Vincent, *Two-Timing Modernity: Homosocial Narrative in Modern Japanese Fiction* (Cambridge, MA: Harvard University Asia Center, 2012), 3.

8. Kim Yunsik, *Yi Kwangsu wa kŭ ŭi sidae* (Seoul: Sol, 1999), 220–21. "Ai ka" is available in two English translations: "Maybe Love," trans. John Whittier Treat, *Azalea: Journal of*

Korean Literature and Culture 4, no. 1 (2011): 321–27, and "Is This Love? (Ai ka)," trans. Janet Pool, in *Queer Subjects in Modern Japanese Literature: Male Love, Intimacy, and Erotics, 1886–2014*, ed. Stephen D. Miller (Ann Arbor: University of Michigan Press, 2022), 63–70.

9. Han Sŭng'ok, "Tongsŏng'aejŏk kwanjŏm esŏ pon *Mujŏng*," *Hyŏndae sosŏl yŏngu* 20 (2003): 10.

10. Sin Chiyŏn, "Yi Kwangsu ŭi t'eksŭt'ŭ e nat'ananŭn tongsŏng kan kwangye wa kamjŏng ŭi ŏnŏhwa pangsik," *Sanghŏ hakbo* 21 (October 2007): 190–91. See also Sin Chiyŏn, "1920–30 nyŏndae 'tongsŏng(yŏn)ae' kwallyŏn kisa ŭi susajŏk maengnak," *Minjok munhwa yŏngu* 45 (2006): 265–92.

11. On the particular role of nationalism in shaping modern sexuality and vice versa in the case of Europe, see George Mosse, *Nationalism and Sexuality* (New York: Howard Fertig, 1985). In the case of colonial Korea, see Yi Hyeryŏng, "Singminjuŭi ŭi naemyŏnhwa wa naebu singminji: 1920–30 nyŏndae sosŏl ŭi sekshuŏllit'i, jendŏ, kyegŭp," *Sanghŏ hakbo* 8 (February 2002): 269–93.

12. Lee Namho et al., *Twentieth Century Korean Literature*, ed. Brother Anthony of Taizé, trans. Youngju Ryu (Norwalk, CT: EastBridge, 2005), 6.

13. See, for instance, Kwŏn Podŭrae, *Yŏn'ae ŭi sidae: 1920 nyŏndae ch'oban ŭi munhwa wa yuhaeng* (Seoul: Hyŏnsil Munhwa Yŏngu, 2003), 25–27.

14. David Halperin, *Saint Foucault: Towards a Gay Hagiography* (New York: Oxford University Press, 1997), 66.

15. The unreachability of the norm is certainly not unique to colonial Korea. See, for example, Audre Lorde on "the mythical norm" in "Age, Race, Class and Sex: Women Redefining Difference," in *Sister Outsider: Essays and Speeches* (Trumansburg, NY: Crossing Press, 1984), 114–23.

16. Janet Jakobsen, "Queer Is? Queer Does? Normativity and the Problem of Resistance," *GLQ* 4, no. 4 (1998): 523–524.

17. Jakobsen, "Queer Is? Queer Does?," 528.

18. Yi Kwangsu [Ch'unwŏn], "Mujŏng," *Maeil sinbo*, 1 January–14 June 1917. Hereafter cited parenthetically, with numbers referring to the installment. Translations from Ann Sung-hi Lee, *Yi Kwang-su and Modern Korean Literature: Mujŏng* (Ithaca, NY: Cornell University East Asia Program, 2005).

19. The narrative suggests that perhaps this is only an attempted rape, but either way, both she and Hyŏngsik perceive her purity as lost, her body defiled.

20. Jennifer Robertson, "The Politics of Androgyny in Japan: Sexuality and Subversion in the Theater and Beyond," *American Ethnologist* 19, no. 3 (August 1992): 427.

21. It should be noted that the dichotomy between "Korean" and "modern" is itself a product of colonial discourse. Rather than accepting it on its own terms, I am gesturing toward the impossibilities this dichotomy creates and queer practice as a tool for overcoming them.

22. Complicating this line of thinking, however, is the generally accepted theory that Yi's original manuscript for *Mujŏng* was written in mixed script and then translated into hangŭl-only style, either by Yi himself or an editor at the newspaper. See Hatano Setsuko, "*Mujō* [*Mujŏng*] no hyōki to buntai ni tsuite," *Chōsen gakuhō* 236 (July 2015): 1–28.

23. On the role of translation (through Japanese) in the formation of modern Korean literature, see Heekyoung Cho, *Translation's Forgotten History: Russian Literature, Japanese*

Mediation, and the Formation of Modern Korean Literature (Cambridge, MA: Harvard University Press, 2016).

24. For the Japanese analogue to this problem, see Komori Yōichi, *Nihongo no kindai* (Tokyo: Iwanami Shoten, 2000), 65–67.

25. It is worth noting that much of this material, especially the lines spoken in Japanese, is removed (censored) from later published versions of the text, such as the version appearing in *Yi Kwangsu chŏnjip* (*The Complete Works of Yi Kwangsu*, Samjungdang: 1962–64). The erasure of this messy multilingualism from Yi's work, as well as from postwar Korean vernacular style in general, illustrates the loss entailed in the interest of greater coherence or legibility.

26. Kwŏn, *Yŏn'ae ŭi sidae*, 31.

27. Kwŏn, *Yŏn'ae ŭi sidae*, 25–31.

28. Judith Butler, *Gender Trouble: Feminism and the Subversion of Identity* (London: Routledge Classics, 2006), 186–89. Obviously her broader theorization of gender, normativity, and performativity is illuminating in thinking through gender, sexuality, and language in *Mujŏng*.

29. At the time of *Mujŏng*'s publication, the standard orthography for Hyŏngsik's surname was "Ri," though in later South Korean versions of the text it is written as "Yi" (이).

30. For a discussion of this kind of imperialist organization of temporalities, see Stefan Tanaka, *New Times in Modern Japan* (Princeton, NJ: Princeton University Press, 2004), especially "Prelude" (1–25).

31. Ellie Choi, "Space and National Identity: Yi Kwangsu's Vision of Korea during the Japanese Empire" (PhD diss., Harvard University, 2009), 2.

32. That said, a major caveat is in order in the case of Yi Kwangsu's own position within Korean literary history, where he is at once acknowledged as the pioneer of Korean modern vernacular style, but also denounced as a collaborator for eventually taking a Japanese name and supporting imperial subjectification and expansion. It is only relatively recently that his career has been reconsidered and his image somewhat resuscitated. See John Whittier Treat, "Choosing to Collaborate: Yi Kwang-su and the Moral Subject in Colonial Korea," *The Journal of Asian Studies* 71, no. 1 (2012): 81–102.

3. THE POWER TO KNOW: KIM SARYANG AND THE WORLD AS ADDRESSEE

1. Kim Saryang, "Haha e no tegami," in *Kim Saryang zenshū*, vol. 4 (Tokyo: Kawade Shobō, 1973), 104–7.

2. Quoted in Kim Saryang, "Haha e no tegami," 104. Nayoung Aimee Kwon examines Kim's relationship with I-novel discourse in Japan, analyzing "Into the Light" as the quintessential example of what she calls the "colonized I-novel." See *Intimate Empire: Collaboration and Colonial Modernity in Korea and Japan* (Durham, NC: Duke University Press, 2015), 54–57.

3. Kim Saryang, "Haha e no tegami," 104.

4. Kim Saryang, "Haha e no tegami," 104–5.

5. See, for instance, Nam Pujin, *Kindai bungaku no "Chōsen" taiken* (Tokyo: Bensei Shuppan, 2001), 55; Piao Yinji, "Kim Saryang no 'Kusa fukashi' o yomu: Tekusuto bunseki ni yoru kokoromi," *Arīna* 12 (2011): 318; Kwon, *Intimate Empire*, 55.

6. Kim Saryang, "Haha e no tegami," 107.

7. David Damrosch, *What Is World Literature?* (Princeton, NJ: Princeton University Press, 2003), 15–17.

8. The best sources for background on Kim's life and career are the timeline included in his collected works (An Usik, "Kim Saryang nenpu," in *Kim Saryang zenshū*, vol. 4 (Tokyo: Kawade Shobō, 1973), 383–93) and An Usik's somewhat hagiographic biography, *Hyōden Kim Saryang* (Tokyo: Sōfūkan, 1983).

9. An, "Kim Saryang nenpu," 383.

10. Kim Saryang Zenshū Henshū Iinkai, ed., *Kim Saryang zenshū*, 4 vols. (Tokyo: Kawade Shobō, 1973).

11. Notably, it is also at this time, in the early 1970s, that Kim Sŏkpŏm began to develop his notion of *Nihongo bungaku* (Japanese-language literature) as distinct from *Nihon bungaku* (Japanese literature), a topic I take up in chapter 4.

12. Shirakawa Yutaka's *Shokuminchiki Chōsen no sakka to Nihon* (Okayama: Daigaku Kyōiku Shuppan, 1995) is pioneering in this respect.

13. Kim Sŏkpŏm, *Kotoba no jubaku: "Zainichi Chōsenjin bungaku" to Nihongo* (Tokyo: Chikuma Shobō, 1972), 108–9. Kim also wrote a book-length polemic on collaboration, in which he similarly disavows Yi Kwangsu: *Tenkō to shinnichiha* (Tokyo: Iwanami Shoten, 1993).

14. Theodore Hughes identifies a similar disavowal in the making of South Korean national literature in the context of the Cold War; see *Literature and Film in Cold War South Korea: Freedom's Frontier* (New York: Columbia University Press, 2012).

15. The premise of Kwon, *Intimate Empire*, is that national literary traditions in Japan and Korea are built on the mutual disavowal of collaboration and other imperial intimacies, though she reads Kim Saryang as emblematic of the entanglements that necessitated disavowal. In the case of Zainichi Korean literature, however, he is canonized rather than excluded.

16. Another direct cause is the increased attention to Kim Saryang in Korean and Japanese studies in recent decades, particularly within English-language scholarship. Three of the English-language monographs that have most significantly impacted my own thinking—Nayoung Aimee Kwon's *Intimate Empire*, Travis Workman's *Imperial Genus*, and Christina Yi's *Colonizing Language*—all pay sustained attention to Kim's work.

17. See Christopher P. Hanscom, *The Real Modern: Literary Modernism and the Crisis of Representation in Colonial Korea* (Cambridge, MA: Harvard University Asia Center, 2013) on the perception of crisis in the Korean language and Korean literature in the colonial period.

18. Christina Yi, *Colonizing Language: Cultural Production and Language Politics in Modern Japan and Korea* (New York: Columbia University Press, 2018), xxi.

19. C. Yi, *Colonizing Language*, xxii. Yi also notes that despite the common understanding of this moment of crisis as a complete elimination of the Korean language from public media, a small number of outlets continued to publish in Korean up until 1945 (13–14). Kim Saryang himself published a long serialized novel in Korean (*Pada ŭi norae*) in the pages of the *Maeil sinbo* in 1943–44.

20. Kim Saryang, "Chōsen bungaku fūgetsuroku," in *Kim Saryang zenshū*, vol. 4 (Tokyo: Kawade Shobō, 1973), 9.

21. Kim Saryang, "Chōsen bungaku fūgetsuroku," 9.

22. Kwon, *Intimate Empire*, 155–56.

23. Kim Saryang, "Chōsen bungaku fūgetsuroku," 9.

24. Kim Saryang, "Chōsen bungaku fūgetsuroku," 9.

25. Emily Apter, *Against World Literature: On the Politics of Untranslatability* (New York: Verso, 2013), 8.

26. Apter, *Against World Literature*, 2.

27. Kim Saryang, "Chōsen bungaku fūgetsuroku," 11, emphasis added.

28. Quoted in Kim Sŏkpŏm, *Kotoba no jubaku*, 71.

29. Kim Talsu echoes both writers in describing his own motivation for writing in Japanese in the postwar: "I decided I wanted to write about Koreans and their lives. And I wanted to inform others, I wanted to appeal to them. In particular, I wanted to inform—I thought I had to inform—the Japanese people who still held various feelings or ideas (almost all of them mistaken) about Koreans and their lives" (*Waga bungaku* [Tokyo: Chikuma Shobō, 1976], 10–11; translation from Yi, *Colonizing Language*, 102–3).

30. See Travis Workman, *Imperial Genus: The Formation and Limits of the Human in Modern Korea and Japan* (Berkeley: University of California Press, 2016). On the participation of Korean colonial subjects in this reconciliation of fascism with the multiethnic space of the empire, see Janet Poole, *When the Future Disappears: The Modernist Imagination in Late Colonial Korea* (New York: Columbia University Press, 2014).

31. Chang Munsŏk, "Kim Saryang to Doitsu bungaku," trans. Yanagawa Yōsuke, *Gengo shakai* 14 (March 2020): 84.

32. In fact, Kim argues that Korean literature is more directly influenced by European literature than Japanese literature, pointing again to the multifarious cultural influences that constituted the conditions of Korean (literary) colonial modernity. See Kim Saryang, "Chōsen no sakka o kataru," in *Kim Saryang zenshū*, vol. 4 (Tokyo: Kawade Shobō, 1973), 17.

33. Chang, "Kim Saryang to Doitsu bungaku," 84.

34. Johann Peter Eckermann, *Conversations of Goethe*, trans. John Oxenford (London: Smith, Elder & Co., 1850), 351.

35. Damrosch, *What Is World Literature?*, 15–17.

36. On Japanese as vehicular language, see Travis Workman, "Locating Translation: On the Question of Japanophone Literature," *PMLA* 126, no. 3 (May 2011): 701–8.

37. An, "Kim Saryang nenpu," 387.

38. Kwak Hyŏngdŏk, "Kim Saryang saku 'Kusa fukashi' ni okeru 'igengo' no taema: 'Hon'yaku' sareta shokuminchi okuchi kikō," *Bungei to hihyō* 11, no. 8 (November 2013): 109–10.

39. For a detailed overview of the incident and the references to it in Kim Saryang's fiction, see Nam Pujin, "Kim Saryang bungaku ni arawareta Hakuhakukyō jiken no kage," *Nihongo to Nihon bungaku* 31 (August 2000): 31–41.

40. Kim Saryang, "Kusa fukashi," in *Hikari no naka ni: Kim Saryang sakuhinshū* (Tokyo: Kōdansha Bungei Bunko, 1999), 168. Hereafter cited parenthetically.

41. See Andre Haag, "The Passing Perils of Korean Hunting: Zainichi Literature Remembers the Kantō Earthquake Korean Massacres," *Azalea: Journal of Korean Literature and Culture* 12 (2019): 257–99.

42. Suh also explores these dynamics through a reading of the opening scene of "Kusa fukashi." Serk-Bae Suh, *Treacherous Translation: Culture, Nationalism, and Colonialism in*

Korea and Japan from the 1910s to the 1960s (Berkeley: University of California Press, 2013), 2–4.

43. Piao Yinji, "Kim Saryang no 'Kusa fukashi' o yomu," 319–23.

44. The *Chŏnggamnok* had ties to the Tonghak movement, out of which the Paekbaekkyo arose. Japanese authorities initially promoted the text as it seemed to predict the downfall of the dynasty they overthrew, but later it was reappropriated, interpreted as predicting the downfall of the Japanese. In the context of the campaign to promote dyed clothing, its references to the Korean people as the "white-wearing race" became particularly problematic for colonial authorities. See Seok-hee Kim, "Joseon in Color: 'Colored Clothes Campaign' and the 'White Clothes Discourse,'" *The Review of Korean Studies* 14, no. 1 (March 2011): 7–34.

4. REPRESENTING RADICAL DIFFERENCE: KIM SŎKPŎM'S KOREA(N) IN JAPAN(ESE)

1. Kim Sŏkpŏm, *Kotoba no jubaku: "Zainichi Chōsenjin bungaku" to Nihongo* (Tokyo: Chikuma Shobō, 1972), 82.

2. Fredric Jameson, "Third-World Literature in the Era of Multinational Capitalism," *Social Text*, no. 15 (1986): 69.

3. Aijaz Ahmad, "Jameson's Rhetoric of Otherness and the 'National Allegory,'" *Social Text*, no. 17 (1987): 3–25.

4. Fredric Jameson, "A Brief Response," *Social Text*, no. 17 (1987): 26–27.

5. Recent entries include Serk-Bae Suh, *Treacherous Translation: Culture, Nationalism, and Colonialism in Korea and Japan from the 1910s to the 1960s* (Berkeley: University of California Press, 2013), 104–34, and Nayoung Aimee Kwon, "A Minor Modernist's Conundrum of Representation: Kim Saryang and the Colonized I-Novel," in *The Routledge Companion to Korean Literature*, ed. Heekyoung Cho (New York: Routledge, 2022), 245–56.

6. See, for example, Shu-mei Shih, "Global Literature and the Technologies of Recognition," *PMLA* 119, no. 1 (January 2004): 16–30; Margaret Hillenbrand, "The National Allegory Revisited: Writing Private and Public in Contemporary Taiwan," *positions* 14, no. 3 (2006): 633–62; Ian Buchanan, "National Allegory Today: A Return to Jameson," in *On Jameson: From Postmodernism to Globalization*, ed. Caren Irr and Ian Buchanan (Albany: State University of New York Press, 2006), 173–88; and Erin Graff Zivin, *Anarchaeologies: Reading as Misreading* (New York: Fordham University Press, 2020), 107–20.

7. See Gilles Deleuze and Félix Guattari, *Kafka: Toward a Minor Literature* (Minneapolis: University of Minnesota Press, 1986), 26–27.

8. Incidentally, many readers see in Kim's characters the figure of Lu Xun's Ah Q, which Jameson takes up in his "national allegory" essay; see Isogai Jirō, *Shigen no hikari: Zainichi Chōsenjin bungaku ron* (Tokyo: Sōjusha, 1979), 83–126; Takeda Seiji, *"Zainichi" to iu konkyo* (Tokyo: Chikuma Shobō, 1995), 103–11; Takazawa Shūji, "Kim Sŏkpŏm ron: 'Zainichi' diasupora no 'Nihongo bungaku,'" *Bungakukai* 67, no. 9 (September 2013): 171. Other examples of allegorical readings of Kim's work include, in English, Elise Foxworth, "The Trope of the Ghost and Cultural Hybridity in Kim Sok Pom's *Mandogi yūrei kitan (The Extraordinary Ghost Story of Mandogi)*, (1971)," in *Recentring Asia: Histories, Encounters, Identities*, ed. Jacob Edmond, Henry Johnson, and Jacqueline Leckie (Boston: Global Oriental,

2011), 237–55; Christopher Scott, "Invisible Men: The Zainichi Korean Presence in Postwar Japanese Culture" (PhD diss., Stanford University, 2006), 100–42. In Japanese, see Yoon Keun Cha, "Henyō gainen to shite no Zainichisei: Zainichi Chōsenjin bungaku/Zainichi bungaku o kangaeru," *Shakai bungaku* 26 (2007): 59–71.

9. For a more thorough reading of the original debate, see an earlier version of this chapter appearing as "Representing Radical Difference: Kim Sŏkpŏm's Korea(n) in Japan(ese)," *positions: asia critique* 27, no. 3 (August 2019): 499–529.

10. Ahmad, "Jameson's Rhetoric of Otherness," 14.

11. Buchanan, "National Allegory Today," 185–86.

12. Here again, it is worth noting that the Korean and Japanese terms do not map easily onto the English "Korea."

13. For more on Korea as a nation or *minjok*, see Henry Em, "Minjok as a Modern and Democratic Construct: Sin Ch'aeho's Historiography," in *Colonial Modernity in Korea*, ed. Gi-Wook Shin and Michael Robinson (Cambridge, MA: Harvard University Press, 1999), 336–61.

14. Isogai Jirō, "Henyō to keishō: 'Zainichi' bungaku no rokujū nen," *Shakai bungaku* 26 (2007): 36.

15. Kim is an exception to his own claim here, as he was proficient enough to publish in Korean for several years. Nevertheless, he is still clearly conscious of Japanese as his first or primary language, which becomes a source of anxiety and suffering for him, as is clear in these essays. He also explores these emotions in fiction: see Kim Sŏkpŏm, "Kyomutan," in *Kim Sŏkpŏm sakuhinshū* (Tokyo: Heibonsha, 2005), 1:135–55.

16. He explores this issue in more depth in a separate essay, "Minzoku no jiritsu to ningen no jiritsu" ("National Autonomy and Personal Autonomy") in *Kotoba no jubaku*, 45–63. In many ways, his ideas here anticipate Jameson's claims about formerly colonized writers and their inextricable position vis-a-vis the collective.

17. Kim Sŏkpŏm, *Kotoba no jubaku*, 85.

18. Kim Sŏkpŏm, *Kotoba no jubaku*, 80.

19. This point is echoed by Naoki Sakai; see *Translation and Subjectivity: On Japan and Cultural Nationalism* (Minneapolis: University of Minnesota Press, 1997), 153–76. Interestingly, Kim's handling of the universal and the particular is eerily similar to that espoused by Kyoto School philosopher Tanabe Hajime, used to justify the subsumption of particularity under a universal fascist state. On Tanabe's imperial ideology of the universal and the particular, see Naoki Sakai, "Subject and Substratum: On Japanese Imperial Nationalism," *Cultural Studies* 14, no. 3/4 (2000): 462–530.

20. Kim Sŏkpŏm, *Kotoba no jubaku*, 89.

21. Kim Sŏkpŏm, *Kotoba no jubaku*, 102.

22. Kim Sŏkpŏm, *Kotoba no jubaku*, 135–56.

23. See Gayatri Chakravorty Spivak, "Subaltern Studies: Deconstructing Historiography," in *In Other Worlds: Essays in Cultural Politics* (New York: Methuen, 1987), 197–221.

24. For a detailed account of the events of the uprising, see John Merrill, "The Cheju-Do Rebellion," *Journal of Korean Studies* 2 (1980): 139–97.

25. Elise Foxworth, "A Tribute to the Japanese Literature of Korean Writers in Japan," *New Voices* 1 (December 2006): 48–49. Foxworth also makes a similar claim about Mandogi; see "The Trope of the Ghost," 237–38.

26. Scott, "Invisible Men," 105.

27. Scott, "Invisible Men," 105–6.

28. Shih, "Global Literature," 21.

29. The notion of nations as imagined constructs is of course familiar; see Benedict Anderson, *Imagined Communities: Reflections on the Origin and Spread of Nationalism* (London: Verso, 1983). In this sense any Korea, not only Kim's Korea, is a fiction. What distinguishes Kim's Korea is that it is assumed fictive at the outset rather than concealing its constructed origins. This is perhaps what Kim means by the "jiyū" (liberty, autonomy) of his essay's title—that is, the freedom to choose (or reject) an affective connection with an imagined entity that comes with the awareness that it is imagined.

30. Nayoung Aimee Kwon, *Intimate Empire: Collaboration and Colonial Modernity in Korea and Japan* (Durham, NC: Duke University Press, 2015), 7–8.

31. Kim Sŏkpŏm, "Karasu no shi," in *Karasu no shi; Yume, kusa fukashi* (Tokyo: Shōgakukan, 1999), 46; hereafter cited in text. "Karasu no shi" is also available in English: Kim Sok-pom, "Death of a Crow," in *Death of a Crow*, trans. Christina Yi (Irvine, CA: Seoul Selection, 2022), 111–230.

32. Kim Sŏkpŏm, "Mandogi yūrei kitan," in *Mandogi yūrei kitan; Sagishi* (Tokyo: Kodansha, 1991), 11, 110; hereafter cited in text. Translations are based on Kim Sŏk-pŏm, *The Curious Tale of Mandogi's Ghost*, trans. Cindi Textor (New York: Columbia University Press, 2010).

33. Nishi Masahiko discusses this history of bilingual literature in *Bairingaruna yume to yūutsu* (Kyoto: Jinbun Shoin, 2014).

34. Kim Sŏkpŏm, "Kansha Paku-soban," in *Kim Sŏkpŏm sakuhinshū*, vol. 1 (Tokyo: Heibonsha, 2005), 7–42. In English: Kim Sok-pom, "Bak-seobang, Jailer," in *Death of a Crow*, trans. Christina Yi (Irvine, CA: Seoul Selection, 2022), 15–110.

5. SPEAKING INTERSECTIONALLY: DISABILITY, ETHNICITY, AND (NON-)REPRESENTATION IN KIN KAKUEI'S *KOGOERU KUCHI*

1. Also known by the Korean pronunciation of his name, Kim Hagyŏng. Here I use the Japanese pronunciation of his characters, Kin Kakuei, deferring to his own apparent preference.

2. Feminist critic Chŏng Yŏnghye notes Kin's criticism of the patriarchal oppression internal to Zainichi nationalism. See Chŏng Yŏnghye, "Aidentiti o koete," in *Sabetsu to kyōsei no shakaigaku*, ed. Inoue Shun et al. (Tokyo: Iwanami Shoten, 1996), 9–10; and Melissa Wender, *Lamentation as History: Narratives by Koreans in Japan, 1965–2000* (Stanford, CA: Stanford University Press, 2005), 54.

3. Anpo (安保) is an abbreviation of "security treaty" in Japanese, and is used to refer to the US–Japan Security Treaty. Popular demonstrations against its revision and renewal in 1959–60 and again in 1970 brought hundreds of thousands of protestors into the streets.

4. John Lie, *Zainichi (Koreans in Japan): Diasporic Nationalism and Postcolonial Identity* (Berkeley: University of California Press, 2008), 117–18; Takeda Seiji, *"Zainichi" to iu konkyo* (Tokyo: Chikuma Shobō, 1995), 121–96.

5. Ozawa Nobuo et al., "'Kyōkaisen' no bungaku: Zainichi Chōsenjin sakka no imi," *Shin Nihon bungaku* 25, no. 9 (September 1970): 56–57. This particular remark belongs to Kobayashi Masaru, speaking in a roundtable setting.

6. Most notably, Takeda, *"Zainichi" to iu konkyo*, 121–96.

7. "Sai" is read "Ch'oi" in Korean. It is unclear which way the name should be read, which will be discussed in further detail later on. I use the term "stutterer" throughout this chapter as a translation of the Japanese *kitsuonsha* (rather than preferable people-first language) in order to reflect the stigma attached to stuttering at issue in Kin's work.

8. Kin Kakuei, "Kogoeru kuchi," in *Kin Kakuei*, "Zainichi" bungaku zenshū 6, (Tokyo: Bensei Shuppan, 2006), 85; hereafter cited parenthetically.

9. Such readings include Takeda, *"Zainichi" to iu konkyo*, 126–33; Pak Yuha's interpretations in Kim Sŏkpŏm et al., "Zainichi Chōsenjin bungaku: Nihongo bungaku to Nihon bungaku," *Subaru* 23, no. 10 (October 2001): 239; and views espoused by the participants in the roundtable discussion recorded in Ozawa et al., "'Kyōkaisen' no bungaku," 56.

10. This immediately signals to the reader that the novel is operating in the mode of an I-novel. I discuss Kin's use and subversion of the I-novel form below.

11. Tobin Siebers, "Tender Organs, Narcissism, and Identity Politics," in *Disability Studies: Enabling the Humanities*, ed. Sharon Snyder, Brenda Jo Brueggemann, and Rosemarie Garland-Thomson (New York: The Modern Language Association of America, 2002), 47–49.

12. Siebers, "Tender Organs," 49.

13. On the pitfalls and potentials of identity politics from the perspective of intersectionality, see Anna Carastathis, *Intersectionality: Origins, Contestations, Horizons* (Lincoln, NE: University of Nebraska Press, 2016), chapter 5.

14. Kyeong-Hee Choi, "Impaired Body as Colonial Trope: Kang Kyŏng'ae's 'Underground Village,'" *Public Culture* 13, no. 3 (2001): 431–58.

15. Choi, "Impaired Body," 434.

16. David Mitchell and Sharon Snyder, *Narrative Prosthesis: Disability and the Dependencies of Discourse* (Ann Arbor: University of Michigan Press, 2001).

17. David Mitchell, "Narrative Prosthesis and the Materiality of Metaphor," in *Disability Studies: Enabling the Humanities*, ed. Sharon Snyder, Brenda Jo Brueggemann, and Rosemarie Garland-Thomson (New York: The Modern Language Association of America, 2002), 20.

18. Mitchell, "Narrative Prosthesis," 23.

19. Paula-Irene Villa, "Embodiment Is Always More: Intersectionality, Subjection and the Body," in *Framing Intersectionality: Debates on a Multi-Faceted Concept in Gender Studies*, ed. Helma Lutz, Maria Teresa Herrera Vivar, and Linda Supik (Burlington, VT: Ashgate, 2011), 181.

20. Mitchell, "Narrative Prosthesis," 24.

21. Mitchell, "Narrative Prosthesis," 28.

22. For in-depth discussions of the trope of confession and its involvement in the making of the canon of modern Japanese literature, particularly the form of the I-novel (discussed below), see Karatani Kōjin, *Origins of Modern Japanese Literature*, trans. Brett de Bary (Durham, NC: Duke University Press, 1993); Edward Fowler, *The Rhetoric of Confession: Shishōsetsu in Early Twentieth-Century Japanese Fiction* (Berkeley: University of California Press, 1988); Tomi Suzuki, *Narrating the Self: Fictions of Japanese Modernity* (Stanford, CA: Stanford University Press, 1996). Notably, one common thread in criticism of Kin Kakuei is that he wrote in the "I-novel" mode, associated as it is with "Japanese

literature" and the trope of confession. For a discussion of this issue, see Kim Sŏkpŏm et al., "Zainichi Chōsenjin bungaku," 235–37.

23. Stuart Hall, "Fantasy, Identity, Politics," in *Cultural Remix: Theories of Politics and the Popular*, ed. Erica Carter, James Donald, and Judith Squires (London: Lawrence and Wishart, 1995), 65.

24. Jacques Lacan, *The Four Fundamental Concepts of Psycho-Analysis*, ed. Jacques-Alain Miller, trans. Alan Sheridan, The Seminar of Jacques Lacan, Book XI (New York: W.W. Norton and Company, 1978), 138–41. See also Homi K. Bhabha's discussion of the implications of the "enunciative split" for questions of cultural difference in "The Commitment to Theory," in *Cultural Remix: Theories of Politics and the Popular*, ed. Erica Carter, James Donald, and Judith Squires (London: Lawrence and Wishart, 1995), 22–24.

25. This rupture is obscured by modern phonocentric notions of language. See Jacques Derrida, *Of Grammatology*, trans. Gayatri Chakravorty Spivak, 40th anniversary ed. (Baltimore: Johns Hopkins University Press, 2016), 6–18.

26. Gayatri Chakravorty Spivak, "Can the Subaltern Speak?," in *Colonial Discourse and Post-Colonial Theory: A Reader* (New York: Columbia University Press, 1994), 66–111.

27. Rosalind C. Morris, "Introduction," in *Can the Subaltern Speak? Reflections on the History of an Idea* (New York: Columbia University Press, 2010), 4.

28. Spivak, "Can the Subaltern Speak?," 103–4.

29. Morris, "Introduction," 6.

30. The collapse of agency into speech also effaces those who do not experience the world first and foremost in terms of speech. See Michael Davidson, "Hearing Things: The Scandal of Speech in Deaf Performance," in *Disability Studies: Enabling the Humanities*, ed. Sharon Snyder, Brenda Jo Brueggemann, and Rosemarie Garland-Thomson (New York: The Modern Language Association of America, 2002), 76–87.

31. I explore the possibility of agency without speech with reference to Spivak's essay in the context of contemporary Okinawan fiction in "Implicated Reading: Medoruma Shun's *Me no oku no mori* and the Ethics of Narrative Transmission," *The Asia-Pacific Journal: Japan Focus* 20, no. 18 (November 15, 2022): Article ID 5748.

32. Christina Yi and Christopher Scott have written in depth on the fraught position of Zainichi literature with respect to what Tomi Suzuki has termed "I-novel discourse." See Christina Yi, *Colonizing Language: Cultural Production and Language Politics in Modern Japan and Korea* (New York: Columbia University Press, 2018), 103–17; Christopher Scott, "Invisible Men: The Zainichi Korean Presence in Postwar Japanese Culture" (PhD diss., Stanford University, 2006), 14–57.

33. Melissa Wender suggests that the narrative itself "stutters," interrupted as it is by long passages of inscrutable scientific terminology and uncited passages from books Sai is reading (*Lamentation as History*, 59). This would also presumably interrupt the smooth flow of knowledge from narrator to reader that the I-novel purports.

34. Quoted from Exodus 6:12, in the King James translation: "And Moses spake before the LORD, saying, Behold, the children of Israel have not hearkened unto me; how then shall Pharaoh hear me, who am of uncircumcised lips?" In the Japanese, it is not "lips" but "mouth" (*kuchi*) that appears in the translation, the same "*kuchi*" as in the title of the novel.

35. I would also be remiss not to note the masculinism of using the foreskin as universal metaphor for human isolation.

36. I thank Nate Heneghan for drawing my attention to the various doppelgängers in *Kogoeru kuchi*, including most notably Sai and Isogai, and Sai and Sai (the narrator/protagonist and the Sai from Isogai's childhood).

37. The "Ch'oi" reading is also suggested within the narrative itself, which implies that the Sai/Ch'oi from Isogai's past preferred the reading "Ch'oi" without ever actually referencing the sound itself: "While the other Korean workers at the shop used two-character Japanese names, only Sai/Ch'oi called himself 'Sai/Ch'oi' in public, and never sought to hide the fact that he was Korean the way others would" (69). He never reveals how this character would pronounce his one-character name, and either reading would acknowledge his identity as Korean, but if the point is that the man was proud and open about his Korean heritage, then "Ch'oi" seems more likely. Again, the presence of this Korean "sound" in the text, without its ever actually being present, is perhaps a more nefarious corruption of "pure" Japanese text.

38. In considering these issues, I have benefited from conversations with Christopher Lowy on what he calls "invisible rubies," the glosses supplied by readers for all *kanji* in the absence of an actual gloss.

6. WORDS THAT HURT: YI YANGJI'S *YUHI* AND THE EMBODIED SUBJECT IN TRANSIT

1. Kuroko Kazuo, "Zainichi Chōsenjin bungaku no genzai—'Zainichi' suru koto no imi," *Kikan Zainichi bungei mintō* 1 (November 1987): 89.

2. Kuroko, "Zainichi Chōsenjin bungaku no genzai," 96–97.

3. For a critique of the conventional wisdom that contemporary Japanese literature has declined into political quietism, see Paul Roquet, *Ambient Media: Japanese Atmospheres of Self* (Minneapolis: University of Minnesota Press, 2016).

4. An early intervention in this area was Chŏng Yŏnghye, "Aidentiti o koete," in *Sabetsu to kyōsei no shakaigaku*, ed. Inoue Shun et al. (Tokyo: Iwanami Shoten, 1996), 1–33. Other feminist studies of Zainichi literature include Yi Sun'ae, *Nisei no kigen to "sengo shisō": Zainichi, josei, minzoku* (Tokyo: Heibonsha, 2000) and Kim Hun'a, *Zainichi Chōsenjin josei bungaku ron* (Tokyo: Sakuhinsha, 2004).

5. The title character's name would be romanized as "Yuhŭi" from Korean, but has conventionally appeared as "Yuhi" in English-language scholarship, following the katakana gloss of the pronunciation in the Japanese text.

6. The Korean word for "older sister," also often used more generally as a term of endearment. It is consistently rendered in katakana in the story (オンニ), but its meaning is not glossed in Japanese.

7. Yi Yangji, "Yuhi," in *Yi Yangji*, "Zainichi" bungaku zenshū 8 (Tokyo: Bensei Shuppan, 2006), 308. Hereafter cited parenthetically. Translations are adapted from Lee Yangji, *Nabi T'aryŏng and Other Stories*, trans. Cindi Textor and Lee Soo Mi (Irvine, CA: Seoul Selection, 2022).

8. Hino Keizō offers one version of this interpretation in a contemporary review of the novel, suggesting that viewing Yuhi through this Korean woman's eyes offers not only an outsider's perspective, but a sort of "absolute" (*zettaiteki*) perspective that makes the story more believable as an objective account of Yuhi's experience; see "*Yuhi* Yi Yangji—

Aru hiyaku," *Shinchō* 86, no. 5 (May 1989): 205. Carol Hayes also argues that this outside perspective allows Yi Yangji "to construct a narrative position which speaks for Korean natives, for Koreans in Japan, and for Koreans resident in Japan returning to live in Korea" and "to dispute the 'fixing' which categories such as ethnicity and geography exert on the formation of identity"; see "Cultural Identity in the Work of Yi Yang-ji," in *Koreans in Japan: Critical Voices from the Margin*, ed. Sonia Ryang (New York: Routledge, 2000): 127.

9. Yi Yangji, "Kotoba no tsue o motomete," in *Yi Yangji zenshū*, (Tokyo: Seikōsha, 1993), 647. Quoted in Carol Hayes, "Cultural Identity in the Work of Yi Yang-ji," 138.

10. Ueda Atsuko, "'Moji' to iu 'kotoba'—Yi Yangji *Yuhi* o megutte," *Nihon kindai bungaku* 62 (May 2000): 128.

11. Naoki Sakai, "How Do We Count a Language? Translation and Discontinuity," *Translation Studies* 2, no. 1 (2009): 85.

12. Sakai, "How Do We Count a Language?," 86.

13. Ueda, "'Moji' to iu 'kotoba,'" 133.

14. Catherine Ryu, "Beyond Language: Embracing the Figure of 'the Other' in Yi Yang-ji's *Yuhi*," in *Representing the Other in Modern Japanese Literature: A Critical Approach*, ed. Rachael Hutchinson and Mark Williams (New York: Routledge, 2007), 327.

15. Sakai, "How Do We Count a Language?," 85.

16. See Eve Kosofsky Sedgwick, *Between Men: English Literature and Male Homosocial Desire* (New York: Columbia University Press, 1985), 201–2.

17. Yi explores this dynamic of the female subject opting out of reproduction in much more depth in *Kazukime* (*The Diver*, 1983). See Nobuko Ishitate-Oku(no)miya Yamasaki, "Body as Battlefield," *Azalea: Journal of Korean Literature and Culture* 12, no. 12 (May 22, 2019): 391–414.

7. WHAT WAS ZAINICHI LITERATURE? TEMPORALITIES OF SILENCE AND THE INCOHERENT FUTURE IN YŪ MIRI'S *HACHIGATSU NO HATE*

1. Another example of a young Korean woman (or in this case, "half" Korean) discovering her background unwittingly appears in the widely distributed documentary film *Hāfu* (directed by Megumi Nishikura and Lara Perez Takagi, 2013), which sketches a cross section of mixed-race people in and outside multicultural Japan.

2. Kaneshiro Kazuki and Oguma Eiji, "Sore de boku wa 'shiteiseki' o kowasu tame ni *GO* o kaita (kōhen)," *Chūō kōron* 116, no. 12 (December 2001): 334–36.

3. Isogai Jirō and Kuroko Kazuo, eds., *"Zainichi" bungaku zenshū*, 18 vols. (Tokyo: Bensei Shuppan, 2006).

4. The prize has since been awarded to a fourth Zainichi writer, Gen Getsu, in 2000.

5. Kenneth W. Warren, *What Was African American Literature?* (Cambridge, MA: Harvard University Press, 2011). Warren's title in turn echoes Leslie Fiedler's *What Was Literature? Culture and Mass Society* (New York: Simon and Schuster, 1982), the argument of which points to a rupture between elite literary tastes and the reading public they are purported to represent. The "end," in all of these cases, is defined by just such a breakdown in the logic of representation. For Warren's discussion of Fiedler see pp. 64–67.

6. Warren, *What Was African American Literature?*, 10.

7. Warren, *What Was African American Literature?*, 2.

8. Warren, *What Was African American Literature?*, 146.

9. John Lie points out several more instances of popular fiction being excluded from the Zainichi literary canon in *Zainichi (Koreans in Japan): Diasporic Nationalism and Postcolonial Identity* (Berkeley: University of California Press, 2008), 117–18.

10. Melissa Wender, *Lamentation as History: Narratives by Koreans in Japan, 1965–2000* (Stanford, CA: Stanford University Press, 2005) is a notable exception, taking up earlier female writers such as Chong Ch'uwŏl and Kim Ch'angsaeng.

11. Song Hyewŏn, *"Zainichi Chōsenjin bungaku shi" no tame ni: Koe naki koe no porifonī* (Tokyo: Iwanami Shoten, 2014). The author renders the English title of her book as *A Literary History of Zainichi Koreans: Revealing the Polyphony of Silent Voices*, but I am using a more literal translation of her Japanese title, which implies that the writing of a Zainichi Korean literary history is an ongoing project.

12. Song, *"Zainichi Chōsenjin bungaku shi" no tame ni*, 37.

13. Lisa Yoneyama, "Reading Against the Bourgeois and National Bodies: Transcultural Body-Politics in Yū Miri's Textual Representations," in Sonia Ryang, ed., *Koreans in Japan: Critical Voices From the Margins* (New York: Routledge, 2000), 106.

14. Ri Kaisei and Yū Miri, "Taidan: Kazoku, minzoku, bungaku," *Gunzō* 52, no. 4 (April 1997): 126–46.

15. Ri and Yū, "Taidan," 127–28.

16. See Rebecca Solnit, *Men Explain Things to Me* (Chicago: Haymarket Books, 2014).

17. Ri and Yū, "Taidan," 135.

18. Quoted in Yoneyama, "Reading Against the Bourgeois and National Bodies," 116.

19. See Edward Mack, "Paracolonial Literature: Japanese-Language Literature in Brazil," *Ilbon yŏngu* 16 (2016): 113.

20. See, for example, Michael I. Norton and Samuel R. Sommers, "Whites See Racism as a Zero-Sum Game That They Are Now Losing," *Perspectives on Psychological Science* 6, no. 3 (2011): 215–18.

21. See Priya Elan, "Why Pharrell Williams Believes in 'The New Black,'" *The Guardian*, April 22, 2014, https://www.theguardian.com/music/shortcuts/2014/apr/22/trouble-with-pharrell-williams-new-black-theory.

22. Tei Taikin, *Zainichi Kankokujin no shūen* (Tokyo: Bungei Shunjū, 2001).

23. See Leslie G. Carr, *"Color-Blind" Racism* (Thousand Oaks, CA: Sage Publications, 1997).

24. Patricia Williams, *Seeing a Color-Blind Future: The Paradox of Race* (New York: The Noonday Press, 1997), 4.

25. Carr, *"Color-Blind" Racism*, 114–16.

26. Williams, *Seeing a Color-Blind Future*, 3.

27. See Adrian Piper, "Passing for White, Passing for Black," *Transition* 58 (1992): 4–32, for example.

28. Eunjung Kim, *Curative Violence: Rehabilitating Disability, Gender, and Sexuality in Modern Korea* (Durham, NC: Duke University Press, 2017).

29. The historical part of the narrative cuts off abruptly when Yi Uch'ŏl dies, coincidentally on the cusp of the Kwangju Massacre, an unrepresentable trauma in South Korean history.

30. Yū Miri, *Hachigatsu no hate* (Tokyo: Shinchōsha, 2004), 7. Hereafter cited parenthetically.

31. Notably, the *ssikkim-kut* as a tradition was in danger of being lost until its designation as "intangible cultural property" in 1980, which generated interest in the ritual both domestically and abroad, but also brought with it a decline in fidelity to earlier formats in favor of more creative artistic expression within the performance. See Mikyung Park, "Korean Shaman Rituals Revisited: The Case of Chindo *Ssikkim-kut* (Cleansing Rituals)," *Ethnomusicology* 47, no. 3 (2003): 355–75. Yū Miri's inclusion of such a performance can be seen as a result of both of these trends: shamanistic ceremonies officially designated and calcified as "representative" of Korean culture, but nevertheless subject to creative license. See also Hyung Il Pai, *Heritage Management in Korea and Japan: The Politics of Antiquity and Identity* (Seattle: University of Washington Press, 2013).

32. Although the passengers are presumably cheering in Korean, the text leaves the reading of these characters ambiguous, yet another gesture at the unrecoverable silences of the past.

33. On the politics of redress see Lisa Yoneyama, *Cold War Ruins: Transpacific Critique of American Justice and Japanese War Crimes* (Durham, NC: Duke University Press, 2016).

34. On the echoes of *sōshi kaimei* in *Hachigatsu no hate* see Kang Yun'i, "Yū Miri *Hachigatsu no hate* ni okeru hi-'honmyō': Sōshi kaimei no kage toshite no gō to genjina," *Shōwa bungaku kenkyū* 74 (March 2017): 157–71.

35. This is yet another refrain in the novel. Not only Ugŭn and Yŏnghŭi, but Uch'ŏl and others refer to their original Korean names in this manner, reflecting the patriarchy inherent in the novel's conception of family and identity formation.

EPILOGUE: GLOBAL ZAINICHI LITERATURE

1. Kim Sŏkpŏm, *Hwasando*, trans. Kim Hwangi and Kim Hakdong, 12 vols. (P'aju: Pogosa, 2015); Kim Chaeyong and Kwak Hyŏngdŏk, eds., *Kim Saryang chakp'um kwa yŏngu*, 5 vols. (Seoul: Yŏngnak, 2008–2016).

2. Kim Sŏkpŏm, *Mandŏk yuryŏng kidam*, trans. Cho Suil and Ko Ŭn'gyŏng (P'aju: Pogosa, 2022); Kim Sŏkpŏm, *Ŏnŏ ŭi kulle*, trans. O Ŭn'yŏng (P'aju: Pogosa, 2022).

3. John Lie, ed., *Zainichi Literature: Japanese Writings by Ethnic Koreans* (Berkeley: Institute of East Asian Studies, University of California, Berkeley, 2018); Melissa Wender, ed., *Into the Light: An Anthology of Literature by Koreans in Japan* (Honolulu: University of Hawai'i Press, 2011).

4. Kaneshiro Kazuki, *GO: A Coming of Age Novel*, trans. Takami Nieda (Seattle: Amazon Crossing, 2018).

5. Yu Miri, *Tokyo Ueno Station*, trans. Morgan Giles (London: Tilted Axis Press, 2019).

6. Yu Miri, *The End of August*, trans. Morgan Giles (New York: Riverhead Books, 2023).

7. Yu Miri, *Tok'yo Ueno Sŭt'eishŏn*, trans. Kang Panghwa (Seoul: Somi Midiŏ, 2021).

8. Kim Tal-su, *The Trial of Pak Tal and Other Stories*, trans. Christopher D. Scott (Irvine, CA: Seoul Selection, 2022); Kim Sok-pom, *Death of a Crow*, trans. Christina Yi (Irvine, CA: Seoul Selection, 2022); Yang Seok-il, *Blood and Bones*, trans. Adhy Kim, 2 vols. (Irvine, CA: Seoul Selection, 2022); Lee Yangji, *Nabi T'aryŏng and Other Stories*, trans. Cindi Textor and Lee Soo Mi (Irvine, CA: Seoul Selection, 2022).

9. David S. Roh, "Kaneshiro Kazuki's *GO* and the American Racializing of Zainichi Koreans," *Verge: Studies in Global Asias* 2, no. 2 (2016): 178.

10. Donna Haraway, "Situated Knowledges: The Science Question in Feminism and the Privilege of Partial Perspective," in *Feminist Theory Reader: Local and Global Perspectives*, ed. Carole McCann and Seung-kyung Kim, 4th ed. (New York: Taylor and Francis, 2016), 442.

11. Min Jin Lee, *Pachinko* (New York: Grand Central Publishing, 2017), 3. Hereafter cited parenthetically.

12. Christina Yi, "Intersecting Korean Diasporas," in *The Routledge Companion to Korean Literature*, ed. Heekyoung Cho (New York: Routledge, 2022), 399–411.

13. Joe Fassler, "What Writers Can Take Away From the Bible," *The Atlantic*, December 20, 2017, https://www.theatlantic.com/entertainment/archive/2017/12/min-jin-lee-by-heart/548810.

14. The absence of Zainichi activism in the novel is pointed out by Sakasai Akito in his review of the Japanese translation of the novel: "Minjin Ri, *Pachinko*: Kōzōteki sabetsu to no tatakai to hon'yaku no jisa ni tsuite (Zainichi, korona, #BLM)," *Gendai shisō* 48, no. 11 (September 2020): 150–54.

15. Fassler, "What Writers Can Take Away From the Bible."

16. Lee, *Pachinko*, 240; see also similar instances on 142, 339, and 413–14.

17. Ikezawa Natsuki, "*Pachinko* (Min Jin Lee cho, Ikeda Makiko yaku)," *Mainichi shinbun*, September 19, 2020, Chōkan edition.

18. Kang Yujin, "Yŏksa ka uri rŭl mangch'ŏnwajjiman, kŭraedo sanggwan ŏpda: Yi Minjin, Yi Mijŏng omgim (2018), *P'ach'ink'o* munhak sasang," *Kyoyanghak yŏngu* 9 (June 2019): 257–58.

19. David Roh interrogates a similar teleology in *Minor Transpacific: Triangulating American, Japanese, and Korean Fictions* (Stanford, CA: Stanford University Press, 2021), chapter 4.

20. Lee, *Pachinko*, 148; attributed to Park Wan-suh.

21. Again, another way of saying this is that the Korean diaspora does not cohere. I have critiqued elsewhere the ethnonationalism inherent in South Korea's newfound "embrace" of the diaspora: "Whose Korea Is It? Reading Zainichi Literature Intersectionally," in *The Routledge Companion to Korean Literature*, ed. Heekyoung Cho (New York: Routledge, 2022), 412–24. On South Korea's "embrace" of the diaspora, see Jaeeun Kim, *Contested Embrace: Transborder Membership Politics in Twentieth-Century Korea* (Stanford, CA: Stanford University Press, 2016).

22. Andrea Mendoza, "Nonencounter as Relation: Cannibals and Poison Women in the Consumption of Difference," *Verge: Studies in Global Asias* 3, no. 2 (Fall 2017): 118–43.

23. Yi Minjin, *P'ach'ink'o*, trans. Yi Mijŏng (Seoul: Munhak Sasang, 2018), 2:314.

WORKS CITED

Ahmad, Aijaz. "Jameson's Rhetoric of Otherness and the 'National Allegory.'" *Social Text*, no. 17 (1987): 3–25.

An Usik. *Hyōden Kim Saryang*. Tokyo: Sōfūkan, 1983.

———. "Kim Saryang nenpu." In *Kim Saryang zenshū*, by Kim Saryang, 383–93. Tokyo: Kawade Shobō, 1973.

Anderson, Benedict. *Imagined Communities: Reflections on the Origin and Spread of Nationalism*. London: Verso, 1983.

Apter, Emily. *Against World Literature: On the Politics of Untranslatability*. New York: Verso, 2013.

Atkins, E. Taylor. *Primitive Selves: Koreana in the Japanese Colonial Gaze, 1910–1945*. Berkeley: University of California Press, 2010.

Avelar, Idelber. "The Ethics of Interpretation and the International Division of Intellectual Labor." *SubStance* 29, no. 1 (2000): 80–103.

Befu, Harumi. *Ideorogī to shite no Nihon bunkaron*. Tokyo: Shisō no Kagakusha, 1987.

Bernheimer, Charles, ed. *Comparative Literature in the Age of Multiculturalism*. Baltimore, MD: Johns Hopkins University Press, 1995.

Bhabha, Homi K. "The Commitment to Theory." In *Cultural Remix: Theories of Politics and the Popular*, edited by Erica Carter, James Donald, and Judith Squires, 3–27. London: Lawrence and Wishart, 1995.

Bridges, Will. *Playing in the Shadows: Fictions of Race and Blackness in Postwar Japanese Literature*. Ann Arbor: University of Michigan Press, 2020.

Buchanan, Ian. "National Allegory Today: A Return to Jameson." In *On Jameson: From Postmodernism to Globalization*, edited by Caren Irr and Ian Buchanan, 173–88. Albany: State University of New York Press, 2006.

Burgess, Chris. "Multicultural Japan? Discourse and the 'Myth' of Homogeneity." *The Asia-Pacific Journal: Japan Focus* 5, no. 3 (March 1, 2007): Article ID 2389.

Butler, Judith. *Gender Trouble: Feminism and the Subversion of Identity*. London: Routledge Classics, 2006.

Caprio, Mark E. *Japanese Assimilation Policies in Colonial Korea, 1910–1945*. Seattle: University of Washington Press, 2011.

Carastathis, Anna. *Intersectionality: Origins, Contestations, Horizons*. Lincoln: University of Nebraska Press, 2016.

Carr, Leslie G. *"Color-Blind" Racism*. Thousand Oaks, CA: Sage Publications, 1997.

Chang Munsŏk. "Kim Saryang to Doitsu bungaku." Translated by Yanagawa Yōsuke. *Gengo shakai* 14 (March 2020): 80–97.

Chapman, David. *Zainichi Korean Identity and Ethnicity*. New York: Routledge, 2008.

Ching, Leo. *Becoming "Japanese": Colonial Taiwan and the Politics of Identity Formation*. Berkeley: University of California Press, 2001.

Cho, Heekyoung. *Translation's Forgotten History: Russian Literature, Japanese Mediation, and the Formation of Modern Korean Literature*. Cambridge, MA: Harvard University Asia Center, 2016.

Choi, Ellie Y. "Space and National Identity: Yi Kwangsu's Vision of Korea During the Japanese Empire." PhD diss., Harvard University, 2009.

Choi, Kyeong-Hee. "Impaired Body as Colonial Trope: Kang Kyŏng'ae's 'Underground Village.'" *Public Culture* 13, no. 3 (2001): 431–58.

Chŏng Yŏnghye. "Aidentiti o koete." In *Sabetsu to kyōsei no shakaigaku*, edited by Inoue Shun, Ueno Chizuko, Ōsawa Masachi, Mita Munesuke, and Yoshimi Shunya, 1–33. Tokyo: Iwanami Shoten, 1996.

Collins, Patricia Hill. *Black Feminist Thought: Knowledge, Consciousness, and the Politics of Empowerment*. 2nd ed. New York: Routledge, 2000.

Combahee River Collective. "A Black Feminist Statement." In *This Bridge Called My Back: Writings by Radical Women of Color*, edited by Cherríe Moraga and Gloria Anzaldúa, 4th ed., 210–18. Albany: State University of New York Press, 2015.

Crenshaw, Kimberlé. "Demarginalizing the Intersection of Race and Sex: A Black Feminist Critique of Antidiscrimination Doctrine, Feminist Theory, and Antiracist Politics." *University of Chicago Legal Forum* 1 (1989): 139–67.

———. "Mapping the Margins: Intersectionality, Identity Politics, and Violence against Women of Color." *Stanford Law Review* 43, no. 6 (1991): 1241–99.

Critchley, Simon. *The Ethics of Deconstruction: Derrida and Levinas*. 3rd ed. Edinburgh: Edinburgh University Press, 2014.

Curtis, Paula R., ed. "Virtual Roundtable: The 'Rebirth' of Japanese Studies." Association of Asian Studies, 2020. http://prcurtis.com/events/AAS2020/.

Dale, Peter. *The Myth of Japanese Uniqueness*. New York: St. Martin's Press, 1986.

Damrosch, David. *What Is World Literature?* Princeton, NJ: Princeton University Press, 2003.

Davidson, Michael. "Hearing Things: The Scandal of Speech in Deaf Performance." In *Disability Studies: Enabling the Humanities*, edited by Sharon Snyder, Brenda Jo Brueggemann, and Rosemarie Garland-Thomson, 76–87. New York: The Modern Language Association of America, 2002.

Davis, Kathy. "Intersectionality as Buzzword: A Sociology of Science Perspective on What Makes a Feminist Theory Successful." *Feminist Theory* 9, no. 1 (April 1, 2008): 67–85.

Deleuze, Gilles, and Félix Guattari. *Kafka: Toward a Minor Literature*. Minneapolis: University of Minnesota Press, 1986.

Denoon, Donald, Mark Hudson, Gavan McCormack, and Tessa Morris-Suzuki, eds. *Multicultural Japan: Palaeolithic to Postmodern*. Cambridge, UK: Cambridge University Press, 1996.

Derrida, Jacques. *Of Grammatology*. Translated by Gayatri Chakravorty Spivak. 40th Anniversary ed. Baltimore: Johns Hopkins University Press, 2016.

———. "Violence and Metaphysics: An Essay on the Thought of Emmanuel Levinas." In *Writing and Difference*, translated by Alan Bass, 97–192. London: Routledge Classics, 2001.

Driscoll, Mark. *Absolute Erotic, Absolute Grotesque: The Living, Dead, and Undead in Japan's Imperialism, 1895–1945*. Durham, NC: Duke University Press, 2010.

Eckermann, Johann Peter. *Conversations of Goethe*. Translated by John Oxenford. London: Smith, Elder & Co., 1850.

Elan, Priya. "Why Pharrell Williams Believes in 'The New Black.'" *The Guardian*, April 22, 2014. https://www.theguardian.com/music/shortcuts/2014/apr/22/trouble-with-pharrell-williams-new-black-theory.

Em, Henry. "Minjok as a Modern and Democratic Construct: Sin Ch'aeho's Historiography." In *Colonial Modernity in Korea*, edited by Gi-Wook Shin and Michael Robinson, 336–61. Cambridge, MA: Harvard University Press, 1999.

Fassler, Joe. "What Writers Can Take Away From the Bible." *The Atlantic*, December 20, 2017. https://www.theatlantic.com/entertainment/archive/2017/12/min-jin-lee-by-heart/548810.

Felski, Rita. *The Limits of Critique*. Chicago: University of Chicago Press, 2015.

Fiedler, Leslie A. *What Was Literature?: Class Culture and Mass Society*. New York: Simon and Schuster, 1982.

Floyd, Nikki Dejan. "Bridging the Colonial Divide: Japanese-Korean Solidarity in the International Proletarian Literature Movement." PhD diss., Yale University, 2011.

Foucault, Michel. *The History of Sexuality, Volume I: An Introduction*. Translated by Robert Hurley. New York: Pantheon Books, 1978.

Fowler, Edward. *The Rhetoric of Confession: Shishōsetsu in Early Twentieth-Century Japanese Fiction*. Berkeley: University of California Press, 1988.

Foxworth, Elise. "A Tribute to the Japanese Literature of Korean Writers in Japan." *New Voices* 1 (December 2006): 46–55.

———. "The Trope of the Ghost and Cultural Hybridity in Kim Sok Pom's *Mandogi yūrei kitan (The Extraordinary Ghost Story of Mandogi)*, (1971)." In *Recentring Asia: Histories, Encounters, Identities*, edited by Jacob Edmond, Henry Johnson, and Jacqueline Leckie, 237–55. Boston: Global Oriental, 2011.

Fukuoka, Yasunori. *Lives of Young Koreans in Japan*. Melbourne: Trans Pacific Press, 2000.

Gates, Henry Louis, Jr. "Beyond the Culture Wars: Identities in Dialogue." *Profession* 1993 (1993): 6–11.

Glade, Jonathan. "Occupied Liberation: Transforming Literary Boundaries in Japan and Southern Korea, 1945–1952." PhD diss., University of Chicago, 2013.

Graff Zivin, Erin. *Anarchaeologies: Reading as Misreading*. New York: Fordham University Press, 2020.

Haag, Andre. "The Passing Perils of Korean Hunting: Zainichi Literature Remembers the Kantō Earthquake Korean Massacres." *Azalea: Journal of Korean Literature and Culture* 12 (2019): 257–99.

Hall, Stuart. "Fantasy, Identity, Politics." In *Cultural Remix: Theories of Politics and the Popular*, edited by Erica Carter, James Donald, and Judith Squires, 63–69. London: Lawrence and Wishart, 1995.

Halperin, David. *Saint Foucault: Towards a Gay Hagiography*. New York: Oxford University Press, 1997.

Han Sŭng'ok. "Tongsŏng'aejŏk kwanjŏm esŏ pon *Mujŏng*." *Hyŏndae sosŏl yŏngu* 20 (2003): 7–29.

Hanscom, Christopher P. *The Real Modern: Literary Modernism and the Crisis of Representation in Colonial Korea*. Cambridge, MA: Harvard University Asia Center, 2013.

Hara Hitoshi, ed. *Yū Miri: 1991–2010*. Tokyo: Kanrin Shobō, 2011.

Haraway, Donna. "Situated Knowledges: The Science Question in Feminism and the Privilege of Partial Perspective." In *Feminist Theory Reader: Local and Global Perspectives*, edited by Carole McCann and Seung-kyung Kim, 4th ed., 440–51. New York: Taylor and Francis, 2016.

Hatano Setsuko. "*Mujō [Mujŏng]* no hyōki to buntai ni tsuite." *Chōsen gakuhō* 236 (July 2015): 1–28.

Hayes, Carol. "Cultural Identity in the Work of Yi Yang-ji." In *Koreans in Japan: Critical Voices from the Margin*, edited by Sonia Ryang, 119–39. New York: Routledge, 2000.

Heneghan, Nathaniel. "Floating Signifiers: Tracing Zainichi Korean Identity in Postcolonial Literature and Visual Media." PhD diss., University of Southern California, 2015.

Hillenbrand, Margaret. "The National Allegory Revisited: Writing Private and Public in Contemporary Taiwan." *positions: east asia cultures critique* 14, no. 3 (2006): 633–62.

Hino Keizō. "*Yuhi* Yi Yangji—Aru hiyaku." *Shinchō* 86, no. 5 (May 1989): 202–5.

Hughes, Theodore. *Literature and Film in Cold War South Korea: Freedom's Frontier*. New York: Columbia University Press, 2012.

Igarashi, Yoshikuni. *Bodies of Memory: Narratives of War in Postwar Japanese Culture, 1945–1970*. Princeton, NJ: Princeton University Press, 2000.

Ikezawa Natsuki. "*Pachinko* (Min Jin Lee cho, Ikeda Makiko yaku)." *Mainichi shinbun*, September 19, 2020, Chōkan edition.

Inokuchi, Hiromitsu. "Korean Ethnic Schools in Occupied Japan, 1945–1952." In *Koreans in Japan: Critical Voices from the Margin*, edited by Sonia Ryang, 140–56. New York: Routledge, 2000.

Isogai Jirō. "Henyō to keishō: 'Zainichi' bungaku no rokujū nen." *Shakai bungaku* 26 (2007): 32–46.

———. *Shigen no hikari: Zainichi Chōsenjin bungaku ron*. Tokyo: Sōjusha, 1979.

———. *"Zainichi" bungakuron*. Tokyo: Shinkansha, 2004.

Isogai Jirō and Kuroko Kazuo, eds. *"Zainichi" bungaku zenshū*. 18 vols. Tokyo: Bensei Shuppan, 2006.

Jakobsen, Janet R. "Queer Is? Queer Does? Normativity and the Problem of Resistance." *GLQ: A Journal of Lesbian and Gay Studies* 4, no. 4 (1998): 511–36.

Jameson, Fredric. "A Brief Response." *Social Text*, no. 17 (1987): 26–27.

———. "Third-World Literature in the Era of Multinational Capitalism." *Social Text*, no. 15 (1986): 65–88.

Kaneshiro Kazuki [Kanesiro Kajŭk'i]. *GO*. Translated by Yang Yun'ok. Seoul: Habillisŭ, 2023.
———. *GO: A Coming of Age Novel*. Translated by Takami Nieda. Seattle: Amazon Crossing, 2018.
Kaneshiro Kazuki and Oguma Eiji. "Sore de boku wa 'shiteiseki' o kowasu tame ni *GO* o kaita (kōhen)." *Chūō kōron* 116, no. 12 (December 2001): 324–36.
Kang Yujin. "Yŏksa ka uri rŭl mangch'ŏnwajjiman, kŭraedo sanggwan ŏpda: Yi Minjin, Yi Mijŏng omgim (2018), *P'ach'ink'o* munhak sasang." *Kyoyanghak yŏngu* 9 (June 2019): 253–61.
Kang Yun'i. "Yū Miri *Hachigatsu no hate* ni okeru hi-'honmyō': Sōshi kaimei no kage to shite no gō to genjina." *Shōwa bungaku kenkyū* 74 (March 2017): 157–71.
Karatani Kōjin. *Origins of Modern Japanese Literature*. Translated by Brett de Bary. Durham, NC: Duke University Press, 1993.
Kashiwazaki, Chikako. "The Politics of Legal Status: The Equation of Nationality with Ethnonational Identity." In *Koreans in Japan: Critical Voices from the Margin*, edited by Sonia Ryang, 13–31. New York: Routledge, 2000.
Kawamura Minato. *Umaretara soko ga furusato: Zainichi Chōsenjin bungakuron*. Tokyo: Heibonsha, 1999.
Kim Chaeyong and Kwak Hyŏngdŏk, eds. *Kim Saryang chakp'um kwa yŏngu*. 5 vols. Seoul: Yŏngnak, 2008.
Kim, Eunjung. *Curative Violence: Rehabilitating Disability, Gender, and Sexuality in Modern Korea*. Durham, NC: Duke University Press, 2017.
Kim Hun'a. *Zainichi Chōsenjin josei bungaku ron*. Tokyo: Sakuhinsha, 2004.
Kim, Jaeeun. *Contested Embrace: Transborder Membership Politics in Twentieth-Century Korea*. Stanford, CA: Stanford University Press, 2016.
Kim Saryang. "Chōsen bungaku fūgetsuroku." In *Kim Saryang zenshū*, 4:9–16. Tokyo: Kawade Shobō, 1973.
———. "Chōsen no sakka o kataru." In *Kim Saryang zenshū*, 4:17–20. Tokyo: Kawade Shobō, 1973.
———. "Haha e no tegami." In *Kim Saryang zenshū*, 4:104–7. Tokyo: Kawade Shobō, 1973.
———. "Kusa fukashi." In *Hikari no naka ni: Kim Saryang sakuhinshū*, 168–204. Tokyo: Kōdansha Bungei Bunko, 1999.
Kim Saryang Zenshū Henshū Iinkai, ed. *Kim Saryang zenshū*. 4 vols. Tokyo: Kawade Shobō, 1973.
Kim, Seok-hee. "Joseon in Color: 'Colored Clothes Campaign' and the 'White Clothes Discourse.'" *The Review of Korean Studies* 14, no. 1 (March 2011): 7–34.
Kim, So Hye. "Questioning Authenticity: On the Documentary Film Reclaiming Our Names." *Azalea: Journal of Korean Literature and Culture* 12 (2019): 335–63.
Kim Sŏkpŏm [Kim Sok-pom]. *Death of a Crow*. Translated by Christina Yi. Irvine, CA: Seoul Selection, 2022.
———. *Hwasando*. Translated by Kim Hwangi and Kim Hakdong. 12 vols. P'aju: Pogosa, 2015.
———. "Ima, 'Zainichi' ni totte 'kokuseki' to wa nani ka: Ri Kaisei-kun e no tegami." *Sekai* 653 (October 1998): 131–42.
———. "Kansha Paku-soban." In *Kim Sŏkpŏm sakuhinshū*, 1:7–42. Tokyo: Heibonsha, 2005.
———. "Karasu no shi." In *Karasu no shi; Yume, kusa fukashi*, 5–102. Tokyo: Shōgakukan, 1999.

———. *Kotoba no jubaku: "Zainichi Chōsenjin bungaku" to Nihongo*. Tokyo: Chikuma Shobō, 1972.
———. "Kyomutan." In *Kim Sŏkpŏm sakuhinshū*, 1:135–55. Tokyo: Heibonsha, 2005.
———. "Mandogi yūrei kitan." In *Mandogi yūrei kitan; Sagishi*, 7–172. Tokyo: Kodansha, 1991.
———. *Mandŏk yuryŏng kidam*. Translated by Cho Suil and Ko Ŭn'gyŏng. P'aju: Pogosa, 2022.
———. "'Nihongo bungaku' to rekishisei." *Kokyō: Nihongo bungaku kenkyū (Border Crossings: The Journal of Japanese-Language Literature Studies)* 2, no. 1 (June 2015): 4–6.
———. *Ŏnŏ ŭi kulle*. Translated by O Ŭn'yŏng. P'aju: Pogosa, 2022.
———. *Tenkō to shinnichiha*. Tokyo: Iwanami Shoten, 1993.
——— [Kim Sŏk-pŏm]. *The Curious Tale of Mandogi's Ghost*. Translated by Cindi Textor. New York: Columbia University Press, 2010.
Kim Sŏkpŏm, Pak Yuha, Inoue Hisashi, and Komori Yōichi. "Zainichi Chōsenjin bungaku: Nihongo bungaku to Nihon bungaku." *Subaru* 23, no. 10 (October 2001): 210–54.
Kim Talsu [Kim Tal-su]. *The Trial of Pak Tal and Other Stories*. Translated by Christopher D. Scott. Irvine, CA: Seoul Selection, 2022.
———. *Waga bungaku*. Tokyo: Chikuma Shobō, 1976.
Kim Tong'in. "Ch'unwŏn yŏngu." *Samch'ŏlli* 6, no. 7 (July 1934), no. 8 (August 1935).
Kim Yunsik. *Yi Kwangsu wa kŭ ŭi sidae*. 2 vols. Seoul: Sol, 1999.
Kin Kakuei. "Kogoeru kuchi." In *Kin Kakuei*, 5–97. "Zainichi" bungaku zenshū 6. Tokyo: Bensei Shuppan, 2006.
Kleeman, Faye Yuan. *Under an Imperial Sun: Japanese Colonial Literature of Taiwan and the South*. Honolulu: University of Hawai'i Press, 2003.
Ko Youngran. *"Sengo" to iu ideorogī: rekishi, kioku, bunka*. Tokyo: Fujiwara Shoten, 2010.
Komori Yōichi. *Nihongo no kindai*. Tokyo: Iwanami Shoten, 2000.
Kono, Kimberly. *Romance, Family, and Nation in Japanese Colonial Literature*. New York: Palgrave Macmillan, 2010.
Kuroko Kazuo. "Zainichi Chōsenjin bungaku no genzai—'Zainichi' suru koto no imi." *Kikan Zainichi bungei mintō* 1 (November 1987): 86–97.
Kwak Hyŏngdŏk. "Kim Saryang saku 'Kusa fukashi' ni okeru 'igengo' no taema: 'Hon'yaku' sareta shokuminchi okuchi kikō." *Bungei to hihyō* 11, no. 8 (November 2013): 109–20.
Kwon, Nayoung Aimee. "A Minor Modernist's Conundrum of Representation: Kim Saryang and the Colonized I-Novel." In *The Routledge Companion to Korean Literature*, edited by Heekyoung Cho, 245–56. New York: Routledge, 2022.
———. *Intimate Empire: Collaboration and Colonial Modernity in Korea and Japan*. Durham, NC: Duke University Press, 2015.
———. "Japanophone Literature? A Transpacific Query on Absence." *MFS Modern Fiction Studies* 64, no. 3 (Fall 2018): 537–58.
Kwŏn Podŭrae. *Yŏn'ae ŭi sidae: 1920 nyŏndae ch'oban ŭi munhwa wa yuhaeng*. Seoul: Hyŏnsil Munhwa Yŏngu, 2003.
Lacan, Jacques. *The Four Fundamental Concepts of Psycho-Analysis*. Edited by Jacques-Alain Miller. Translated by Alan Sheridan. The Seminar of Jacques Lacan, Book XI. New York: W.W. Norton and Company, 1978.

Lee, Ann Sung-hi. *Yi Kwang-su and Modern Korean Literature: Mujŏng*. Ithaca, NY: Cornell University East Asia Program, 2005.

Lee, Changsoo, and George A. De Vos, eds. *Koreans in Japan: Ethnic Conflict and Accommodation*. Berkeley: University of California Press, 1981.

Lee, Min Jin. *Pachinko*. New York: Grand Central Publishing, 2017.

——— [Yi Minjin]. *P'ach'ink'o*. Translated by Yi Mijŏng. 2 vols. Seoul: Munhak Sasang, 2018.

Lee, Minsook. "The Japan-Korea Solidarity Movement in the 1970s and 1980s: From Solidarity to Reflexive Democracy." *The Asia-Pacific Journal: Japan Focus* 12, no. 38 (September 21, 2014): Article ID 4187.

Lee Namho, Wu Chan Je, Lee Kwangho, and Kim Mi Hyun. *Twentieth Century Korean Literature*. Edited by Brother Anthony of Taizé. Translated by Youngju Ryu. Norwalk, CT: EastBridge, 2005.

Lee, Soo Mi. "Performing Postcolonial Feminine Identity as Shaman: Building Narrative Bridges Between Two Worlds." PhD diss., University of California, Berkeley, 2015.

Levinas, Emmanuel. *Totality and Infinity: An Essay on Exteriority*. Translated by Alphonso Lingis. 4th ed. Dordrecht: Kluwer Academic Publishers, 1991.

Lie, John. *Multiethnic Japan*. Cambridge, MA: Harvard University Press, 2001.

———. *Zainichi (Koreans in Japan): Diasporic Nationalism and Postcolonial Identity*. Berkeley: University of California Press, 2008.

———, ed. *Zainichi Literature: Japanese Writings by Ethnic Koreans*. Berkeley: Institute of East Asian Studies, University of California, Berkeley, 2018.

Liu, Lydia. *Translingual Practice: Literature, National Culture, and Translated Modernity—China, 1900–1937*. Stanford, CA: Stanford University Press, 1995.

Lorde, Audre. "Age, Race, Class, and Sex: Women Redefining Difference." In *Sister Outsider: Essays and Speeches*, rev. ed., 114–23. Berkeley, CA: Crossing Press, 2007.

Mack, Edward. "Paracolonial Literature: Japanese-Language Literature in Brazil." *Ilbon yŏngu* 16 (2016): 89–128.

Mackie, Vera, Brian Dowdle, Joshua Fogel, Stefano Romagnoli, and Davinder Bhowmik. "The Death of Japanese Studies (Roundtable Discussion)." Association for Asian Studies, Denver, Colorado, 2019.

Maher, John, and Gaynor Macdonald, eds. *Diversity in Japanese Culture and Language*. New York: Kegan Paul International, 1995.

May, Vivian. "Intellectual Genealogies, Intersectionality, and Anna Julia Cooper." In *Feminist Solidarity at the Crossroads: Intersectional Women's Studies for Transracial Alliance*, edited by Kim Marie Vaz and Gary L. Lemons, 59–71. New York: Routledge, 2012.

Mendoza, Andrea. "Nonencounter as Relation: Cannibals and Poison Women in the Consumption of Difference." *Verge: Studies in Global Asias* 3, no. 2 (Fall 2017): 118–43.

Merrill, John. "The Cheju-Do Rebellion." *Journal of Korean Studies* 2 (1980): 139–97.

Migraine-George, Thérèse. *From Francophonie to World Literature in French: Ethics, Poetics, and Politics*. Lincoln: University of Nebraska Press, 2013.

Mitchell, David. "Narrative Prosthesis and the Materiality of Metaphor." In *Disability Studies: Enabling the Humanities*, edited by Sharon Snyder, Brenda Jo Brueggemann, and Rosemarie Garland-Thomson, 15–30. New York: The Modern Language Association of America, 2002.

Mitchell, David, and Sharon Snyder. *Narrative Prosthesis: Disability and the Dependencies of Discourse*. Ann Arbor: University of Michigan Press, 2001.

Mitchell, Richard H. *The Korean Minority in Japan*. Berkeley: University of California Press, 1967.

Mizuno Naoki. *Sōshi kaimei: Nihon no Chōsen shihai no naka de*. Tokyo: Iwanami Shinsho, 2008.

Mobius, J. Mark. "The Japan-Korea Normalization Process and Korean Anti-Americanism." *Asian Survey* 6, no. 4 (April 1966): 241–48.

Morris, Rosalind C. "Introduction." In *Can the Subaltern Speak? Reflections on the History of an Idea*, 1–18. New York: Columbia University Press, 2010.

Mosse, George. *Nationalism and Sexuality*. New York: Howard Fertig, 1985.

Murphy, David. "Literature after Empire: A Comparative Reading of Two Literary Manifestos." *Contemporary French and Francophone Studies* 14, no. 1 (January 2010): 67–75.

Nam Pujin. "Kim Saryang bungaku ni arawareta Hakuhakukyō jiken no kage." *Nihongo to Nihon bungaku* 31 (August 2000): 31–41.

———. *Kindai bungaku no "Chōsen" taiken*. Tokyo: Bensei Shuppan, 2001.

Nash, Jennifer. *Black Feminism Reimagined: After Intersectionality*. Durham, NC: Duke University Press, 2019.

Nishi Masahiko. *Bairingaruna yume to yūutsu*. Kyoto: Jinbun Shoin, 2014.

Nishikura, Megumi, and Lara Perez Takagi, dirs. *Hāfu*. New York: Third World Newsreel, 2013.

Norton, Michael I., and Samuel R. Sommers. "Whites See Racism as a Zero-Sum Game That They Are Now Losing." *Perspectives on Psychological Science* 6, no. 3 (2011): 215–18.

Oguma Eiji. *Tan'itsu minzoku shinwa no kigen: "Nihonjin" no jigazō no keifu*. Tokyo: Shin'yōsha, 1995.

Ozawa Nobuo, Kijima Hajime, Kobayashi Masaru, and Kitamura Hisashi. "'Kyōkaisen' no bungaku: Zainichi Chōsenjin sakka no imi." *Shin Nihon bungaku* 25, no. 9 (September 1970): 46–65.

Pai, Hyung Il. *Heritage Management in Korea and Japan: The Politics of Antiquity and Identity*. Seattle: University of Washington Press, 2013.

Pak Chungho. "'Zainichi' bungaku wa shōmetsusuru no ka." *Shakai bungaku* 26 (2007): 187–90.

Palais, James. "A Search for Korean Uniqueness." *Harvard Journal of Asiatic Studies* 55, no. 2 (December 1995): 409–25.

Park, Mikyung. "Korean Shaman Rituals Revisited: The Case of Chindo *Ssikkim-kut* (Cleansing Rituals)." *Ethnomusicology* 47, no. 3 (2003): 355–75.

Perry, Samuel. *Recasting Red Culture in Proletarian Japan: Childhood, Korea, and the Historical Avant-Garde*. Honolulu: University of Hawai'i Press, 2014.

Piao Yinji. "Kim Saryang no 'Kusa fukashi' o yomu: Tekusuto bunseki ni yoru kokoromi." *Arīna* 12 (2011): 318–28.

Piper, Adrian. "Passing for White, Passing for Black." *Transition* 58 (1992): 4–32.

Poole, Janet. *When the Future Disappears: The Modernist Imagination in Late Colonial Korea*. New York: Columbia University Press, 2014.

Ri Kaisei. "'Mukokusekisha' no yuku michi: Kim Sŏkpŏm-shi e no hentō." *Sekai* 657 (January 1999): 257–69.

——— [Yi Hoe-song]. "The Woman Who Fulled Clothes." In *Flowers of Fire: Twentieth-Century Korean Stories*, edited by Peter Lee, translated by Beverly Nelson, rev. ed., 344–72. Honolulu: University of Hawai'i Press, 1986.

Ri Kaisei and Yū Miri. "Taidan: Kazoku, minzoku, bungaku." *Gunzō* 52, no. 4 (April 1997): 126–46.

Ri Rika, ed. *Chōsenseki to wa nani ka: Toransunashonaru no shiten kara*. Tokyo: Akashi Shoten, 2021.

Ri Yuhwan. *Nihon no naka no sanjūhachidosen: Mindan, Chōsōren no rekishi to genjitsu*. Tokyo: Yōyōsha, 1980.

Ricoeur, Paul. *Freud and Philosophy*. New Haven, CT: Yale University Press, 1970.

Robertson, Jennifer. "The Politics of Androgyny in Japan: Sexuality and Subversion in the Theater and Beyond." *American Ethnologist* 19, no. 3 (August 1992): 419–42.

Roh, David S. "Kaneshiro Kazuki's *GO* and the American Racializing of Zainichi Koreans." *Verge: Studies in Global Asias* 2, no. 2 (2016): 163–87.

———. *Minor Transpacific: Triangulating American, Japanese, and Korean Fictions*. Stanford, CA: Stanford University Press, 2021.

Roquet, Paul. *Ambient Media: Japanese Atmospheres of Self*. Minneapolis: University of Minnesota Press, 2016.

Rushdie, Salman. "'Commonwealth Literature' Does Not Exist." In *Imaginary Homelands: Essays and Criticism 1981–1991*, 61–70. London: Granta Books, 1991.

Ryang, Sonia, ed. *Koreans in Japan: Critical Voices from the Margin*. New York: Routledge, 2000.

———. *North Koreans in Japan: Language, Ideology, and Identity*. Boulder, CO: Westview Press, 1997.

———. "The North Korean Homeland of Koreans in Japan." In *Koreans in Japan: Critical Voices from the Margin*, edited by Sonia Ryang, 32–54. New York: Routledge, 2000.

———. *Writing Selves in Diaspora: Ethnography of Autobiographics of Korean Women in Japan and the United States*. Lanham, MD: Lexington Books, 2008.

Ryang, Sonia, and John Lie, eds. *Diaspora Without Homeland: Being Korean in Japan*. Berkeley: University of California Press, 2009.

Ryu, Catherine. "Beyond Language: Embracing the Figure of 'the Other' in Yi Yang-ji's *Yuhi*." In *Representing the Other in Modern Japanese Literature: A Critical Approach*, edited by Rachael Hutchinson and Mark Williams, 312–31. New York: Routledge, 2007.

———. "Introduction to Chong Ch'u-wŏl's 'Ningo.'" *Azalea: Journal of Korean Literature and Culture* 12 (2019): 415–23.

Sakai, Naoki. "How Do We Count a Language? Translation and Discontinuity." *Translation Studies* 2, no. 1 (2009): 71–88.

———. "Subject and Substratum: On Japanese Imperial Nationalism." *Cultural Studies* 14, no. 3–4 (2000): 462–539.

———. *Translation and Subjectivity: On Japan and Cultural Nationalism*. Minneapolis: University of Minnesota Press, 1997.

Sakai, Naoki, and Hyon Joo Yoo, eds. *The Trans-Pacific Imagination: Rethinking Boundary, Culture and Society*. Singapore: World Scientific Publishing Company, 2012.

Sakasai Akito. "Minjin Ri, *Pachinko*: Kōzōteki sabetsu to no tatakai to hon'yaku no jisa ni tsuite (Zainichi, korona, #BLM)." *Gendai shisō* 48, no. 11 (September 2020): 150–54.

Schmid, Andre. *Korea Between Empires, 1895–1919*. New York: Columbia University Press, 2002.

Scott, Christopher. "Invisible Men: The Zainichi Korean Presence in Postwar Japanese Culture." PhD diss., Stanford University, 2006.

Sedgwick, Eve Kosofsky. *Between Men: English Literature and Male Homosocial Desire*. New York: Columbia University Press, 1985.

Shigematsu, Setsu, and Keith L. Camacho, eds. *Militarized Currents: Toward a Decolonized Future in Asia and the Pacific*. Minneapolis: University of Minnesota Press, 2010.

Shih, Shu-mei. "Against Diaspora: The Sinophone as Places of Cultural Production." In *Global Chinese Literature: Critical Essays*, edited by Jing Tsu and David Der-wei Wang, 29–48. Leiden: Brill, 2010.

———. "Global Literature and the Technologies of Recognition." *PMLA* 119, no. 1 (January 2004): 16–30.

Shin, Michael. "Interior Landscapes: Yi Kwangsu's 'The Heartless' and the Origins of Modern Literature." In *Colonial Modernity in Korea*, edited by Gi-Wook Shin and Michael Robinson, 248–87. Cambridge, MA: Harvard University Press, 1999.

Shirakawa Yutaka. *Shokuminchiki Chōsen no sakka to Nihon*. Okayama: Daigaku Kyōiku Shuppan, 1995.

Siebers, Tobin. "Tender Organs, Narcissism, and Identity Politics." In *Disability Studies: Enabling the Humanities*, edited by Sharon Snyder, Brenda Jo Brueggemann, and Rosemarie Garland-Thomson, 40–55. New York: The Modern Language Association of America, 2002.

Simon, Daniel, trans. "Toward a 'World-Literature' in French." *World Literature Today* 83, no. 2 (April 2009): 54–56.

Sin Chiyŏn. "1920–30 nyŏndae 'tongsŏng(yŏn)ae' kwallyŏn kisa ŭi susajŏk maengnak." *Minjok munhwa yŏngu* 45 (2006): 265–92.

———. "Yi Kwangsu ŭi t'eksŭt'ŭ e nat'ananŭn tongsŏng kan kwangye wa kamjŏng ŭi ŏnŏhwa pangsik." *Sanghŏ hakbo* 21 (October 2007): 181–221.

Solnit, Rebecca. *Men Explain Things to Me*. Chicago: Haymarket Books, 2014.

Song Hyewŏn. *"Zainichi Chōsenjin bungaku shi" no tame ni: Koe naki koe no porifonī*. Tokyo: Iwanami Shoten, 2014.

Spivak, Gayatri Chakravorty. "Can the Subaltern Speak?" In *Colonial Discourse and Post-Colonial Theory: A Reader*, 66–111. New York: Columbia University Press, 1994.

———. *Death of a Discipline*. New York: Columbia University Press, 2003.

———. "Subaltern Studies: Deconstructing Historiography." In *In Other Worlds: Essays in Cultural Politics*. New York: Methuen, 1987.

Suh, Serk-Bae. *Treacherous Translation: Culture, Nationalism, and Colonialism in Korea and Japan from the 1910s to the 1960s*. Berkeley: University of California Press, 2013.

Sullivan, Mecca Jamilah. *The Poetics of Difference: Queer Feminist Forms in the African Diaspora*. Champaign: University of Illinois Press, 2021.

Suzuki, Tomi. *Narrating the Self: Fictions of Japanese Modernity*. Stanford, CA: Stanford University Press, 1996.

Takazawa Shūji. "Kim Sŏkpŏm ron: 'Zainichi' diasupora no 'Nihongo bungaku.'" *Bungakukai* 67, no. 9 (September 2013): 168–219.

Takeda Seiji. *"Zainichi" to iu konkyo*. Tokyo: Chikuma Shobō, 1995. Previously published as Takeda Seiji, *"Zainichi" to iu konkyo: Ri Kaisei, Kim Sŏkpŏm, Kin Kakuei* (Tokyo: Kokubunsha, 1983).

Tanaka, Stefan. *New Times in Modern Japan*. Princeton, NJ: Princeton University Press, 2004.

Tei Taikin. *Zainichi Kankokujin no shūen*. Tokyo: Bungei Shunjū, 2001.

Textor, Cindi. "Implicated Reading: Medoruma Shun's *Me no oku no mori* and the Ethics of Narrative Transmission." *The Asia-Pacific Journal: Japan Focus* 20, no. 18 (November 15, 2022): Article ID 5748.

———. "Representing Radical Difference: Kim Sŏkpŏm's Korea(n) in Japan(ese)." *positions: asia critique* 27, no. 3 (August 2019): 499–529.

———. "Whose Korea Is It? Reading Zainichi Literature Intersectionally." In *The Routledge Companion to Korean Literature*, edited by Heekyoung Cho, 412–24. New York: Routledge, 2022.

———. "Zainichi Writers and the Postcoloniality of Modern Korean Literature." In *Routledge Handbook of Modern Korean Literature*, edited by Yoon Sun Yang, 225–38. New York: Routledge, 2020.

Thornber, Karen. *Empire of Texts in Motion: Chinese, Korean, and Taiwanese Transculturations of Japanese Literature*. Cambridge, MA: Harvard University Asia Center, 2009.

Tierney, Robert. *Tropics of Savagery: The Culture of Japanese Empire in Comparative Frame*. Berkeley: University of California Press, 2010.

Ting, Grace En-Yi. "Negativity and Hope, or Addressing Gender and Race in Japanese Studies." *Gender and Sexuality* 15 (2020): 67–81.

Treat, John Whittier. "Choosing to Collaborate: Yi Kwang-su and the Moral Subject in Colonial Korea." *The Journal of Asian Studies* 71, no. 1 (2012): 81–102.

———. "Japan Is Interesting: Modern Japanese Literary Studies Today." *Japan Forum* 30, no. 3 (March 2018): 421–40.

———. *The Rise and Fall of Modern Japanese Literature*. Chicago: University of Chicago Press, 2018.

Ueda, Atsuko. *Concealment of Politics, Politics of Concealment: The Production of "Literature" in Meiji Japan*. Stanford, CA: Stanford University Press, 2007.

Ueda Atsuko. "'Moji' to iu 'kotoba'—Yi Yangji *Yuhi* o megutte." *Nihon kindai bungaku* 62 (May 2000): 128–43.

Villa, Paula-Irene. "Embodiment Is Always More: Intersectionality, Subjection and the Body." In *Framing Intersectionality: Debates on a Multi-Faceted Concept in Gender Studies*, edited by Helma Lutz, Maria Teresa Herrera Vivar, and Linda Supik, 171–86. Burlington, VT: Ashgate, 2011.

Vincent, J. Keith. *Two-Timing Modernity: Homosocial Narrative in Modern Japanese Fiction*. Cambridge, MA: Harvard University Asia Center, 2012.

Warren, Kenneth W. *What Was African American Literature?* Cambridge, MA: Harvard University Press, 2011.

Weiner, Michael, ed. *Japan's Minorities: The Illusion of Homogeneity*. New York: Routledge, 1997.

Wender, Melissa, ed. *Into the Light: An Anthology of Literature by Koreans in Japan*. Honolulu: University of Hawai'i Press, 2011.

———. *Lamentation as History: Narratives by Koreans in Japan, 1965–2000*. Stanford, CA: Stanford University Press, 2005.

Williams, Patricia. *Seeing a Color-Blind Future: The Paradox of Race*. New York: The Noonday Press, 1997.

Workman, Travis. *Imperial Genus: The Formation and Limits of the Human in Modern Korea and Japan*. Berkeley: University of California Press, 2016.

———. "Locating Translation: On the Question of Japanophone Literature." *PMLA* 126, no. 3 (May 2011): 701–8.

Yamasaki, Nobuko Ishitate-Oku(no)miya. "Body as Battlefield." *Azalea: Journal of Korean Literature and Culture* 12 (2019): 391–414.

Yang Seok-il. *Blood and Bones*. Translated by Adhy Kim. 2 vols. Irvine, CA: Seoul Selection, 2022.

Yang, Yoon Sun. *From Domestic Women to Sensitive Young Men: Translating the Individual in Early Colonial Korea*. Cambridge, MA: Harvard University Asia Center, 2017.

Yi, Christina. *Colonizing Language: Cultural Production and Language Politics in Modern Japan and Korea*. New York: Columbia University Press, 2018.

———. "Intersecting Korean Diasporas." In *The Routledge Companion to Korean Literature*, edited by Heekyoung Cho, 399–411. New York: Routledge, 2022.

Yi, Christina, and Jonathan Glade. "The Politics of Passing in Zainichi Cultural Production." *Azalea: Journal of Korean Literature and Culture* 12 (2019): 235–56.

Yi Hyeryŏng. "Singminjuŭi ŭi naemyŏnhwa wa naebu singminji: 1920–30 nyŏndae sosŏl ŭi sekshuŏllit'i, jendŏ, kyegŭp." *Sanghŏ hakbo* 8 (February 2002): 269–93.

Yi Kwangsu. "Is This Love? (Ai ka)." Translated by Janet Poole. In *Queer Subjects in Modern Japanese Literature: Male Love, Intimacy, and Erotics, 1886–2014*, edited by Stephen D. Miller, 63–70. Ann Arbor: University of Michigan Press, 2022.

———. "Maybe Love (Ai ka, 1909)." Translated by John Whittier Treat. *Azalea: Journal of Korean Literature and Culture* 4, no. 1 (2011): 321–27.

——— [Ch'unwŏn]. "Mujŏng." *Maeil sinbo*, January 1–June 14, 1917.

——— [Ch'unwŏn]. "Munhak iran hao." *Maeil sinbo*, November 10–23, 1916.

——— [Ch'unwŏn]. "Ŏrin pŏt ege." *Chŏngch'un* 9–11 (1917).

———. "What Is Literature? (Munhak iran hao)." Translated by Jooyeon Rhee. *Azalea: Journal of Korean Literature and Culture* 4 (2011): 293–313.

Yi Sun'ae. *Nisei no kigen to "sengo shisō": Zainichi, josei, minzoku*. Tokyo: Heibonsha, 2000.

Yi Yangji. "Kotoba no tsue o motomete." In *Yi Yangji zenshū*, translated by An Usik, 647. Tokyo: Seikōsha, 1993.

———. "Watashi wa Chōsenjin." In *Yi Yangji zenshū*, 579–91. Tokyo: Seikōsha, 1993.

———. "Yuhi." In *Yi Yangji*, 275–336. "Zainichi" bungaku zenshū 8. Tokyo: Bensei Shuppan, 2006.

——— [Lee, Yang Ji]. "Yu-Hee." In *New Japanese Voices: The Best Contemporary Fiction From Japan*, edited by Helen Mitsios, translated by Constance Prener, 55–68. New York: Atlantic Monthly Press, 1991.

——— [Lee Yangji]. *Nabi T'aryŏng and Other Stories*. Translated by Cindi Textor and Lee Soo Mi. Irvine, CA: Seoul Selection, 2022.

Yoneyama, Lisa. *Cold War Ruins: Transpacific Critique of American Justice and Japanese War Crimes*. Durham, NC: Duke University Press, 2016.

———. "Reading against the Bourgeois and National Bodies: Transcultural Body-Politics in Yu Miri's Textual Representations." In *Koreans in Japan: Critical Voices from the Margin*, edited by Sonia Ryang, 103–18. New York: Routledge, 2000.

———. "Toward a Decolonial Genealogy of the Transpacific." *American Quarterly* 69, no. 3 (September 2017): 471–82.

Yoon Keun Cha. "Henyō gainen to shite no Zainichisei: Zainichi Chōsenjin bungaku/Zainichi bungaku o kangaeru." *Shakai bungaku* 26 (2007): 59–71.

———. *"Zainichi" no seishinshi*. Vol. 3. Tokyo: Iwanami Shoten, 2015.

Yū Miri [Yu Miri]. *Gold Rush*. Translated by Stephen Snyder. New York: Welcome Rain, 2002.

——— [Yu Miri]. *The End of August*. Translated by Morgan Giles. New York: Riverhead Books, 2023.

——— [Yu Miri]. *Tokyo Ueno Station*. Translated by Morgan Giles. London: Tilted Axis Press, 2019.

——— [Yu Miri]. *Tok'yo Ueno Sŭt'eishŏn*. Translated by Kang Panghwa. Seoul: Somi Midiŏ, 2021.

Yū Miri. *Hachigatsu no hate*. Tokyo: Shinchōsha, 2004.

INDEX

affect, 92, 97, 125, 128, 131, 133
African American literature, 140–41, 146
Ahmad, Aijaz, 82–83, 85
Akutagawa Prize, 27, 59, 61–62, 139, 142, 157
allegory, 82–84, 87–89, 91, 98–99, 102
Allied occupation of Japan, 24–28, 164
anglophone. *See* English language
Anpo, 29, 101
Apter, Emily, 65–66
area studies, 8–10, 159
assimilation, 23, 30–31, 71–72, 81–82, 85–86, 116–17, 120, 137, 138, 144, 149

bilingual, 63–64, 92–94, 126
black feminism, 12–14
bundan, 31–33, 59–63, 138–39
Butler, Judith, 56

canon, 5–8, 24, 62–63, 66, 80, 101, 109
"Can the Subaltern Speak?," 114
censorship, 23, 73–75, 78, 84, 106–7
Chaeil, 2–3, 37, 158. *See also* Zainichi
Chainich'i, 2–3, 37, 158. *See also* Zainichi
Chang Hyŏkju, 19, 24, 61, 63, 66–67
Cheju-do, 87–88, 93, 157
Che Sil, 36, 158
Ch'ongryŏn, 28–30, 101, 162, 165
Chōsen, 25, 27. *See also* Chōsenjin
Chōsen bungaku. *See* Korean literature
"Chōsen bungaku fūgetsuroku," 64
Chōsenjin, 2–3, 24, 165
Chōsen-seki, 30–31, 36, 84, 101
Chosŏn, 25, 27
Chosŏnin. *See* Chōsenjin
Chosŏn munhak. *See* Korean literature
Ch'unwŏn. *See* Yi Kwangsu
citizenship, 26, 30–31, 84, 101, 120, 141, 164. *See also* naturalization
class, 28, 35, 65, 68–69, 73, 80, 140
Cold War, 2–4, 7–8, 24–26, 28–30, 90, 101, 135
colonial Korea, 18–23, 39–41, 106, 137, 144, 150, 158, 163–64. *See also* Japanese empire
colorblindess, 140, 146–49. *See also* post-racial
comfort women, 140, 147, 151–54
Commonwealth literature, 6–7
confession, 109–13, 115–16, 129–30
Crenshaw, Kimberlé, 12–13
Curious Tale of Mandogi's Ghost, The. See *Mandogi yūrei kitan*

Death of a Crow. See *Karasu no shi*
decolonization, 25, 84
deimperialization, 25
disability, 32, 100, 102–3, 105–16, 118, 120, 135, 147–49
division of Korean peninsula, 3, 25, 27–28, 30, 33, 89, 101, 135, 143, 150

End of August, The. See *Hachigatsu no hate*
English language, 1–4, 6–8, 11, 14, 21, 34, 36–37, 80, 157–61, 164–66

ethics, 11, 13–15, 53, 66–68, 127, 129, 149, 156, 160, 166
ethnicity, 32–33, 73–74, 89–90, 100, 102–3, 107–8, 116–18, 145, 148, 159, 161, 163
ethnic literature, 19, 141
ethnonation, 35, 42, 58, 67, 82, 84, 89–90, 102–3, 119. *See also* minjok; minzoku

4.3 Incident, 87–88, 92–93, 157
francophone, 6
Frozen Mouth. See *Kogoeru kuchi*
furigana. *See* gloss

genbun itchi, 22, 47
gender, 33, 39, 54–58, 73–74, 100, 105, 114, 120, 134, 140, 142, 159, 162–64
General Association of Korean Residents in Japan. *See* Ch'ongryŏn
Gen Getsu, 157, 187n4
"Gengo to jiyū," 81, 85–86, 94
gloss, 71–72, 93–97, 117–18, 123–24, 126, 128, 131–32, 152
GO, 36, 158
Goethe, Johann Wolfgang von, 67–68
Great Kantō Earthquake, 71, 148, 153
Gunzō, 142

Hachigatsu no hate, 16, 140, 149–56, 158
"Haha e no tegami," 59–60, 70
Hall, Stuart, 110–11
Hangugin. *See* Kankokujin
Hanguk, 25
hangul, 46–48, 51–52, 55–57, 64, 97, 126–28, 131
hanja, 47, 51–52
Harraway, Donna, 159
hate speech, 147
Hayashi Mariko, 144–45
heteronormativity, 40–43, 45, 49, 58
"Hikari no naka ni," 59–60, 80
"Hontō no natsu," 158

identity politics, 12, 105
illegibility, 11, 46, 61, 77, 114, 126–30, 160
imperialism, 16, 20–21, 39, 42, 57, 61, 100, 159. *See also* Japanese empire; neo-imperialism
incoherence, 4–5, 10–11, 13–16, 36–38, 45–47, 57–58, 63, 89–90, 99, 100, 120–21, 140–42, 159–60
I-novel, 59, 115–16, 150
intersectionality: and difference, 6–8, 18, 33, 35, 37, 65, 68, 78, 80; of empires, 20–24, 26–27, 29, 39, 100, 107, 135, 158–60, 164; theory, 4, 8–9, 11–14, 41–42, 46, 73, 103, 105, 107–9, 114, 120, 140–42, 145, 166
"Into the Light." *See* "Hikari no naka ni"
Isogai Jirō, 27

Jameson, Fredric, 82–83, 85, 87–88, 98
Japanese empire, 18–23, 64–65, 71–73, 82, 85, 90, 92, 106, 149–50, 152–53, 158–59, 163–64. *See also* colonial Korea
Japanese-language literature. *See* Nihongo bungaku
Japanese literature, 5, 8–9, 20, 109, 119–20
Japanese studies, 5, 7–8, 18
Japanophone. *See* Nihongo bungaku
Jini no pazuru, 36, 158
JR Ueno-eki Kōenguchi, 36, 158

Kaneshiro Kazuki, 16, 34–36, 139, 142, 158
Kang Yun'i, 31–32
Kankoku, 25, 27. *See also* Kankokujin
Kankokujin, 1–3, 165
Kankoku-seki, 30–31, 36, 101
"Kansha Paku Soban," 93–94
Kantō Earthquake. *See* Great Kantō Earthquake
Karasu no shi, 15, 87, 89–97
Kawamura Minato, 19–20
Kazantō, 157
Kim Hagyŏng. *See* Kin Kakuei
Kim Masumi, 36, 158
Kim Saryang, 15, 17, 19–20, 24, 35, 59–68, 80, 85, 100, 157, 166
Kim Shijong, 157
Kim Sŏkpŏm, 9, 15, 17, 27, 30–32, 35–36, 62–63, 81–90, 98–99, 100–101, 119–20, 126, 138
Kim Talsu, 62, 142
Kin Kakuei, 15–16, 17, 27, 32, 35, 84, 100–103, 105, 119–20, 144
knowledge production, 1, 8–11, 65, 79, 82, 159, 161, 164, 166
Kogoeru kuchi, 15, 100, 102–18
kōminka, 23, 64
Korean-Japanese. *See* Korian-Japanīzu; Zainichi
Korean language, 32, 37, 84, 90, 100, 117, 128, 130–33, 137, 142, 164
Korean literature, 15, 21–24, 39–42, 47, 58, 64–65, 67, 100, 120, 137
Korean school, 28, 138, 164
Koreans in Japan. *See* Zainichi
Korean studies, 7–8, 18, 82
Korean War, 26, 62, 89, 150
Korian-Japanīzu, 2–3, 34, 139
koseki, 92, 98, 154–56
Kotoba no jubaku, 15, 85–86, 157

kukhanmun, 46. *See also* mixed script
Kuroko Kazuo, 119–20
"Kusa fukashi," 15, 61, 65, 68–80

Lacan, Jacques, 111
language politics, 28, 33–34, 64, 70, 73–74, 84–85, 87, 90, 93, 103
League of Koreans in Japan, 28
Lee Hoesung. *See* Ri Kaisei
Lee Yangji. *See* Yi Yangji
Levinas, Emmanuel, 11
Lie, John, 19, 30, 101
literary establishment. *See* bundan
literary history, 17–19, 24, 27, 35, 39, 137, 140–42, 146
literary taxonomy, 6–7, 14–15, 17–19, 23–24, 63, 90, 100, 138–39, 145, 150, 158–59, 166

Mandogi yūrei kitan, 15, 36, 87–98, 157
Mendoza, Andrea, 164
Michel Foucault, 40, 110, 114
Mindan, 28–30, 101
Min Jin Lee, 16, 36, 157, 161–162, 164, 166
minjok, 22, 40, 84. *See also* ethnonation; minzoku
Minjŏn. *See* Minsen
Minsen, 28
minzoku, 35, 40, 59, 67, 84, 119. *See also* ethnonation; minjok
mixed script, 47, 51, 55
modernity, 20–21, 40–43, 45, 47, 58
"Moeru Sōka," 36, 158
Mujŏng, 15, 22, 39, 41–58
multiculturalism, 7–8, 24, 34, 162
munhak, 21
"Munhak iran hao," 21, 40

naichi, 20, 24–25, 60, 64, 73
naichigo, 60, 70
names, 19, 31–32, 54–56, 92–93, 96–98, 117–18, 138, 148, 153–55
narrative prosthesis, 107–9, 121
national literature, 5–6, 22–23, 41, 63, 67, 158
naturalization, 31, 120, 138, 143–44
neo-imperialism, 9, 24, 26, 29
Nihongo bungaku, 9, 18–19, 60, 80, 88, 146
Nihonjinron, 7, 9
norm, 21, 27, 40–42, 44–48, 51, 52, 55–58, 105, 107–8, 134–35, 156
normalization of Japan-South Korean relations, 29–30, 81, 101–2
North Korea, 27–30, 62, 81, 101, 135, 162, 165

occupation. *See* Allied occupation of Japan

Pachinko, 16, 36, 157–58, 160–66
pan-Asianism, 21, 23
passing, 30–31, 54–55, 87–88, 113, 138, 148, 153
patriarchy, 42–43, 45, 49–51, 135, 143–44, 162–63
popular literature, 33–35, 142
postcolonial studies, 9, 60, 86
post-racial, 140, 142, 144–49, 154. *See also* race
post-Zainichi, 142, 144–46, 147, 149
pure literature, 35, 141–42

queer, 14–15, 39, 41–42, 45, 47–48, 50–51, 53, 55–56, 58

repatriation, 28, 81
Republic of Korea Residents Union in Japan. *See* Mindan
reunification of Korean peninsula, 30, 101, 119, 138–39
Ri Kaisei, 27, 31–32, 62, 84, 86, 101–2, 139, 142–45
rubies. *See* gloss

Sagisawa Megumu, 158
Sakai, Naoki, 122, 130
Sedgwick, Eve Kosofsky, 40
Seeing a Colorblind Future, 147–48
sexuality, 39–42, 45–46, 48, 134–35, 142, 159, 164
Shih, Shu-mei, 88
Siebers, Tobin, 105
Sinophone Studies, 5–6
Song Hyewŏn, 19, 142, 149
Sōren. *See* Ch'ongryŏn
sōshi kaimei, 32, 96–97, 153–55
South Korea, 28–31, 81, 101, 135, 143, 145, 147, 150–51, 157–59, 164–65
Spivak, Gayatri Chakravorty, 86, 114
Suh, Serk-Bae, 72

taishū bungaku. *See* popular literature
Takeda Seiji, 32
Tanaka Yoshie. *See* Yi Yangji
Tei Taikin, 147
Tokyo Ueno Station. See *JR Ueno-eki Kōenguchi*
translation, 15–16, 51–53, 55, 65–70, 79–80, 86, 96, 121–25, 127–32, 157–58, 161
transnational, 7–10, 36–37, 159–60
transpacific studies, 9–10

United Democratic Front for Koreans in Japan. *See* Minsen
US-Japan Security Treaty. *See* Anpo

vernacular, 21–22, 40, 42, 46–48, 51, 53, 56
Vietnam War, 29, 101

Warren, Kenneth, 140–41
What Was African American Literature?, 140–41
Williams, Patricia, 147–48
World Literature, 15, 61, 65–68, 146

Yi, Christina, 64, 160–61
Yi Hoesŏng. *See* Ri Kaisei
Yi Kwangsu, 15, 17, 19–22, 24, 35, 39–42, 47, 61, 100, 137, 166
Yi Sang, 137
Yi Yangji, 16, 33, 36, 100, 119–22, 138–39, 142, 144, 157–58
Yuhi, 16, 36, 121–37, 157
Yū Miri, 16, 17, 33, 36, 100, 139–40, 142–50, 157–58

zainichi (literal translation), 22, 24, 34, 120
Zainichi (proper noun), 24–26, 33–34, 36–38
"Zainichi" bungaku, 5, 14–16, 23–24, 33, 35–36, 62–63, 80, 81, 83–85, 100, 102–3, 117, 119, 138–42, 144–45, 157–61, 166. *See also* Zainichi Chōsenjin bungaku
"Zainichi" bungaku zenshū, 5–6, 16, 34, 139
Zainichi Chōsenjin. *See* Chōsenjin
Zainichi Chōsenjin bungaku, 5, 14–15, 17, 19, 27–28, 31, 33, 59, 62–63, 66, 117, 119–20. *See also* "Zainichi" bungaku
"Zainichi Chōsenjin bungaku shi" no tame ni, 142, 149
Zainichi Chōsen-Kankokujin, 2–3, 33–34
Zainichi ideology, 30–33, 35, 101–2
Zainichi Kankokujin. *See* Kankokujin
Zainichi Korean literature. *See* "Zainichi" bungaku; Zainichi Chōsenjin bungaku
Zainichi Korian, 2, 34
Zainichi literature. *See* "Zainichi" bungaku; Zainichi Chōsenjin bungaku
Zainichi organizational politics, 28–29, 101
Zainichi studies, 8, 159
"Zainichi" to iu konkyo, 32

Founded in 1893,
UNIVERSITY OF CALIFORNIA PRESS
publishes bold, progressive books and journals on topics in the arts, humanities, social sciences, and natural sciences—with a focus on social justice issues—that inspire thought and action among readers worldwide.

The UC PRESS FOUNDATION
raises funds to uphold the press's vital role as an independent, nonprofit publisher, and receives philanthropic support from a wide range of individuals and institutions—and from committed readers like you. To learn more, visit ucpress.edu/supportus.

www.ingramcontent.com/pod-product-compliance
Ingram Content Group UK Ltd.
Pitfield, Milton Keynes, MK11 3LW, UK
UKHW020031220325
456593UK00005B/78

9 780520 398726